Pioneers of "

OTHER MCFARLAND TITLES
FROM RICHARD IRVIN

*Film Stars' Television Projects: Pilots and Series
of 50+ Movie Greats, 1948–1985* (2017)

*George Burns Television Productions:
The Series and Pilots, 1950–1981* (2014)

Pioneers of "B" Television

Independent Producers, Series and Pilots of the 1950s

RICHARD IRVIN

McFarland & Company, Inc., Publishers
Jefferson, North Carolina

All illustrations are from the author's collection.

ISBN (print) 978-1-4766-8996-8
ISBN (ebook) 978-1-4766-4770-8

LIBRARY OF CONGRESS AND BRITISH LIBRARY
CATALOGUING DATA ARE AVAILABLE

Library of Congress Control Number 2022048550

Front cover image: Little boy cowboy watching a vintage TV show,
The Howdy Doody Show (NBC/Photofest)

Printed in the United States of America

*McFarland & Company, Inc., Publishers
Box 611, Jefferson, North Carolina 28640
www.mcfarlandpub.com*

Acknowledgments

The author would like to thank the following for their contributions to this work:

- Staff from the Thousand Oaks Library for summarizing information for *Challenge of the Yukon* from the Broadcasting Collection.
- Staff from the New York Public Library for the Performing Arts for information from the Vincent J. Donehue Papers;
- Staff from the Motion Picture and TV Reading Room at the Library of Congress for videos of several early 1950s pilots.
- Staff from the UCLA TV Archives for access to videos of unsold TV pilots as well as staff from UCLA's Charles E. Young Research Library for information about certain television projects.
- Staff from the American Heritage Center, University of Wyoming, for documentation from the Center's various collections.
- The National Cowboy & Western Heritage Museum for material from the Walter Brennan Papers.
- Beinecke Rare Book and Manuscript Library, Yale University, for material from the Steven H. Scheuer Collection of Television Scripts, Yale Collection of American Literature.
- Mary Huelsbeck from the Wisconsin Center for Film and Theater Research of the Wisconsin Historical Society for copies of scripts and other material from the Walter Wanger collection, the Kirk Douglas collection, the United Artists collection, and the David Victor collection.
- Nancy Randle for summarizing various pilots from the UCLA Film and Television Archives.
- Jerome Coopersmith for his recollections about working with producer Martin Stone.

- Evelyn Rudie for her comments about making the Hal Roach Jr. pilot *Cindy*.
- Julie Newmar for her reminiscences about *My Living Doll* and Garry Settimi for proofing and editing the manuscript.

Table of Contents

Preface

The focus of this book is on a sample of producers who strived to make popular, filmed "B" television series in the 1950s. "B" television shows offer pure entertainment to viewers with well-known storylines and characters with whom the audience is familiar. The characters are usually adapted from other media like radio, comic strips, movies or pulp magazines.

As television grew more prevalent in the 1950s, several independent producers began filming shows for the comparably young medium. Since major movie studios like MGM and Warner Brothers saw television, in the early 1950s, as a competitor and wanted nothing to do with it, individuals with some knowledge of making low-cost movies or radio shows transferred their skills to producing TV shows. Such producers saw the advantage in filming TV series since filmed shows, unlike those done live, could be rerun, resulting in large financial returns.

This work profiles the following early independent producers: Hal Roach Sr. and Jr., who went from making comedy shorts for the movies to situation comedies and crime dramas for television; Roland Reed, who not only co-produced sitcoms like *My Little Margie* with Hal Roach Jr. but also made one of the first filmed science fiction series for juveniles, *Rocky Jones, Space Ranger*; Jack Chertok, who filmed the *Lone Ranger* and *Sky King* series as well as the comedies *Private Secretary* and *My Favorite Martian*; Jerry Fairbanks, who developed a camera system to reduce the costs of filming TV series; Bernard J. Prockter, who turned stories of real-life crime into television shows; Martin Stone, who produced the popular kids' series *The Howdy Doody Show*; William F. Broidy, who filmed the iconic Western *The Adventures of Wild Bill Hickok*; Frederick W. Ziv, who syndicated several television series including *The Cisco Kid*, *Highway Patrol* and *Sea Hunt*; Edward Lewis, one of the pioneers of introducing back-door pilots as episodes of an anthology series; Albert Gannaway, who introduced viewers to country and Western music singers on TV; Leon Fromkess, who helped to

1

produce adventure series such as *Ramar of the Jungle, Lassie* and *Fury*; and Walter Wanger, a movie producer who tried and failed at launching B television series.

Early producers of B television series often started their careers in radio or in movies making short subjects for the cinema. While primarily making B TV shows, many also aspired to producing critically acclaimed anthologies or TV specials.

In addition, this work covers the attempts of movie stars such as Bing Crosby, Gene Autry and Mickey Rooney who organized their own production companies to film Westerns, anthologies and adventure series in the '50s. A few female producers who attempted to launch crime dramas, melodramas and comedies are profiled in the final chapter.

Introduction

In describing one of the series profiled in this book, Tim Brooks and Earle Marsh wrote,

> Boston Blackie, hero of more than a dozen 1940s B movies, a B radio series, and B-grade magazine stories dating back decades, appeared in a memorable B-grade television series in the early 1950s. The term "B" is used in all the best senses: a certain vitality and sense of humor substituted more than adequately for the normal criteria of expensive production and famous stars.[1]

This book celebrates the early producers of B-grade television series during the 1950s as TV production moved from live presentations on the East Coast to filmed series made on the West Coast by men (and sometimes women) who sought to make a profit from adapting B-grade radio series and other potboiler material for TV. Some of the producers were successful in launching television shows that many people grew up with in the 1950s (*The Lone Ranger, My Little Margie, The Cisco Kid*). Several other producers tried to launch similar series but failed.

B television series' main goal, other than attempting to sell a sponsor's product, is to provide pure entertainment to viewers with familiar storylines but with some uniqueness so that the show is not entirely bland. The characters on B TV series are generally stereotypical, as are the plots, but the characters usually have some type of "hook" to entice viewers to watch from week to week.

The description of B movies also applies to B television series. B TV shows were usually adapted from preexisting material with which most television viewers would be familiar. As with B movies, B television shows provided training for young actors awaiting their show business break, gave writers and directors the chance to improve their skills, and offered aging actors or those whose movie careers were in decline the opportunity to continue to appear before the public.

The period from the late 1940s through the 1950s is often described as the Golden Age of Television because of the fine dramatic anthologies

3

presented by the networks. Series like *Kraft Television Theatre*, *Philco Television Playhouse* and *Playhouse 90* aired mostly live dramas from New York City. There were also broadcasts of "cultural" shows such as Shakespearean plays, Tchaikovsky ballets, and the first opera produced especially for television: *Amahl and the Night Visitors*. Initially, the new medium was confined to large cities and to urban viewers who could afford to pay for a television set.

But as television expanded across the country and as more people bought TV sets, many West Coast producers not affiliated with major movie studios entered television with cheaply made filmed fare, often bypassing the major networks to sell their series directly to advertisers and/or to local television stations. These series, among the first B TV ones, were like comfort food for viewers. The viewing audience always saw good triumphing over bad on Western series and crime dramas; viewers were transported to different countries and different time periods on adventure shows. Anthologies and other melodramas played on viewers' emotions of fear, joy and sympathy, while comedy series were either heartwarming or just plain silly. As film and television historian Allen Glover wrote,

> The "B" movie never died; it simply moved to television, an exodus encouraged not only by the glaring conundrum of too much airtime and too little product to fill it, but by a surge in the number of television-equipped households. No longer the high-luxury totem it had been in the immediate postwar years, television by the early 1950s was a staple in the homes of many blue-collar and middle-class families—the target audience of the genre fare down at the local bijou.[2]

B Television Genres

The most popular genres for B TV series were adventure shows, Westerns, science fiction, sitcoms, crime dramas, mysteries, melodramas and variety series. Each of these genres can be divided between television series that appealed primarily to juveniles and those chiefly targeted towards adult viewers.

Many adventure series for juveniles are either built around a young person with a faithful companion such as a canine or horse, or they feature a hero set in a time period before the 1800s. Adult adventure series usually are centered around a contemporary American hero overcoming a variety of dangerous situations and/or evil characters somewhere in the world. Westerns and science fiction series could be considered a subgenre of adventure shows, with Westerns set in the nineteenth century in territory west of the Mississippi River. Science fiction series take place sometime in the future, usually in outer space. However, in this book, they are treated as their own genres.

Kids' Westerns ordinarily have a hero with a comic sidekick and, in particular, a trusty steed with a name. While some adult Western heroes may have a sidekick that elicits laughs from viewers, they always ride unnamed horses.

Science fiction series for juveniles are of the fantasy type, taking youthful viewers to cartoon-like planets with one-dimensional characters in outrageous costumes who, amazingly, speak English. In the 1950s, adult science fiction series were more science-based, using scientific logic and accuracy as the starting point for their storylines.

Crime and mystery dramas are normally for adult viewers with the lead character either being a police officer or a private detective. Sometimes a mystery drama may be for juvenile viewers if the main character is a teenage detective like Nancy Drew or the Hardy Boys, or if the series is a hybrid comedy-detective show.

If a B television drama series did not involve a crime of some kind, then it would no doubt be a melodrama highlighting emotional stories of love, romance or family issues. Many times, B TV dramas were presented in the form of an anthology with a different story and cast in each installment. But unlike A television anthologies that featured a wide variety of drama types and even comedies, B TV anthologies normally centered around a single theme such as suspense, horror or empathic individuals.

Situation comedies are the one genre where there is not a great distinction between those oriented toward adults and those for kids, especially those comedies centered on a family. Nevertheless, there is some distinction between sitcoms where a child or teenager is the main character or where adults act like children in their escapades, and those comedies involving two married or single adults encountering situations that may be too sophisticated for children.

If a variety series features clowns, puppets and/or circus acts, it is ordinarily aimed at kids, while a variety series with adult male and female singers or comics is targeted toward adults. Also, B TV variety series for adults often use original songs presented by the singers so as to eliminate the costs of royalties for popular hits.

The Basis for B Television Series

In the 1950s, many B TV series were adapted from other media, particularly radio. A popular radio series—Westerns, adventures, comedies, etc.—had a built-in fan base that producers thought would translate into television viewers. In turn, many radio series had originally begun as movies or novels.

In addition to adaptations from other media, B TV series, especially those with a documentary feel, were repackaged movie newsreel footage focusing on a single theme such as sports, disasters or newsworthy personages. Producers Jerry Fairbanks and Frederick Ziv entered television with such series.

Several B TV series could be described as "variations on a theme." In the Western genre, series were often based on a real historical personage with a name well-known to the public. There were fictionalized shows about such heroes as Wild Bill Hickok, Annie Oakley, Kit Carson and Bat Masterson along with attempts to bring Calamity Jane and other popular Western heroes or heroines to the small screen.

Several crime dramas were built around real-life incidents as a way of attracting viewer interest. If a crime drama based on the files of local police departments became a success, producers would launch other dramas based on the files of federal agencies, newspapers, international crime enforcement organizations and other similar entities.

If a popular drama centered on adventures on the sea, then the same producer might try a similar series set on land or in the air. Likewise, if a show featured police patrolling the highways of America, then the producer could seek to launch a crime drama with police patrolling U.S. waterways.

Another source of B television shows could be titled "old wine in new bottles." Here, movie actors with long careers who had developed a popular persona with the public could be signed as lead actors on a television drama or comedy. If an actor had portrayed a bumbling character in several movies, then why not make a TV series starring the actor as a bumbling father or detective? Likewise, if an actor often appeared in films as an authority figure, then in a television series that actor would play a detective, a lawyer or a doctor. As television matured, the medium created its own stars who, after an initial success with a particular TV series, would try to recreate their success with a new series featuring a character similar to the one they portrayed earlier. A prime example of this is Lucille Ball who, after *I Love Lucy*, replayed her Lucy character in her succeeding sitcoms.

In the mid– to late 1950s, producers began launching TV series that were reboots, sequels or spin-offs of prior television shows. An early television series that was done live could be brought back as a filmed entry. For example, Frederick Ziv relaunched the comedy *Meet Corliss Archer* on film; a few years earlier, it had been presented live.

Sequels were a way of presenting a beloved television character in a new setting or situation, while spin-offs took a popular character from an established show and made the character the focus of a new series.

Some Early, Unsuccessful B-TV Producers

The late 1940s and early 1950s could be termed the "Wild West" of television production companies with most of the major movie studios staying away from making TV series. Almost anyone with an idea for a series and enough money could make a pilot knowing that a hit show could reap tremendous rewards, particularly in reruns.

As noted in Christopher Anderson's book *Hollywood TV: The Studio System in the Fifties*, more than 800 telefilm producers sought riches before 1952. "As a result, more than two thousand unsold pilots languished on storage shelves or rotted in trash bins, having failed to attract sponsors.... Neglected studios, empty warehouses, supermarkets and family garages were transformed into temporary soundstages...."[3]

Some early, unsuccessful television production companies from the late 1940s included:

Bell International: Founded by a man named Jack Gilson, this 1948 firm attempted several TV projects, none of which ever became a series.

One of the company's first initiatives involved making 26 musical shorts for television starring Johnny Carpenter and his group of blind musicians, the Blind Rhythm Riders. The group consisted of a five-piece band made up of members of the Braille "Seeing Horses" club organized by Carpenter. The "Seeing Horses" club performed equestrian acts.

An ABC radio series served as the basis for a 1948 project titled *Retribution*. This planned anthology filmed two episodes, "One Witness" and "Operation-Murder." While the storylines of these episodes could not be found, the first episode starred Helene Stanley and John Lawrence; the second one featured Marjorie Woodworth, Robert Dane and Marta Mitrovitch.

In that same year, the company attempted to launch a musical comedy romance series with June Preisser and Gene Reynolds, *Hollywood Harmony House*, as well as a community sing-a-long show, *Sing with the Stars*.

In 1949, the company wanted to introduce a dramatic series, *Dark Venture*. From 1945 to 1947, ABC radio broadcast a psychological drama called *Dark Venture* that presented stories about people thinking of committing a crime and then actually doing it and being caught. Bell

International adapted this series for TV. Sixty stories were to be made, but apparently only the pilot was filmed.

Bonded Television: Founded by Anson Bond and Allen Kent in 1948, this company produced a few TV pilots that never became series, including a pilot for an anthology titled *Road to Gold*, based on true stories of lost and buried treasure. Basing TV series episodes on supposedly true stories to capture viewer interest is one of the hallmarks of B television.

The *Road to Gold* pilot, completed in mid–1948, starred Robert Shayne, Stanley Andrews, Byron Foulger, Bernardene Hayes, Dorinda Clifton, Julian Rivero, Alan Hale Jr. and Barney Phillips. It concerned the story of the Lost Dutchman Gold Mine in Arizona's Superstition Mountains. The storyline dealt with the search for the lost mine and its original discovery. The 30-minute pilot was made in two days.

While some filming was done in Arizona, Bond told reporters, "Under the existing Arizona workingmen's compensation law, it was not feasible for us to bring our entire cast into the state. We would have preferred to do so, instead of filming much of the strip in Hollywood. Arizona has outstanding advantages in scenery and climate, and its residents are most cooperative. But until the law is modified, our work in Arizona locations will be limited."[4]

Anson Bond was the son of Charles Anson Bond, the founder of Bond Stores. In 1948, Anson teamed up with actress Ida Lupino and her husband Collier Young to make another TV pilot, *The Judge*, with Jonathan Hale as the judge. This potential series had a recurring character relating stories about the court cases and lawyers with whom he has been involved in his position as a judge.

Lupino and Bond penned the pilot script in two days and filmed it in five days at a cost of $40,000. The project starred a pre–*Gunsmoke* Milburn Stone as a criminal defense attorney known for having the charges against accused murders dismissed over legal technicalities.

The judge relates the story of attorney Martin Strang (Stone), married to an unloving wife, Lucille (Katherine DeMille). She is having an affair with a police psychiatrist, Dr. James Anderson (Stanley Waxman). Not well thought of by his colleagues, Strang makes big money by getting his clients freed after they committed crimes. One day, Strang sees a pickpocket, William Jackson (Paul Guilfoyle), shoot a police officer. Strang decides to defend Jackson on the condition that the pickpocket does everything that Strang demands. Jackson is accused of murdering the cop, but Strang is able to have the charges dismissed because, technically, the police officer was not a cop at the time, having failed to pay a bond required of policemen. After Jackson is freed, Strang has him play an intense game of Russian roulette using both real bullets and blanks. Both Jackson and Strang survive the contest, but then an irate Jackson shoots Strang using a gun owned by Dr. Anderson that Strang had stolen. Anderson is arrested for the murder and commits suicide in jail. Jackson is then re-indicted for the murder of the police officer after the fallen officer is classified as a civilian. Jackson also confesses to the murder of Strang.

When the pilot didn't become a series, Emerald Productions released it as a feature film in 1949. Releasing failed pilots as well as episodes of ongoing television series as movies during the 1950s is another hallmark of B television producers seeking to recoup some of the costs of production.

Telepak: Formed by Charles Robert Longenecker in 1948, Telepak was created to produce filmed television shows. Longenecker had worked as a radio producer at CBS's KNX in Los Angeles as well as a talent agent for Myron Selznick and Co. Joining Longenecker in the firm were Ben Finney, an independent film producer, and art director William Cameron Menzies.

Pacesetters in the world of filmed TV drama, Telepak made two 15-minute installments of classic horror stories. One, "A Terribly Strange Bed" starring Richard Greene and Roman Bohnen, concerned an English college student who visits a Paris gambling house, wins big and decides to stay overnight in the building. He is almost killed by a specially constructed four-poster bed whose canopy slowly descends to suffocate him. The other story, Edgar Allan Poe's "The Tell-Tale Heart," focused on a murderer who dismembers his victim and hides the body parts under the floorboards in his apartment. He then hears the thumping of the victim's heart beneath the floor. This installment starred Richard Hart. In reviewing the two films, *Variety* noted,

> For grisly, terrifying effect the closeups of agonized faces and devices of destruction will curdle the corpuscles of viewers but the kiddies will have to leave the room lest they want to grapple with nightmares.... What gives the films their new tele look are the simple sets with a strong contrast of light and shadows. Narration rides over the dialog at times and eerie sound effects creep and crawl with the flesh.[5]

Both films were made in a single day. "A Terribly Strange Bed" eventually aired as a segment of *Fireside Theatre* on June 21, 1949. Richard Hart signed with Telepak for six more 16mm installments if a series had resulted from the initial pilots.

Other Telepak projects that failed to turn into series included:

Two Girls for Iowa, starring sisters Joan and Betty Caulfield, dealing with two gals who make their way to New York to become fashion models; *Uncle Gilbert,* a comedy featuring character actor Victor Moore; *Yankee Spy,* an adventure series starring Richard Hart, Bob Cummings and Douglas Fairbanks Jr. The series attempt, based on the *Leatherstocking* tales by James Fenimore Cooper, was to be produced and directed by Menzies; *Opportunity Playhouse,* a talent discovery program, which would be part filmed interviews with Hollywood stars describing how they broke into show business and a live portion, airing from a different city each week, featuring new talent; *Your Witness* with Regis Toomey, a unique mystery series in which members of a studio audience had a chance to quiz suspects of a crime near the end of the show whose pilot was titled "The Marionette Mystery"; *Gilbert and Sullivan,* a planned 30-minute musical series; and *Adventures of Guignol and Barbarin,* a 26-week puppet series made in France which Telepak would dub in English.

After Longenecker left the company in July 1949, Gifford Phillips took over and renamed the firm TeeVee Films. Merrill Pye, who had worked with Longenecker at Telepak, became vice-president in charge of production at the new company. Longenecker eventually returned to the talent agent business.

Failing to turn any of its pilots into TV series, the firm struck a deal with Hal Roach Jr. to show "The Tell-Tale Heart," "A Terribly Strange Bed" and "The Marionette Mystery" as a single film in theaters and to air each of them on television.

Eclipse Productions: Formed in 1948 by Michael and Dorothy Colins, this company's first and apparently only attempt at a TV series was *Fireside Detective.* The comedy-mystery show featured a husband-and-wife team and a missing clue gimmick for audience participation. It was made on 16mm with the use of 36mm sound equipment, Lee Loeb wrote the pilot. Twenty-six episodes were planned.

Made in 1948 but not aired until April 1952 on KECA-TV in Los Angeles, the test show told the story of a detective lieutenant (Keith Hetherington) whose wife (Kay Christopher) hopes to make him famous through her writing. His involvement in a sensational murder case finally brings him fame. The pilot ends with audience participation in picking out clues that lead to the murderer's identity.

Eclipse Productions, desperate to have their film televised so a potential sponsor might buy it, offered *Fireside Detective* free to local stations. If a TV station scheduled the pilot for airing, Eclipse planned to send cards to contacts asking them to view the program.

CHAPTER 1

Hal Roach Sr. and Jr.

From Movie Shorts to B TV Series

Hal Roach, born on January 14, 1892, began producing comedy shorts in Hollywood in 1915. His most popular comedies starred the team of Laurel and Hardy, comic actor Charley Chase and the young actors in the *Our Gang* films. He also made some feature-length movies, including *Of Mice and Men* (1939) and *One Million B.C.* (1940).

With a recession in the film industry in 1948, Hal Roach Studios were in grave financial trouble. Unlike other independent studios that operated with little overhead, Roach had buildings with stages and equipment that he had to maintain. Roach Sr. attempted to sell his 14-acre studio to the U.S. Air Force, which rejected his offer. The only option he found to avoid bankruptcy was television production.

Roach Sr. produced many 30-minute pilots in the late 1940s, none of which ever became series. He had hopes of producing nine hours of TV programming a week at his studio. To reduce the costs of filming series, Roach planned to use experienced movie actors willing to forego high salaries in hopes of achieving fame in the new medium. He also wanted to use new talent in his TV projects. Writers were recruited from radio, the movies and pulp fiction, while directors and camera technicians were mainly old-time Roach associates.

Commenting on his venture into television, Roach said, "I am convinced that the insatiable desire to be entertained will find its greatest satisfaction through television. Accordingly, we are converting all of our efforts into production for the television field, and our entire studio will be devoted to fashioning films for this medium."[1]

Roach Sr.'s Unsold Television Pilots

In many respects, each of Hal Roach Sr.'s early TV pilots served as a blueprint for the types of shows on television today. He made a domestic, character-centered family comedy, a mismatched roommates show, a slapstick workplace sitcom, a crime satire, a kids' comedy, a melodrama and a comedy sketch show.

The Brown Family concerned a typical American family with hardworking father Mortimer Brown (John Eldredge), devoted mother, Lois (Ann Doran) and two teenagers, 17-year-old Sheila (Carol Brandon), who aspires to be an actress, and a young son, Stanley (Billy Gray), who seems to always be in trouble.

Made over a two-day period in December 1948, the pilot's title was "Man's Best Friend." Stanley and his classmates jointly own a dog named Community with each boy taking care of the dog one day a month. When Stanley brings the dog home, Community refuses to eat a plate of Lois' homemade stew which all the family is having for dinner. When the dog won't eat, the entire family loses its appetite for the stew. In the middle of the night, unbeknownst to one another, each family member awakes and feeds the dog some ground beef from the refrigerator. Later, they find that the dog did eventually eat the plate of stew.

Made in December 1948, *Sadie and Sally*, a "beauty" vs. "brains" comedy, featured Sadie (Joi Lansing) as the not-too-bright Southern beauty stranded in New York City with the intelligent Sally (Lois Hall).

Hal Roach Sr. in 1963. Roach passed away at age 100.

Sadie moves in with Sally and takes advantage of her hospitality. Sadie takes over most of Sally's clothes closet and drawer space. She puts her nylons in Sally's bathroom sink, with Sally having to wash them, and then she asks Sally to iron her clothes. At night, Sadie ties a rope around her leg and Sally's leg, saying that she walks in her sleep and the rope will prevent her from getting out of bed. Before going to sleep, Sadie makes herself a hamburger. Sally finally gets a measure of revenge by informing

Sadie, after she eats the burger, that it consists of horse meat for Sally's dog.

Joi Lansing was known more for her looks than her acting talent. *Sadie and Sally* was her first appearance in a TV project. She later appeared on episodes of *The Bob Cummings Show* and *The Beverly Hillbillies.*

In the *Botsford's Beanery* episode "Botsford Wakes Up," made in December 1948, Montgomery Botsford (Don Barclay), owner of a restaurant–pool hall, wakes up on one of his pool tables and prepares to serve customers. Some tough guys visit to install a slot machine in his establishment despite Montgomery's objections. He starts playing the machine, but it doesn't pay off until a customer comes in, puts a coin in the slot and wins a jackpot. Botsford hopes to win money from the customer by betting on a pool game, but the customer beats him at that as well. Botsford has to put up the slot machine to cover the customer's $100 bet. When the customer wants to take the machine out of the restaurant, the tough guys return. A custard pie fight ensues with the hoods vs. Botsford, his waitress Agnes (Anne Triola) and Joe (Candy Candido), the barber from the shop next door. A police officer arrests the gangsters.

Foo Young starred Richard Loo and Maria Sen-Yung in a satire of Oriental private detectives like Charlie Chan. The pilot, entitled "The Curtin Case," featured a fumbling private eye and his clever niece. It aired on *Summer Theatre* during the summer of 1953.

Our Main Street had a cast that included Sandra Gould as Lola, Bill Thompson as a grocer, John Brown as Doc and Norma Varden as Genevieve Olyphant. A cross between a situation comedy and a sketch show, it portrayed a supposedly typical afternoon in a small town. The proposed series presented vignettes of the interactions between store proprietors and their customers.

One segment featured a young couple at a drug store soda fountain, the girl trying to decide what to order. She orders vanilla ice cream which the soda jerk places in a bowl, but then she changes her mind and orders chocolate ice cream. This goes on for a while with the clerk finally offering her the "imbecile special" which she agrees to take. It consists of all the desserts she had ordered and then decided not to take.

Another vignette had beautician Lola wanting to purchase cheese. The grocer says that his uncle in the back room is an expert on different types of Swiss cheese. He goes into the back, puts on a mustache and pretends he is the uncle, and tells Lola what cheese she should buy. The guy returns to the back room, takes off the mustache and comes back to wait on Lola. When he asks for the money for the cheese, Lola says that she already paid his uncle.

An ongoing storyline centered on Mrs. Genevieve Olyphant, who wants to buy stamps from Doc the druggist. He refers to her as "Mrs. Elephant." She next goes to Lola's beauty salon for a manicure, but Lola talks her into having her hair redone. Predictably, Lola makes a mess of Genevieve's hair with some of it falling out. Word of the incident spreads. At the barber shop, the customers and barber begin singing "An Olyphant Never Forgets," but when Mrs. Olyphant comes by, the group switches to "O Genevieve," much to her delight.

Myrt and Marge featured Bernadette Hayes as Myrtle Speer, Phyllis Coates as Marge Minter and Franklin Pangborn as Clarence Tiffingtuffer. The "dramedy" was a co-production between Hal Roach and Matterhorn Productions

The *Myrt and Marge* radio serial, which ran from 1931 to 1946, dealt with a seasoned chorus girl, Myrt Spear, and Marge Minter, a young girl new to the chorus. Given the last names of the lead characters, it is not surprising that Wrigley, the maker of Spearmint chewing gum, sponsored the radio show. Advertisements described the show as "the world of the theater and the world of life, and the story of two women who seek fame in the one and contentment in the other."

Roach produced a television version of the radio series. The pilot presented the story of Marge's initial audition for the chorus in a Broadway show. Myrt, the captain of the chorus, puts her girls through their routine with Marge observing. Marge works up the courage to ask Myrt for a break and then passes out due to hunger. Myrt gives her money for lunch. After eating, Marge performs a dance number for Myrt. When one of the chorus girls slips on some cold cream spilled on the floor and breaks her leg, Myrt decides to hire Marge as the replacement.

Actor Franklin Pangborn, who frequently played stereotypical gay roles in movies, appeared in the pilot as a costume designer. In one scene, typical of the parts written for him, his character is to measure a man's inseam in a horse's costume for a fitting; the man resists the designer's endeavors. The blanket on the horse costume reads PANSY. The pilot aired as an installment of *Summer Theatre* in August 1953.

The Puddle Patch Club attempted to recreate the *Our Gang* comedies for the TV generation. As Louella Parsons reported, "[Hal Roach] wants boys of all types, not just junior slickers. Remember the fat ones, skinny ones, boys with glasses, freckles, etc. of his famous old 'Our Gang' comedies? Well, that's the idea."[2] The pilot starred Jackie Coogan Jr. as Droope, Billy Gray as Pinky and Edward Gargan as Officer Clancey.

In the late '40s, Roach also had two other groups of pilots that he sought to make but apparently never did. Among these were two musical shows, *Melody Lane* and *Serenade for Tonight*; a dramatic series called *Sandy Shor*; *Bob Wire*, a Western; *Café Social*, a satire on New York café society, and *The Blue Yonder*, an adventure story about airplane pilots. The other group included *Mary Holden, Housewife*, a soap opera; the fantasy *Angie and Impie*; *Caballeros*, a Mexican musical; *Fast and Loose*, about an American and a British slicker; *Alkali Albert*, a comedy Western, and *The Glicket Cat*, a children's series.

In November 1953, Roach Sr. contemplated a half-hour series called *Hollywood Four Star Theatre*. Not to be confused with the anthology *Four Star Playhouse* launched by Dick Powell and associates in the early '50s, *Hollywood Four Star Theatre* would feature a permanent stock company of actors with four name actors in rotating star assignments. This anthology never materialized.

Roach Sr.'s Hour-Long Television Ideas

Despite most early TV series being 30 minutes in length, Roach's interest was in hour-long series. He made a pilot with actress Fay Bainter called *The Dramatic Hour*. This proposed anthology, also titled *The Actors' Hour*, had four segments: a screen test with established stars critiquing the test with actors who participated in it; a chapter of a serial, "The Last Days of Pompeii"; a playlet by the Hal Roach Studio Stock Company, and a playlet with a cast headed by Bainter and another star.

In the pilot, the co-star was Onslow Stevens. Publicity stills from the pilot of Stevens made-up to look like George Washington had to be destroyed when producers saw the actor smoking a cigarette in them.

Roach divided *The Dramatic Hour* into four different segments so that each could be sponsored by a separate advertiser instead of a single sponsor for the entire 60 minutes.

While *The Dramatic Hour* never became a series, the producer succeeded in launching the 60-minute series *The Children's Hour*, which consisted of four quarter-hour segments. The sequences were "The Little People," a Bible story titled "The Lost Lamb," "Hal Roach Rascals" and "The Clown." "The Clown" was a pantomime; "Rascals," a reincarnation of the *Our Gang* comedies. "The Little People" featured Angie, who lives on a cloud and has wings but cannot help being mean on occasion, and Impy (Frankie Darro), who isn't quite bad enough to be in Hell because he sometimes does a good deed. Maureen O'Sullivan appeared throughout the four segments as mistress of ceremonies.

In 1950, Roach Studios negotiated a deal with Magnavox to make two one-hour TV "movies" for *The Magnavox Theater*, the company's anthology series. The anthology usually aired live productions (as did most such series in TV's early days) but for the series' final presentations, Roach produced filmed episodes.

The first, airing November 24, 1950, was a TV adaptation of the Alexandre Dumas novel *The Three Musketeers*, starring Robert Clarke as D'Artagnan, John Hubbard as Athos, Mel Archer as Porthos and Keith Richards as Aramis. The production, filmed over four and a half days, used four sets in addition to a ranch location. One camera shot the entire show. Each scene was rehearsed three or four times before being filmed. Shot first was the master scene, and then closer angles and close-ups.

Based on a story from *The Saturday Evening Post*, the second production was filmed in the same way as the first. Titled "Hurricane at Pilgrim Hill," it starred Virginia Grey as Janet Smedley Adams, David Bruce as her husband Tom, an attorney, Cecil Kellaway as Jonathan Huntoon Smith and Clem Bevans as Sam "Bigmouth" Smedley. Sam travels from Wyoming to Pilgrim Hill, Massachusetts, to visit his granddaughter Janet. He discovers that wealthy Smith, Tom's most important client, is causing a lot of stress for the Adamses as well as for his daughter and her blue-collar boyfriend. Grandpa Smedley decides to make Smith "disappear." He performs a rain dance that he learned from Native Americans in Wyoming. A deluge results, and Smith is nowhere to be found. Eventually discovered on an island off the Massachusetts coast, he is rescued by his daughter's boyfriend and Bigmouth. Thankful, Smith no longer objects to his daughter marrying her boyfriend.

Another TV movie, *Tales of Robin Hood* (not shown on *Magnavox Theater*) was a joint venture between Roach's son Hal Roach Jr. and Robert Lippert, who formed R&L Productions. Made in late 1951, it starred Robert Clarke as Robin Hood and Mary Hatcher as Maid Marian. *Tales of Robin Hood* (aka *Robin Hood and the Golden Arrow*) related the origin story of the hero who robbed from the rich and gave to the poor. In the film, Robin Hood's father, the Earl of Chester, is killed. Before he dies, he advises his son to always fight for his country. Robin Hood grows up and battles against the tyranny of Sir Gui (Paul Cavanagh), who imposes taxes on his citizens and confiscates their land if they don't pay. Maid Marian, Friar Tuck (Ben Welden) and Little John (Wade Crosby) join Robin Hood's group. Robin ends up killing Sir Alan (Keith Richards), who had murdered Robin's father, and then Robin and his men fight Sir Gui's soldiers to the point where Sir Gui decides to make Robin the official Earl of Chester, inheriting his father's estate. It was hoped that a television series would evolve from the production; it never materialized. The film was later exhibited in movie theaters.

A *New York Times* article about this project indicated that Roach sought to set a time and low-cost record for making the film:

> Working ten hours a day, the *Tales of Robin Hood* unit has been completing about 20 minutes of film a day compared to the average of five minutes, which is regarded as good. Mr. Roach says the secret lies in thorough pre-production preparation, especially in working out beforehand the placement of sets and such matters as camera angles and lighting which can develop into problems that cost time and money.[3]

Roach Jr. and Roland Reed's *The Trouble with Father* and *My Little Margie*

Not surprisingly, given his father's production of comedy shorts for movie theaters, Hal Roach Jr.'s strong suit in television was producing various comedy series and pilots.

In 1950, Roach Jr., along with Roland Reed, launched the first successful filmed TV situation comedy, *The Trouble with Father* (aka *The Stu Erwin Show*); it ran on ABC for five seasons. Roach Jr. seemed to always have financial problems with his projects, and tried to solve them by entering into partnerships with other producers. The *Trouble with Father* sponsor wanted a $250,000 cash bond to insure delivery of the initial 26 episodes. Roach Jr. asked Reed to attend a meeting concerning the bond and emerged with a signed contract eliminating the bond requirement.

The comedy starred long-time movie actor Stu Erwin playing a high school principal with June Collyer, his real-life wife, as his TV wife June. Sheila James appeared as their daughter Jackie along with Ann E. Todd and then Merry Anders as their other daughter Joyce. The resulting sitcom was similar to the unsuccessful *Brown Family* pilot that Roach Sr. made.

The series concerned a somewhat befuddled father and an understanding wife. During its run, it had other titles, e.g., *Life with the Erwins* and, in its final season, *The New Stu Erwin Show*. The series had "predictable" storylines with the well-meaning plans of the various characters creating confusion because they never explained to others what they had in mind. Erwin portrayed a somewhat similar character (the absent-minded manager of an apartment house) in the radio series *Phone Again Finnegan*.

In one episode, "Contest," Stu gets involved in a popularity contest

The cast of *The Trouble with Father* (left to right): Stu Erwin, Sheila James, Ann E. Todd and June Collyer. Erwin's character often found himself confused by the problems dreamed up by his two growing daughters and his wife on the series.

for high school students being held by the local drug store. As the principal, Stu decides to stop the contest, but Joyce, who is competing against her friend Nancy Johnson, says that Nancy is spreading a rumor that Stu brought a halt to the contest because he knew that Joyce would lose. Stu reconsiders. Joyce then learns that Nancy is way ahead in votes and wants her dad to stop the contest again. However, instead of doing that, Stu and his wife begin buying a lot of items at the drug store since each of their cash register receipts shows a vote for their daughter. Nancy's mother and father begin doing the same for their daughter. Mr. Johnson decides to become a partner in the store for $8000, meaning that his daughter will win. When he informs Nancy of his plan, she begins demanding several items to further enhance her popularity. Stu ends up winning the contest when Johnson applies his $8000 toward votes for Stu's daughter.

In the episode "Spooks," Jackie devises a plan to disrupt her sister's party for an initiate. Since Jackie is not permitted to attend, she takes a skeleton from school to frighten the attendees. At the party, Joyce plans to have a boy dress as a skeleton to scare the initiate. Confusion ensues over which is the real skeleton and which is the person in a skeleton costume.

The episodes were shot in assembly-line fashion to reduce costs; each episode took two days and cost $10,000. The actors reported to work every morning at 8:30 and filmed until 6:00 p.m. Separate sets were made for each room in the Erwin house with all episode scenes involving one set shot at the same time, out of sequence. Action would stop only for the actors to change clothes for the various scenes.

In another partnership with Roland Reed, Roach Jr. produced *My Little Margie*. While most TV comedies featuring funny duos focused on husbands and wives or mismatched roommates, *My Little Margie* concerned the relationship between a widowed father and his adult daughter living under one roof.

Originally, Mona Freeman was to star as Margie; Wanda Hendrix and Marjorie Reynolds were also under consideration for the role before Gale Storm got the part. Charles Farrell played Vern Albright, Margie's widowed father; Clarence Kolb appeared as Mr. Honeywell, Vern's boss; Don Hayden portrayed Freddie, Margie's boyfriend, and Gertrude Hoffman had the role of Mrs. Odets, Margie's neighbor and co-conspirator in many of her schemes.

According to Storm's biographer David Tucker, Roach Jr.'s interactions with his own teenage daughter (he thought she was difficult to handle and wondered what she would be like at 21) partly inspired *My Little Margie*. Roach turned the idea over to writer Frank Fox, who developed the characters. Fox had a secretary named Margie, which is where the character's name came from.[4]

The series started in 1952 as a summer replacement for *I Love Lucy*. It was popular with viewers, so NBC brought it back as a regular series before it was picked up by CBS again.

The premiere, "Reverse Psychology," had Margie attempting to use reverse psychology on her father over his dislike for her boyfriend. Margie begins agreeing with Vern that she doesn't really like Freddie. At the same time, Mr. Honeywell suggests that Vern use reverse psychology on Margie by saying that he really likes Freddie. Both Margie and her dad think that their tactics are working on the other. Margie tells Freddie what she is doing and then discovers that she and her father have been reading the same book on the subject.

Margie sees her dad's girlfriend Roberta (Hillary Brooke), who lives across the hall, carrying a wedding dress and jumps to the conclusion that her dad is getting married. Vern and Roberta board the same train, traveling separately, and Margie and Freddie follow. Vern sees Margie and Freddie and thinks they are eloping. In the end, all misunderstandings are resolved.

The series seemed familiar to viewers probably because the characters and situations were similar to those on *I Love Lucy*. The conflicts between Margie and her dad were like those between Lucy and Ricky. Like the character of Ethel Mertz on *I Love Lucy*, Mrs. Odets was Margie's ally in her misadventures. To illustrate, in "Margie Sings Opera," Margie is asked by her friend Ginny to meet with a family friend, an Italian opera singer, and pretend that she is Ginny since Ginny doesn't have time to visit with him. When meeting with the singer, Margie asks him to attend a party with one of her dad's important clients since the client wants to meet celebrities. However, when she goes to bring the opera singer to the party, Ginny's father is there, and so Margie's attempt to impersonate his daughter ends. With the help of Mrs. Odets, Margie puts on a fat suit and skull cap to pose as the singer. When the guests ask her to sing, she lip-syncs to one of his recordings. The record gets stuck, causing embarrassment, and then her fat suit over-inflates and explodes. At the last moment, Ginny brings the real opera singer to the party.

Roach Jr. contemplated making a musical movie version of *My Little Margie*, to be filmed in 1955, but the project never materialized.

Duffy's Tavern

Roach's TV version of the long-running radio comedy *Duffy's Tavern* was syndicated for one season in 1954. As on the radio show, Duffy, owner of the café where the "elite meet to eat," never appeared. Archie (Ed Gardner), the central character, often spoke to Duffy on the telephone. Others in the cast were Pattie Chapman as Miss Duffy, the owner's daughter, Alan Reed as Finnegan, a dimwitted but faithful customer, and Jimmy Conlin as Charley the waiter.

On the premiere, "Grand Opening," Duffy's Tavern has no customers. Everyone is at the ice cream parlor next door. Archie learns that it is so popular because it is a front for a gambling establishment. He reports the activity to the police. When the boss of the gambling operation comes by, Archie mistakes him for a police detective. The real detective shows up and Archie realizes his error. After the gambling boss threatens him, Archie clams up. Because he still needs to show Duffy that the tavern is making money, Charley comes up with a plan to lure customers back by advertising that a diamond ring has been lost in the tavern's chicken fricassee. All of the ice cream parlor customers come to the tavern ordering the chicken dish. To get even with Archie for taking away his customers, the mob boss moves his gambling equipment to the tavern's kitchen where the police find it. After the detective identifies the mobster from prior encounters with him, he is arrested.

Like the main character in Roach Sr.'s comedy attempt *Botsford's Beanery*, Archie often became involved in crackpot schemes which he believes will benefit him but they have the opposite effect. In "Archie, the Politician," he is convinced to run for alderman by Harrigan the Hipster. He has to give Harrigan $50 for posters, buttons, etc., only to learn from the police that the position of alderman was abolished years ago. Harrigan then suggests that Archie run for state treasurer and asks him for more money for that campaign. The cops tell Archie that Harrigan is a con man. Archie decides to run for the treasurer position on his own and raises money by putting on a pageant presenting his life story and emphasizing that he is against graft. In the final tally, Archie earns a single vote.

Movie Stars Try Television

In the early 1950s, Roach Jr. attempted to launch TV series for several movie actors dipping their toes in the new medium. Most of these comedy attempts were of the "feel-good," warm-hearted variety.

Roach Jr. contemplated a comedy project in 1951 with movie actor William Bendix. Bendix would have reprised his role as McGuerin, a Brooklyn taxi driver who starts his own cab service. The actor had played this role in Roach Sr.'s movie *The McGuerins of Brooklyn* (1942) and its sequels *Brooklyn Orchid* (1942) and *Taxi, Mister* (1943). The project never got off the ground.

A comic movie actor and radio show star, Joe E. Brown played the widowed owner of a general store in 1952's *The Joe E. Brown Show*, a pilot for a gentle syndicated comedy-melodrama produced by Roach Jr. without a laugh track. The planned series co-starred Sally Fraser as Joe's daughter Janie and Anthony Sykes as his young son. Helen Spring appeared as Janie's mentor Laura, who is in love with Joe. George Carlton Brown and Edward E. Seabrook, the long-time Hal Roach Studios writers who scripted series like *Racket Squad* and *My Little Margie*, authored the script for this pilot.

In announcing the pilot, Roach commented, "Joe is one of the great comedians and humanitarians of our time and I am confident his series will quickly establish itself as a favorite and remain so for as long as Joe sees fit to continue it."[5]

The setting for the unsold pilot was Greendale, a typical American small town. Always attempting to help others, Joe relates the tale of new arrivals in town, Steve Bergerman (Steven Geray) and his wife and son. Steve, a mechanic, isn't having any luck finding a job, so Brown hires him to help out at his store. Henry Crockett (Robert Foulk), a factory foreman, dislikes Bergerman because he speaks with an accent. Bergerman decides to quit since he thinks people don't accept him. Joe decides to hold a "basket party" for the Bergerman family where everyone in town brings a covered dish of food so that the townspeople can meet the family. Bergerman impresses everyone when he recites the Preamble to the Constitution when no one else seems to remember it. When a fire breaks out at the factory, Bergerman repairs the fire engine pump in time to save the building, and as a result he gets a job there.

Roach Jr. next produced, with Bert Granet, a pilot for ABC, *The Laraine Day Show* (aka *White Collar Girl*). The 1953 unaired pilot starred the film actress as Nancy Hale, a fashion designer from the Midwest trying to make it in New York City. Mary Beth Hughes played her roommate Jennie Turner. Both lived at the Martha Ross Hotel where Lee Patrick worked as the desk clerk.

The storyline had Nancy arriving in New York where she promptly loses her wallet with all her money in a taxi cab. She meets her roommate Jennie and Jennie's former roommate Jane (Dawn Addams), who was left at the altar by her intended Eddie (Fess Parker). Eddie later stops by the hotel seeking Jane, who is returning to her Montana hometown after the aborted marriage ceremony. Eddie explains that he couldn't make it to his wedding because he was inducted into the Army. Nancy takes him to Penn Station to reunite with Jane. Later, Nancy schedules a job interview with a fashion design company, and her wallet is returned by the cab driver.

In another family comedy attempt by Roach Jr. with plenty of nostalgia, James Lydon, known to movie audiences for playing Henry Aldrich in several films, starred as Andrew Todd in the unsold pilot for a series called *It Seems Like Yesterday*. Mary Anderson played his wife Sue. This 1954 pilot for ABC concerned a couple, married for 20 years, who flash-back to episodes as newlyweds in the early 1930s when a current situation seemed similar to a past one.

When their son quits his job after losing his temper, the son asks if his dad ever lost his temper. The couple relate an incident that happened early in their marriage, during the Great Depression. Sue wants to get a job to help with finances, but Andrew is against it. Saying that she is not married, Sue goes out on her own to seek employment at Carlton's Department Store where Andrew works. Once she is hired, the store manager Mr. Harris (Douglas Fowley) begins flirting with her. Andrew intends to put a stop to the flirtation. He ultimately loses his temper and is fired by Harris.

Andrew gets a job as a flagpole sitter and he will receive $1000 if he breaks the record of 23 days for sitting atop a flagpole. Later, Sue finds out she is pregnant and is late for work. Harris challenges her, but she talks with the store's owner Mr. Carlton (Charles Halton), who lays down the law to Harris. Mr. Carlton tells Andrew that he has his old job back and raises his salary to $30 a week. Returning to the present, the family laughs about the incident.

Film and radio scribe Jean Holloway wrote the pilot. Peter Lind Hayes and his wife Mary Healy were originally considered for the leads in the planned series.

Blondie

Roach Jr. attempted to bring the comic strip *Blondie* to TV with Pamela Britton as Blondie and Hal LeRoy as Dagwood. The proposed 1954 series would co-star Stuffy Singer as Alexander, Mimi Gibson as Cookie, Robert Burton as Mr. Dithers, Isabel Withers as Cora Dithers and Robin Raymond as Tootsie.

In the pilot, Dagwood's boss Mr. Dithers orders Dagwood to buy a gun for his collection and doesn't want his wife Cora to find out about it. While looking for a gift for her husband, Blondie and the kids see Dagwood entering a sporting goods store to purchase the gun. Although Dithers had given Dagwood $50 to buy the weapon, Dagwood wants to see if he can bargain for a lower price. He leaves the store planning to return, hoping for a better deal. Blondie then decides to buy the derringer for her husband's birthday gift and puts $20 down toward the purchase. Unbeknownst to both Blondie and Dagwood, they become involved in a bidding war over the gun. After work, Dagwood returns home for his birthday dinner where the family presents him with the derringer. When Mr. Dithers and his wife Cora show up, Dagwood gives the gun to his boss as a gift so that Cora doesn't think her husband spent money on it.

Prior to Roach's involvement with *Blondie*, producer Stephen Slesinger had sought to bring the comic strip to TV. Slesinger, a New York literary agent, acquired the rights to several iconic literary characters and adapted them to various media. He took out patents for the TV versions of various comic strips and in the late 1940s demonstrated animated versions of *Dick Tracy* and *Otto the King*.

Slesinger had acquired rights to A.A. Milne's Winnie the Pooh in 1930 and created dolls, records, board games and films based on the character. In the late 1930s, he developed the characters of Red Ryder and King of the Royal Mounted, the latter based on Zane Grey's works.

In the late 1940s and early 1950s, Slesinger began producing films and TV pilots based on the characters to which he had acquired the rights. Stephen Slesinger Productions established itself in 1950 to turn Red Ryder, Winnie the Pooh and Blondie into TV series.

Titled *The Blondie Story*, the project starred Arthur Lake as Dagwood Bumstead and his real-life family as the other characters: his wife Patricia as Blondie, daughter Marion as Cookie, and son Arthur Jr. as Alexander. Patricia was either the niece of actress Marion Davies or, as some have reported, the illegitimate daughter of Davies and William Randolph Hearst.

Chic Young, creator of the *Blondie* strip, served as script consultant for the TV series with 52 episodes planned. Upon announcing the expected series, the Lakes remarked, "We've been wanting to do this for a long time. It feels good to know the public wants us, as much as we want to do it. We've received hundreds of letters suggesting it."[6] The pilot cost about $30,000. The William Morris agency scheduled screenings of the film for potential advertisers at Romanoff's in Hollywood, the Waldorf-Astoria in New York City and the Ambassador East in Chicago.

There were apparently no takers because in 1952, Slesinger did another pilot with an all-new cast. He hired Jeff Donnell and John Harvey to play the main characters; they were to appear in both the series and a planned film, but Slesinger's unexpected death in 1953 seemed to bring a halt to these projects.

In 1957, Roach Jr. finally launched a TV version of *Blondie* with Arthur Lake as the dim-witted Dagwood and Pamela Britton as his more level-headed wife. Ann Barnes played Cookie; Stuffy Singer appeared as Alexander; Hal Peary landed the role of Herb Woodley, and Florenz Ames was J.C. Dithers. The series aired on NBC from January to September of '57.

The 1954 pilot described above was remade for the 1957 *Blondie*. The acting, particularly by Lake, was very broad with Dagwood yelling "Blondie!" at the top of his lungs, usually when encountering a problem. The typical episode had Dagwood getting into some type of trouble. For example, in "The Trouble with Birds," a client of the Dithers' company is impressed with Dagwood's critique of the design of a supermarket he wants Dithers to build. The client suggests that Dagwood handle the construction. When the Bumstead family shows up at the site, Cookie sees a bird's nest with eggs in it in a tree that is about to be bulldozed. She pleads with her dad not to have the tree taken down, and he agrees. Herb Woodley snaps a photo of Dagwood and Cookie which is printed in the local newspaper with an article about construction being stopped on the project. When Dithers reads the article, he is enraged and threatens to fire Dagwood. Dagwood permits the foundation to be done but prevents the tree from being removed. He comes up with the idea to build sections of the supermarket offsite and then each section is moved to the site with a courtyard in the center where the tree is.

More '50s Comedy Projects

It's Always Sunday, airing January 11, 1956, was, like the Joe E. Brown pilot, a heart-warming comedy attempt by Roach Jr. about a minister (movie actor Dennis O'Keefe) as the Reverend Charles Parker, who believes in doing good for the unfortunate. Itinerants Eddie (Chick Chandler) and George (Sheldon Leonard) arrive in town. Believing that Parker will provide food to only one of them, George shows up at the Parker house. After feeding him, the reverend gets the idea from George for his next sermon on the subject, "trust thyself and it will follow that you will find trust from your fellow man." Subsequently, the minister learns that today is his wedding anniversary and that he has to perform a wedding ceremony for a young couple. He trusts George to take a sports car and pick up an anniversary gift. Hours go by and no sign of George. The car owner asks the police to find George. A police officer brings the car, George and Eddie back to the preacher's house where George says that he took the car to pick up Eddie, who was inspired by the minister's sermon about trust. Fay Wray played Mary Parker, Charles' wife. The pilot never became a series.

In 1955, Roach Jr. tried to finalize a deal to bring the iconic comedy team of Laurel and Hardy back to the studio. Renewed public interest in the team came about after their films were shown on TV and after their appearance on an episode of Ralph Edwards' *This Is Your Life.* As reported by Erskine Johnson in his March 14, 1955, "Hollywood Today" column: "[T]alks have been going on between Roach and the comedians for weeks. The blueprint calls for six features to be made over a one-year period. Then the footage will be re-edited into two feature-length pictures for European theater showings." Johnson followed up in a May 19, 1955, column: "The first hour-long film for TV starring Stan Laurel and Oliver Hardy goes before Hal Roach Jr.'s cameras as soon as Stan puts finishing touches on his own script. The plot has them playing

Pilgrims."[7] Another account states that there were to be four one-hour specials to be made with the title *Laurel and Hardy's Fabulous Fables* with the shows being comic opera versions of fairy tales.[8]

A few months later, reports were that NBC and Roach were ready to close a deal under which the team would make three 90-minute color films for the network. The films would be presented as NBC spectaculars and then released to theaters.[9] In the end, no such TV specials ever resulted, presumably because of the ill health of the two comedians.

Also in 1955, Roach Jr. sought to make a pilot starring Norwegian figure skater Sonja Henie. After her career as an Olympic skater, Henie starred in several Twentieth Century–Fox movies in the '30s and '40s, most of them comedies. Thirty-nine episodes were envisioned, built around the concept of what goes on behind the scenes as Henie takes her ice show on tour. Liberal doses of Henie on ice were to featured on *The Sonja Henie Show*. Not clear is whether this planned show would be a drama or a comedy. One March 1955 account stated that it would be "a half-hour dramatic series on film."[10] Another news article indicated, "It's another situation comedy idea...."[11] Given that Henie's most successful movies were comedies, one can presume that this project would have been a comedy rather than a drama. It never got off the ground.

In 1957, Roach Jr. tried *Cindy*, a comedy starring child actress Evelyn Rudie. This sitcom focused on an orphan whose parents died in an auto accident. Cindy goes to live with her bachelor uncle (Robert Rockwell). The unrealized show, for ABC, co-starred Margaret Hamilton as Rockwell's housekeeper, who becomes Cindy's nanny.

Reflecting on the unsold pilot, Rudie remarked, "[T]he experience itself was great—everyone was terrific—treated me like a pro (instead of like a 'kid'). Robert Rockwell was charming (I had a huge crush on him). Margaret Hamilton was a dream—she was so nice, we went over our lines together. I really felt as though she and I were part of a family."[12]

Roach subsequently partnered with comedian Ben Blue and Blue J Productions to make a pilot called *Ben Blue's Brothers* featuring the comedian in multiple roles including himself and his four brothers: an unemployed vaudeville entertainer, a henpecked industrialist, a Charlie Chaplin–like tramp and an average guy. Character actress Ruth McDevitt played the brothers' mother. Blue had once worked for Roach's father in the *Taxi Boys* series of comedy shorts. *Ben Blue's Brothers* did not become a series.

In 1958, Roach Jr. co-produced a proposed comedy, *The Fabulous*

Oliver Chantry, starring George Sanders as a New York columnist. Sanders had portrayed a similar character type in the film *All About Eve*. Doris Singleton appeared as Chantry's secretary Sally Parker, and Steven Geray played his butler.

Chantry lives in an ultra-modern apartment with push-button accommodations such as a desk that descends from the ceiling to his bed so that he can work from bed. Chantry's secretary works in a section of his living room.

In the unsold pilot, Rachel (Ellen Corby), a wardrobe mistress whom Chantry knows, is upset that another New York columnist has written that her niece Lois (Ann Baker) will not be appearing in the play *The Grenadier*. Reacting to the column, Lois wants to give up acting and marry Bob (Doug McClure), a farmer from upstate New York. Oliver thinks he can get Lois the lead in the play. The play's director wants an acting couple, Alfred (Ian Keith) and Lynn Barry (Cicely Browne), who had previously appeared in the work, to star in the revival.

Chantry convinces Lois not to give up the stage and throws a party for the Barrys in order to pit the couple against each other. He contacts various other newspaper columnists to spread rumors about the poor relationship between the Barrys. At the party, Alfred talks with Lois about her playing opposite him. Lynn and Alfred argue. She says that she will not be in the play and accuses Alfred of starting the rumors. After Lois lands the female lead in the revival, Chantry learns that she is doing a terrible acting job. He thinks this is because she is still in love with Bob. Later, Lois admits to loving Bob and being distraught over his return home. Bob and Lois reunite, and Chantry goes to see Lynn Barry to convince her to work with Alfred. Lynn reconciles with her husband, and they star in the revival.

Roach Jr. sought to bring Broadway legend Ethel Merman to the small screen in 1958 in *Carnival*, a variety show that would feature both songs and comedy. A pilot was never made, because Merman got the role of Mama Rose in the musical *Gypsy* and asked Roach to release her from the pilot commitment so she could begin preparations for her return to the Great White Way.

Roach's final unsuccessful attempt at launching a comedy series was inspired by the radio show *McGarry and His Mouse*: The planned TV series *McGarry and Me* was set to star movie actors Michael O'Shea and Virginia Mayo. Married in real life, the O'Sheas played Dan and Kitty McGarry—he, a police officer, she, a homemaker. In the pilot, Dan loses two weeks' pay gambling with his colleagues at the police station using confiscated equipment. Kitty investigates how his money disappeared.

Love That Jill

One of the final comedy series launched by Roach Jr., *Love that Jill* starred the husband-wife team of Robert Sterling and Anne Jeffreys, who had become popular playing the ghostly couple on *Topper*. The "battle of the sexes" comedy premiered as a midseason replacement on ABC in January 1958 and lasted until April 1958. Jeffreys appeared as Jill Johnson, the head of a modeling agency who continually tries to recruit models or clients from a rival agency owned by Jack Gibson (Sterling). Gibson likewise competes with the Johnson firm but seems more interested in romancing Jill. The show was originally titled *Jacques and Jill* and then *Me and Jill*. Sterling labeled the series a romantic comedy, "sort of like the Irene Dunne film comedies."[13] Series creator Alex Gottlieb characterized the series as being all about the "chase": "And *not* a Western chase even though I may be laughing with spurs in my eyes. This is the adventurous pursuit of maid by man." He added that the series will present "weekly lessons on how to stalk a girl and how to trap a man. But I'm not going to let them get married unless the sponsor insists on it."[14] Maybe because *Love That Jill* differed from other 1950s comedies (it presented two single characters each operating their own businesses), viewers rejected the somewhat sophisticated (for the era) concept.

The debut of this comedy, titled "Tonight's the Night," had Jack and Jill feuding over two of Jill's top models. Jack is about to win the women to his camp with contracts waiting for their signatures when Jill devises a plan to hold on to them. A subsequent episode had Jack trying to win a week of dates with Jill by stacking the cards on a Unifact computer used on the TV show *Find Your Perfect Mate*. In another episode, Jack persuades Jill to join him and an old Army buddy for dinner. The buddy turns out to be a very pretty girl that Jack hopes will make Jill jealous. In "Hug the Hillbilly," Jill discovers that one of her models is under age and tricks Jack into escorting her home to her father in the Ozarks.

Bringing Back the Stars of *My Little Margie*

Roach premiered *The Gale Storm Show* (aka *Oh, Susanna*), created by Lee Karson, on CBS in September 1956. The series had been sold to Nestlé even before the pilot film was completed. Starring *My Little Margie*'s Gale Storm as Susanna Pomeroy, social director on a cruise ship, the comedy lasted four seasons. ZaSu Pitts appeared as Esmerelda "Nugie" Nugent, operator of the ship's beauty parlor and Susanna's cohort in her misadventures (similar to the character of Mrs. Odets on *Margie*). Roy Roberts played the cruise ship captain whose character, often disapproving of Susanna's antics, was somewhat like Vern Albright on Storm's prior sitcom.

As critic John Crosby put it, "From time to time, there are glints of humor in *Oh, Susanna* as there were glints in *My Little Margie*.... But they all sound not only very much like each other but also very much like dozens of others of these machine-tooled, production-line films that come out of the Hollywood dream factory."

Crosby described a typical episode thusly: "[Gale] is incessantly getting herself in trouble and, when she does that, the captain rolls his eyes Heavenward and says 'Oh, Susanna,' or her roommate (ZaSu Pitts) says 'Oh, Susanna,' or someone else says 'Oh, Susanna.' And then the captain tries to fire her, but it turns out that the chimpanzee that had got into the air-conditioner was really the long-lost pet of the president of the line."[15] Instead of being terminated, Susanna receives a bonus.

As with other sitcoms of the era, several episodes of the series were built around misunderstandings, usually involving mistaken identities. In "Passenger Incognito," Nancy Kulp starred as plain-looking Helga Peterson, looking for romance and adventure on her cruise. At the same time, authorities are searching the ship for a jewel thief known as "The Countess." Susanna has Nugie makeover Miss Peterson into a "woman of mystery" and gives her fake jewelry to wear. The authorities believe that Miss Peterson is the thief after Susanna says that the woman is a countess traveling incognito. When Nugie sees the two detectives searching Peterson's room, she concludes that they are the thieves. Nugie and Susanna enlist Helga's help in capturing the pair with Miss Peterson displaying all of her fake jewels. However, the detectives end up arresting the real thief with Susanna collecting the reward for the thief's capture. A male passenger asks Helga for her hand in marriage.

In 1958, Roach sold past episodes of the series, and the rights to make new ones, to Independent Television Corporation. ITC moved the series to ABC.

Roach also produced a vehicle for *My Little Margie*'s Charles Farrell. Like the *Margie* series, *The Charlie Farrell Show* started out as a temporary replacement for *I Love Lucy* in the summer of 1956. However, unlike *My Little Margie*, it was not that successful; only 12 episodes were made. Farrell played the owner and manager of the Palm Springs Racquet Club, a resort that the actor did actually own. This workplace comedy dealt with the problems Farrell encountered in running the resort. Reviewers were not kind to the show, one writing:

Charles Farrell is a nice guy and his Racquet Club in Palm Springs, Calif., is a nice place. But that pleasant state of affairs is not necessarily just cause for CBS-TV to launch a filmed "situation comedy" series about Farrell and the club.

To me, last week's opener of *The Charlie Farrell Show* was the dullest and most cliche-laden effort at being funny I've seen in a long, long time.

The plot was so absurd, the gags so ancient and bearded, the double-takes of the actors so Mack Sennett that there is absolutely nothing to say about it.[16]

As with many other Roach sitcoms, plots revolved around some type of misunderstanding. In the first episode, Charlie believes that a scandal writer is about to do an exposé on his club for a national magazine. Actually, the club's chef is writing an article about favorite recipes of movie stars. This misunderstanding ends up landing Charlie in the hospital with a fake stomach ache, hiding in a laundry cart and experiencing other misadventures.

About the series, critic John Crosby opined, "If my instinct is at all sound, there will be endless cases in *The Charlie Farrell Show* of con men mistaken for important movie directors and treated royally, and important movie directors being mistaken for con men and thrown, sputtering with rage, into jail."[17]

"Reality" Crime Dramas

Like several other producers profiled in this book, Roach Jr. seemed to specialize in crime dramas based on real-life incidents. In 1950, he began syndicating the police drama *Racket Squad* starring Reed Hadley as Police Captain John Braddock. Hadley had starred in several B movies as well as on various radio series. In June 1951, CBS picked up *Racket Squad*, which ran until 1953. Following the pattern of many subsequent crime dramas, the episodes were based on stories taken from police and similar agency files. Produced by Showcase Productions (co-owned by Roach and Carroll Case), the program dealt with confidence schemes like bogus charities, the selling of fake paintings, peddling phony stocks and bonds, and fraudulent séance schemes.

In 1956, Roach released to movie theaters the feature-length *Mobs, Inc.*, which consisted of three *Racket Squad* episodes cobbled together. It begins at the Los Angeles Police Academy showing Captain Braddock lecturing rookie officers about confidence rackets. One story concerned a dancer and a racketeer masquerading as a writer and photographer tasked by a magazine to do an article on a millionaire's home but really intending to rob it. The second episode involved a wealthy newspaper publisher being swindled by a crooked stock syndicate, and the third related the story of a young man who claims the hot springs on his property cured his arthritis. He tries to get the town council to purchase the property for far more than it is worth until the police arrive with proof that he was never crippled in the first place.

Roach Jr.'s next crime drama attempt, *Code 3* for ABC, planned to present stories based on actual files from the Los Angeles Police Department. "Code 3" signifies a police emergency requiring immediate action. As an advertisement for the series stated. "All policemen know the chilling meaning of those two words: somewhere a cop is in real trouble."[18] Don Siegel directed the 1954 pilot, on which Ted De Corsia made opening and closing remarks about the story. Three years after the pilot, Roach Jr. and Roland Reed made additional episodes with Richard Travis as Sheriff George Barnett taking over the De Corsia role. (Roach presumably resurrected *Code 3* based on the success of the syndicated *Highway Patrol* with Broderick Crawford, described in Chapter 8.) Roach sold the series of 39 episodes to local television stations beginning April 2, 1957.

Code 3 focused on the characterization of the perpetrator and/or victim of the story with police detectives appearing as supporting actors. The first episode, "The Rookie Sheriff," concentrated on the training of deputy sheriff recruits. One of them, a refugee from Czechoslovakia named Rancich (Peter Van Eyck), has lived under both Nazi and Communist dictatorships and has misgivings about American law enforcement practices; he believes that policing involves dominating everyone through physical and mental superiority. Out in the field, Rancich overreacts to a man insulting another officer. Rancich wants to resign from the academy, but the head of the training unit refuses to let him. Rancich then receives high marks for defusing a situation involving a Hungarian man and his wife, who were threatening to shoot officers trying to serve a search warrant. When Rancich tells the man that American police do not use force, he gains the respect of his superiors.

"The Sniper" relayed the story of a phantom gunman terrorizing Los Angeles County killing women. George Thayer, a frustrated realtor having a dry spell in selling properties, is jealous of his wife Marie, an art gallery owner who is more successful than he is. When he is shot at in the driveway of his home, he contacts police saying that the L.A. sniper committed the act. Hidden behind bushes, George then shoots his wife, injuring her leg but not killing her. After she returns home from the hospital, she becomes suspicious of her husband—as do the police. When the police visit the Thayer home again to collect more evidence, they find that the shot fired at Mr. Thayer wasn't fired by the sniper. Mrs. Thayer says that her husband is sick and has been trying to kill her. George used the story of the sniper to cover up his own malicious intent. He is arrested. The real L.A. sniper is later caught and put on trial.

Alias Mike Hercules, an unsold crime drama pilot, starred future *Leave It to Beaver* dad Hugh Beaumont as a character that ABC described as a "hard-talking, quick-thinking private eye who looks for trouble ... and finds it ... on the San Francisco waterfront."[19] Unlike Roach's other crime drama attempts, this one was not based on police files. Like some other private eyes in '50s TV shows who fall into a gray area between the police and law breakers, Mike Hercules (not the character's real name but an alias given to him in prison) had served five years in Alcatraz for a crime he didn't commit. He gained release when the truth came out. Hercules takes the cases of people in trouble because he knows what it's like to be an innocent victim. His friend, the Professor (Reginald Denny), helps the detective solve his cases.

Hercules meets with Vivian Harding (Anne Kimball), daughter of Walter Harding (Roy Roberts); after being incarcerated with Hercules, he is now out of prison. Vivian tells Mike that her now-wealthy father, who has been seeing the attractive Lydia Brady (Marie Windsor), has been kidnapped. Vivian doesn't want to go to the police given her father's criminal history. The kidnappers are demanding a $100,000 ransom. Hercules learns that Max Capallo (Gregg Martell), who worked with Lydia's con-man husband, is behind the kidnapping. Mike and the Professor free Walter and the police are called. Filmed in 1954, the pilot aired in July 1956 on *General Electric Summer Originals*.

Pat O'Brien appeared as Pat Duggan in Roach Jr.'s 30-minute pilot *Parole Chief*, about a caring parole officer who tries to get his parolees on the straight and narrow. Irene Hervey played his wife. Another potential series based on true crime files, *Parole Chief* drew its inspiration from a book by New York State Parole Chief David Dressier concerning cases in that state.

The pilot was filmed in 1954 and eventually aired on *Sneak Preview* as "The Way Back" on July 31, 1956, Duggan, head of the Parole Division, helps Roy Bennett (Robert Arthur), a young man recently released from reform school and attempting to find work. Duggan learns that Roy lives with his aunt and cousin Gene, who is not a good influence. Pat invites Roy home to have dinner with him and his wife and finds the boy a job as a mechanic. Roy soon quits his job, saying that the owner's family doted on him too much. Someone breaks into the garage where Roy had worked, injures the owner and steals a car. Roy confesses that he quit the job because he knew about his cousin's felonious plans. Gene is arrested and Roy returns to work.

At the end of the show, O'Brien makes an impassioned speech to potential sponsors about the importance of parole officers in the community and says that his Pat Duggan character will be similar to his iconic movie characters from the 1930s and 1940s. He also mentions that the next episode will be about a female released from prison.

Producer Roach had made a deal with Vitapix, a television show distribution company owned by 42 stations, to offer *Parole Chief* to national advertisers. Sponsors would pay to advertise on the series at a rate less than what they would pay to sponsor a network show. The idea was to have at least 60 stations involved in the deal. However, no advertisers signed on, and so the pilot never became a series.

Also in 1954, Roach and Carroll Case brought Reed Hadley of *Racket Squad* fame back to television in *Public Defender*. The crime drama, created by Mort Lewis and Sam Shayon, began with Hadley telling viewers what a public defender does:

> A public defender is an attorney employed by the community and responsible for giving legal aid without cost to a person who seeks it and is financially unable to employ private council. It is his duty to defend those accused of a crime until the issue is decided in a court of law. The first public defender's office in the United States was opened in January 1913. Over the years, other offices were opened and today that handful has grown to a network ... a network of lawyers cooperating to protect the rights of our clients.

The first episode, "The Case of the Parolee," had Bart Matthews (Hadley) defending a parolee, Mark Collins, who has been arrested for stealing from his workplace. Collins' girlfriend Alice Parker brings the case to Matthews' attention. In his jail cell, Mark explains to Matthews how he got a job as a bookkeeper at an appliance sales company. There he met Alice, a secretary, along with Fred Davis, a bill collector, and the boss, Mr. Marshall. One day, Davis brought in a considerable amount of cash he collected from customers, and Alice locked the money away. Someone then broke into the office and stole the money. Because Mark served time, the police arrest him.

Matthews learns from Alice that Davis has been receiving calls at the office, supposedly from his brother-in-law. It turns out that Davis bet on the horses and owed money to the caller, who has since been paid. However, the public defender also discovers that Mr. Marshall owed the same fellow and that he, not Collins or Davis, stole from his company.

At the end of each episode, the name of an actual public defender flashed on the screen to salute the individual for outstanding achievement in the cause of justice.

In late 1955, the Ashley-Steiner Agency finalized negotiations with Hal Roach Jr. to produce a TV version of the radio series *Nightwatch*. Similar to the later Fox series *Cops* in concept, this early documentary police series would have been filmed almost entirely on location at night using only whatever light was available. A camouflaged sound truck would follow a police car with cameras shooting actual incidents as they transpire. A pilot scheduled to be filmed around the beginning of February 1956 never was.

Roach Jr. next attempted to launch a 1956 series titled *Probe* starring Wendell Corey as Daniel Padgett, a medical pathologist. The pilot focused on a man accused of murdering his co-worker. Padgett proves that the victim died by inhaling beryllium dust at his workplace. The company assumes responsibility for the death it caused. The story for this unsuccessful crime drama pilot apparently was not derived from a real case.

Anthologies and Melodramas

In 1952, Roach executive-produced a pilot for an anthology series created by Joan Harrison. Titled *The Female of the Species*, it would have presented soap opera–type stories about women. See Chapter 14 for more details.

The following year, Roach produced an anthology pilot called *Guns of Destiny*, a planned series for ABC. Based on actual events, it would dramatize stories about firearms that played a part in history—from the weapon that killed Lincoln to the one that didn't take Napoleon's life. The producer made at least six installments. He continued to try to sell it through 1956. In that year, Roach combined into one new pilot scenes from each of the episodes and hired Ralph Bellamy to portray a gun collector introducing each of the segments. Still the pilot never became a series.

Co-produced by Roach Jr. and Carroll Case for ABC, the anthology *Tales of a Wayward Inn* would have featured melodramatic stories of people who frequented New York City's legendary Algonquin Hotel. It was based on a same-name book by Frank Case, the Algonquin's owner and manager. Brian Aherne played the inn's owner. The pilot "One Minute from Broadway," filmed in 1953, featured the trite story of a small-town girl (Gloria Talbott) who comes to New York to be an actress. She is befriended by the Wayward Inn's owner, who learns that her grandparents are going to visit her, thinking that she knows all the celebrities in the city. He arranges a party for her with many celebrities in attendance. The girl recites some Shakespeare at the party, impressing everyone, and this leads to the launch of her professional acting career. The unsold pilot aired on ABC on September 29, 1954.

Roach Studios premiered what it considered to be a major anthology on NBC in October 1955. With each episode helmed by a major Hollywood director, *Screen Directors Playhouse* consisted of a series of 30-minute dramas and comedies. There had been a radio version of *Screen Directors Playhouse* that aired on NBC from 1949 to 1951 but that program had a format different from the one produced by Roach. The radio version featured adaptations of popular movies like *Stagecoach* and *The Spiral Staircase* with the directors of the films introducing the radio adaptation and talking with the stars who were in the film.

Leo McCarey wrote and directed the initial episode of the television version of *Screen Directors Playhouse*, "Meet the Governor." A comedy, it opens with a courtroom scene about a butler accused of stealing liquor from his employer, J.J. Dirks (Paul Harvey), a candidate for governor. Defending the butler, Clem Waters (Herb Shriner) questions Dirks, who reveals that he drugged the whiskey to teach his butler a lesson. Waters contends that the butler was taking the whiskey on doctor's orders and that the drugs affected his health. After Waters wins the case, political bosses decide to run him against Dirks. Dirks finds that Waters is married to June (Barbara Hale), a woman from Arizona who has a young son. Waters thought that June's father had her earlier marriage annulled. When June shows up, she informs Clem that the marriage had not been annulled because of her pregnancy. Knowing the impact this will have on his political career, particularly after Clem promised to marry a society lady, he broadcasts a speech withdrawing from the race stating he is returning with his wife and son to Arizona. On the way, he hears over the radio that he won the governorship. To show the viewers that the episode was a comedy, it had a laugh track.

Among the directors of other episodes were John Ford, Fred Zinnemann and George Stevens. The series lasted one season.

In the same year as the launch of *Screen Directors Playhouse*, Roach Jr. purchased his father's interest in Hal Roach Studios, becoming the main owner of the studio's stages and library of films. Also, in 1955, Roach attempted to sell a series, presumably an anthology, first called *Point of Crisis* and then *Moment of Crisis*. Sanctioned by the American

Psychiatric Association, the project would deal with the development of mental illness but steer clear of presenting immediate cures.

Roach Jr. sought to premiere another prestige anthology in 1955, *Pulitzer Prize Playhouse,* a reboot of an early 1950s live ABC series featuring adaptations of stories and plays that had won Pulitzers. Roach's version was never picked up as a series.

Roach Jr. partnered with Jerry Stagg to produce a half-hour anthology called *Telephone Time,* which premiered on CBS on April 8, 1956, and moved to ABC a year later. The series ended its run in April 1958. The Bell Telephone System sponsored the series, hence its title. John Nesbitt originally hosted the show, introducing the episodes which were based on his real-life stories of fascinating people. The venture started out with the title *The Stories of John Nesbitt,* before Bell Telephone became the sponsor. Years earlier, Nesbitt had created a radio and movie short series called *Passing Parade* which focused on strange but true historical events.

The debut installment of *Telephone Time* starred Lon Chaney Jr. as Jules Sameian, "The Golden Junkman." Among the items he has collected is an almost complete set of the *Encyclopædia Britannica.* When his wife passes away, he is left to raise his young sons Philip and Alex. While building a successful salvage business, he encourages his sons to read the set of encyclopedias. The sons enroll in a military academy but, while there, become embarrassed by their father's rather uncouth behavior and his occupation. They go on to college, becoming estranged from their father. Sameian begins educating himself by also reading the encyclopedias, enrolls in college and obtains a degree in two years. When his sons learn of his achievement, they attend his graduation where he acknowledges that he has come to understand his offspring, and the sons indicate that they are proud of their father.

In the episode "Stranded," Bette Davis plays Leslie Enter, a teacher in a one-room Minnesota schoolhouse who becomes stranded with her five pupils during a blizzard. At midday, the electricity and phone go out because of the snowstorm. She builds a fire in an old wood stove using books and desks for fuel. A snowplow attempts to open the road leading to the school but is not making much progress through the heavy drifts. With no more fuel for the stove, Miss Enter has her students walk through an old gulley three-quarters of a mile to meet the snowplow and they are all rescued. The real Miss Enter talks with John Nesbitt at the conclusion of the story.

In April 1957, after Davis appeared on *Telephone Time, Variety* indicated that she would star on a weekly half-hour anthology series, *The Bette Davis Show,* to be produced by Jerry Stagg. She would introduce each episode and act in some of them. The project never came to fruition.

The Roach-Stagg partnership also sought to make an anthology with baseball player Joe DiMaggio as host. The project would deal with the drama behind sporting events. The pilot appeared on *Telephone Time* as "Fight for the Title" with George Brenlin playing lightweight champion Benny Leonard. He encounters a young fighter, Kid Lombard (Michael Landon), who wants to be the lightweight champion. Before his fight with Lombard, Lombard's sister asks Leonard to go easy on her brother since he isn't in the best of health. Leonard tries, but the Kid fights on until he is knocked unconscious. Lombard suffers brain damage. Leonard sees the Kid again at a gym: He is punch drunk but still wants to box. Leonard stages a match with him to permit the Kid to win a pretend championship before Lombard is committed to a sanitarium.

The *Telephone Time* installment "The Vestris" was a back-door pilot for a series called *The Veil* hosted by Boris Karloff. In the pilot, set in 1828, the ship *Vestris* is sailing from England to Boston. Captain Norich's (Torin Thatcher) wife is sick and has a vision in which a man directs her to make the ship change course. The captain reluctantly agrees. As a result, they find three shipwreck survivors, one of whom, Dr. Pierre (Karloff), looks exactly like the spirit in the vision. The doctor saves the captain's wife from dying and is as puzzled as everyone else by the woman's vision.

Roach Jr. made a total of 12 episodes of *The Veil* in 1958, all reportedly based on real incidents of supernatural happenings, but the episodes were never broadcast. Other episodes dealt with people having visions, such as a man having a vision of the murder of his brother, and a son having a vision of his late father who helps the son find the father's will.

Roach made another unsold pilot in 1958, *Battles of the Century* (aka *Bob Considine's on the Battleline*). Based on historical events, the proposed series would dramatize actual battles of World War I, World War II and the Korean conflict. The scripts and narration were to be done by Bob Considine.

Partnered with Jerry Stagg, Roach also sought to produce a new anthology series, *Landmark*, scheduled to begin in January 1959. It would dramatize factual stories of well-known landmarks and historic events around the world. In 1958, Roach made a sales pitch for the planned series, to give potential sponsors an idea of what kind of show it would be. The television promo included four filmclips apparently from episodes of *Telephone Time*. For example, one clip featuring Greer Garson came from the *Telephone Time* episode "Revenge," about America's first female juror. The other clips included a scene about the capture of a German U-boat, scenes set in 1840s Oregon starring Chuck Connors, and a segment about the adventures of Emperor Norton from a *Telephone Time* story.

Shows for Kids and for Women

In 1954, Roach made a *Bozo the Clown* pilot starring Gil Lamb as Bozo. The Bozo character originally was portrayed by Pinto Colvig, who narrated a series of records featuring his clown persona. The Roach project directed at young viewers co-starred seven-year-old Jerilyn James. The concept of the never-realized series involved Bozo and the little girl taking shrinking pills and then being able to speak with birds and animals in a take-off on *Alice in Wonderland*. Larry Harmon purchased the rights to the original Bozo the Clown character in 1956 and then franchised a kids' series starring the clown to various television stations across the country.

The following year, Roach Jr. came up with the idea of a daytime show targeted at females: *Magazine of the Air* would have consisted of dramatic sketches, household hints, lectures, fashion parades, musical numbers and comedy skits. Its proposed title had also been used for some daytime radio series aimed at women. This concept never resulted in a series.

Unsuccessful Western Pilots

As noted in profiles of several other B TV producers in this work, the cowboy genre was immensely popular on TV in the 1950s with many producers seeking to launch such series. Roach Jr. tried a few Western pilots.

In *The Brush Roper*, starring movie actor Walter Brennan, the Brennan character Grandpa Atkins attempts to live up to the tales he's told to his grandson "Cowpoke" (Lee Aaker) about life as a young cowboy. Grandpa is now a farmer, but when he learns from Sub Doyal (Edgar Buchanan) and Art Shirley (Chuck Connors) that a bull is on the loose, he takes "Cowpoke" with him to find the animal and collect a $50 reward. His first attempt to rope the bull ends in disaster with Atkins falling off his horse and being dragged by the bull. On the second attempt, he ropes the bull. However, the bull ends up in a canyon while Grandpa and his horse are trapped in a tree. He is rescued by Doyal and Shirley and ultimately receives the reward for capturing the animal. The pilot aired as an installment of *Screen Directors Playhouse* on November 23, 1955.

Partners, a July 4, 1956, installment of *Screen Directors Playhouse*, dealt with a rodeo star (Casey Tibbs as himself) whose vehicle breaks down near a ranch where he encounters a 14-year-old orphan, Terry Johnson (Brandon De Wilde), along with a stern old man and his grumpy nephew for whom Terry works although he has never been compensated. They forbid Terry to go to a rodeo where he wants to enter a bronco riding contest. Tibbs, feeling sorry for the boy who doesn't recognize Tibbs as the world champion rodeo rider, takes him to the Bitter Creek Rodeo. Along with Terry, Tibbs enters the rodeo under an assumed name so that Terry doesn't know his true identity. Terry wins a $30 prize. They return to the ranch where the nephew is upset that Terry went to the event. Tibbs returns Terry to the orphanage and gets legal guardianship of the boy.

Cavalry Surgeon, a back-door pilot that aired January 14, 1958, on *Telephone Time*, starred John Hudson as William Roberts, an assistant surgeon in the Army during the Mexican-American War in 1847. In the episode, Roberts goes up against a cavalry unit captain who wants all the troops, including those who are injured, to help fight the Mexicans in a planned raid on a blockhouse. The surgeon protects the sick men. The attack on the blockhouse proceeds with a small troop of Americans. A Mexican spy captured by the U.S. forces tells Roberts that the troops are riding into a trap with the blockhouse heavily fortified. Roberts goes to the scene and rescues the wounded captain. He then commandeers a covered wagon to crash into the blockhouse, rousting the Mexicans. Roberts dies in the attack. If the pilot had been picked up as a series, presumably it would have chronicled the careers of other cavalry surgeons.

Roach had no luck in turning any of these pilots into a Western series.

Foreign Intrigue and an Outdoor Adventure Series Attempt

Roach Jr. did produce one popular adventure series in the 1950s and made other adventure series attempts. In 1954, along with Jerry Stagg. he launched a syndicated series, *Passport to Danger*, starring Cesar Romero as diplomatic courier Steve McQuinn. The pilot had been made in 1952, but a series of delays held up the production of more episodes. During that time, Romero was offered the lead role in the *Lone*

Wolf TV series. Roach had to pay him $16,000 in option money to turn down the role.

Created by writer Robert C. Dennis, each episode of the series supposedly took place in a different foreign city. Actually, the show, filmed in Hollywood, featured stock footage of the foreign destinations. In Budapest, McQuinn helps a priest arrested for anti–Communist activity; in Damascus, he protects an Arabian sultan from assassination. Flying to Athens, McQuinn encounters a woman in love with a British Intelligence officer. The woman turns out to be Princess Anne Celia (Carolyn Jones). The intelligence agent, Terrance Holden (Mark Dana) is accepting bribes from drug traffickers to allow the chief narcotics smuggler to remain free. McQuinn finds evidence of the bribes and turns it (and the chief) over to the British. On this adventure series, the McQuinn character either protected people from danger or else became entangled in dangerous situations himself.

Roach also sought to launch an outdoor adventure series called *The Forest Ranger* with Dick Foran in the title role. The pilot, filmed in the San Bernardino Nation Forest in California, depicted the adventures of Ranger Will Roberts. The program, planned for the 1956–57 season, would show various phases of forest ranger work such as conservation, fire prevention and law enforcement. Occasionally, the character of a retired ranger would describe accomplishments of rangers in the past.

Ben Fox co-wrote the script for *The Forest Ranger*. As noted in the next chapter, Fox had created the Roland Reed drama *Waterfront*. In 1956, Fox had signed a contract with Roach to make series for the producer as well as series for Fox's own company. Upon signing the contract, Roach had Fox take over the production of *Code 3*, referenced above.

When *The Forest Ranger* was not picked up as a series, Roach commissioned another script by Fox, "Till Death Do Us Part," that focused on a murder case investigated by forest rangers Jim and Dave. In the pocket of the victim, Ranger Al Clements, they find a letter from the Los Angeles Police Department warning Al that a murder had been committed by a man called Jack Nelson. A camper in the forest, Pete Raymond, matches Nelson's description. Residing in a cabin near Raymond's tent are George and Marie Lockton. Although suspicion falls on Raymond, Marie turns out to be the killer.

The revamped project was titled *U.S. Ranger.* I do not known if the project was ever cast or if a pilot was filmed.

In May 1958, Roach Jr. sold his studio to the Scranton Corporation, a subsidiary of the F.L. Jacobs Company that manufactured auto parts. Alexander Guterma, head of the Jacobs Company, was the man behind the acquisition. Roach continued as president of the studio with the deal supposedly allowing the producer sufficient funds to make additional television and movie films. Four months later, Hal Roach Studios bought the radio network, the Mutual Broadcasting System, with the intent of making MBS a new television network with shows produced by Roach. However, the following year, Guterma was arrested for fraud and Roach replaced him as the Jacobs Company's chairman of the board. But, failing to raise sufficient capital, the Mutual Broadcasting Company, the Jacobs Company, the Scranton Corporation and Hal Roach Studios all went into bankruptcy.

Roach Jr., Guterma and a vice-president of the Scranton Corporation were indicted in September 1959 for failing to register as agents of the Dominican Republic after having accepted payments from the dictator of that country to have the Mutual Broadcasting System provide favorable coverage of the Dominican Republic in its newscasts. Roach pleaded no contest to the charge and paid a $500 fine. The Hal Roach Studios were eventually sold as part of the bankruptcy liquidation process and ended up being demolished for commercial development.

In March 1972, Hal Roach Jr. passed away at age 53 from pneumonia. His father lived to be 100. He died of pneumonia on November 2, 1992.

CHAPTER 2

Roland Reed Productions

A Producer of Almost All Genres

A maker of industrial and religious shorts in the 1940s, Roland Reed transitioned his production facilities to television around 1949. Roland Daniel Reed began work at age 19 as Eastern representative for Eagle-Picher Lead Company. He eventually went to Hollywood with hopes of becoming an assistant director.

After he became curious about how a film editor planned to put his footage together, he spent six years as an editor himself. Westinghouse contracted him to produce an industrial film in 1930. In 1937, he made a Technicolor film about U.S. Steel which was so successful it ran in Radio City Music Hall for three weeks as a second feature. By 1938, he had formed Roland Reed Productions and made numerous industrial films.

One of his first projects for television, in 1949, was a series called *Golf Doctor* that starred golfer Olin Dutra in a 15-minute series giving golf instructions.

A Radio Comedy Adaptation and Several Unsold Sitcom Pilots

In addition to the series that Reed produced in association with Hal Roach Jr. (*The Trouble with Father* and *My Little Margie,* discussed in the first chapter), he produced the first TV series with a person of color as the lead.

Beulah, based on the radio show of the same title, premiered on TV in October 1950 with Ethel Waters as Beulah, the maid. She played the part until 1952 when Hattie McDaniel took over the role, which she had performed on the radio version. However, due to illness, McDaniel appeared on only a few episodes. Louise Beavers played Beulah in the comedy's final season.

Beulah was the maid to Mr. and Mrs. Henderson, a white middle-class couple with a son named Donnie. Her friends were her boyfriend Bill Jackson, who ran a fix-it shop, and Oriole. Beulah became involved with attempting to solve the Hendersons' problems and helping Bill with his various ventures such as managing a reducing school, running a matrimonial agent, becoming a fighter, etc.

Reviewing the initial episode, *The New York Times* opined, "With Ethel Waters playing the title role, it had a number of amusing moments, but on the whole the opening installment suffered from a trite story and was regrettably stereotyped in concept."[1] The black characters were woefully stereotypical, particularly Bill, who was portrayed as lazy, and Oriole, who was seen as dim-witted.

Several episodes presented typical comedy situations involving misunderstandings. In "The New Arrival," Donnie is building a soap box derby racer out of spare parts. He needs wheels and so uses his mother's charge account to buy a new baby buggy for its tires. Meanwhile, Alice Henderson wants to surprise her husband with a new barbeque grill. Beulah overhears Mrs. Henderson on the phone talking about a surprise and, when she sees a baby buggy in the kitchen, she concludes that Mrs. Henderson is having a baby. When Harry Henderson comes home, Beulah says that his wife is expecting and word spreads around town. On the day of the barbeque, gifts begin arriving for Alice. The new grill is delivered and is shown to the guests as they learn that Alice is not really pregnant and blame Harry for the miscommunication. Donnie brings in his racer and explains how he got the new wheels.

"Beulah and the Cowboy" satirized the popularity of singing cowboy stars in the 1950s. Donnie is a big fan of TV cowboy Arizona Slim. Harry is upset because he feels he doesn't measure up to Slim in the boy's mind. Having cooked for Slim in the past, Beulah arranges for the cowboy to have dinner with the Hendersons (and build up Mr. Henderson's image). But Slim is more interested in boasting about a new dude ranch he will be opening. Later, while on a hike with the Hendersons, Beulah has Bill and Oriole bring a live bull to their picnic. Slim pretends to be afraid of the animal. To impress his son, Harry steps in to show he does not fear the bull.

Next, Reed attempted to launch a comedy about a bumbling son-in-law. *Meet the O'Briens*, a 1954 comedy pilot, starred Dave O'Brien as himself with Jeff Donnell as his wife Nancy, Emory Parnell as Frank Staple, Dave's father-in-law, and Helen Spring as "Mother Staple." O'Brien played a character who reminded viewers of the antics of Dagwood Bumstead.

Dave lives with his wife's parents and always seems to aggravate his father-in-law Frank. Dave hadn't had a job in months. Using Frank's car, he goes looking for work but is involved in an accident. A tow truck driver attempts to remove the damaged vehicle, but Dave's instructions lead to the car being totaled and taken to a junkyard. He gives the $60 for the junked vehicle to Frank to reimburse him. Since the vehicle was insured, Frank decides to buy a new car. While Frank is at work, Dave goes to the insurance company to pick up the cash to purchase a new automobile. He decides to look at used cars on Frank's behalf. As luck would have it, he unwittingly buys a refurbished convertible, the car he wrecked in the first place. Frank soon realizes that the auto is his old car and, when the brakes don't work, he accidentally drives it into a swimming pool. All is not lost, however, since Dave had entered a sweepstakes and wins a new car for Frank.

Reed produced, in conjunction with MCA, *That Baxter Boy*, an unsold pilot for a teenage comedy with Johnny McGovern as Don Baxter. Frank Wilcox played his father, Ginger Young appeared as Don's girlfriend Julie, and Gary Gray was his friend Mikey. Made in 1955 but not aired until March 1956 on *Heinz Studio 57*, this comedy, set in Crown City, U.S.A., concerned the misadventures of high school student Don and his friends. On the unsold pilot, Don, the program chairman for his school's prom, tries to get a celebrity to attend the event. When Perry Como and Eddie Fisher turn him down, his father, a newspaper editor, suggests he ask actress Mona Freeman whom his father knows. Don's girlfriend is jealous of Mona because of Don's bragging to everyone about how well Mona knows him. When Mona arrives, she mistakes another boy for Don. Greatly embarrassed, Don decides to leave town. His father talks him out of going. Mona tells Julie that one reason Don invited her was to meet his girlfriend. At the dance, Don introduces Mona, who puts on glasses, saying that she is nearsighted and that is why she didn't recognize him initially.

In 1957, Reed attempted to launch his final situation comedy, *Julia Loves Rome*, about a tour guide in the Eternal City, her boyfriend, and her various misadventures. Anna Marie Alberghetti was sought for the title role. The project never resulted in a series.

A Mystery Series and a Legal Drama Attempt

Another Reed production, *Mark Saber Mystery Theatre,* starred B-movie veteran Tom Conway in the title role. The "whodunit" series premiered on ABC in October 1951 and ran for three seasons before being remade with Donald Gray in the lead role and produced in

England by Danziger Productions. In the Tom Conway version, Saber was a homicide detective in an American city with James Burke playing his not-so-bright sidekick, Sgt. Tim Maloney. *A la Perry Mason*, each episode title began with the "The Case of...."

In "The Case of the Locked Room," the program tried its own version of the classic "locked door" mystery. Saber and Maloney investigate the death of Douglas Manning, found in his locked apartment after his mother (Esther Howard) and the building's manager, George Ericson (Stuart Randall), come to the apartment door and hear a gunshot. While Maloney believes the death a suicide, Saber is not so sure. Manning's wife Judith (Virginia Barlow) will inherit her husband's fortune which he just received from his father's estate after a nasty court battle with his mother. The wife suspects that the mother may have killed Manning. On the other hand, the mother suspects Judith. Judith is later shot and killed. Saber finds that Ericson murdered both Manning and his wife because he was in love with Judith, who then fell in love with someone else. He had a key to the Manning apartment and killed both. In each case, he shut off the electricity to the apartment, dumped the body in the kitchen, placed the murder weapon loaded with a blank on top of the stove, and then turned the electricity back on from down in the basement. The heat from the stove made the gun discharge as each body was about to be found. In addition, the apartment had been heated to 95 degrees to complicate the determination of when the individuals were actually killed.

The episodes generally followed the well-worn plot of first a murder; second the detective interviewing the likely suspects, and then the detective identifying the culprit. In "The Case of the Hair of the Dog," Maury Laughton, a gambler and mobster, is found stabbed in the back in his apartment, locked from the inside. Maloney suspects mobster Red Ritter, the last person to see Laughton alive. Saber interviews Billy Griff, Laughton's business partner; Lanie Winters, who was seeing both Laughton and Griff and whose apartment window faced Laughton's window; and a local butcher who owed Laughton a lot of money. With each suspect, Saber discovers dog hair, which was also found at the murder scene. Winters has a small dog. But, in the end, Saber finds that, climbing on the ledge outside Winters' apartment, one can enter Laughton's abode through his window and that Griff committed the murder to inherit Laughton's share of their business. Griff, a skin diver, used a spear gun to kill his partner, retrieving the spear on the string attached to the gun.

In 1956, Reed sought to base a series on Gene Fowler's book *The Great Mouthpiece*, about New York criminal defense attorney William

Fallon, to be portrayed by Brian Donlevy. (Fallon defended Arnold Rothstein and Nicky Arnstein in a trial about the fixing of the 1919 Baseball World Series.) The life and career of Fallon had been the subject of the movie *The Mouthpiece* (1932); its two remakes—*The Man Who Talked Too Much* (1940) and *Illegal* (1955)—used the same storyline.

As Fowler pointed out in his book, "[Fallon] became the Great Mouthpiece for the grand dukes of Racketland."[2] In the '20s, organized crime leaders had huge budgets for legal defense. Fallon's specialty was in hanging a jury. "His device was to address the entire summation to one juror—the one he judged susceptible to that form of flattery. It seems incredible how many times Fallon accomplished a hung jury by the count of 1 to 11."[3]

Nonetheless, Fallon would not take on a client who lied to him. In one example, a diamond thief asked the attorney to defend him but pleaded that he had no money:

> "I'm broke, Bill," the man said. "You're the only one that can save me a long stretch in the sneezer," the thief remarked.
> "But you stole $100,000 in diamonds," Fallon countered.
> "You're all wet, I didn't pull the job," the thief replied.
> "The diamonds are missing; it looks like your work," said Fallon.
> "I didn't do it, Bill. Honest to God."
> "Look here," Fallon said. " I happen to know that you stole the diamonds. Why don't you tell the truth?"
> "I didn't do it, Bill, and I'm flat. You're the only one I can turn to..."
> Mr. Fallon smiled. "My friend, you don't need a lawyer. ... I mean that anybody as innocent as you doesn't need counsel. So don't worry."[4]

Attempting to turn Fallon's life into a TV series presented challenges in the 1950s. First, viewers would probably not have much sympathy for a character who mainly defended gangsters and got them off on technicalities. In the '50s, most series about lawyers portrayed them as basically detectives investigating a crime and usually did not focus on courtroom theatrics. No network picked up the planned Fallon series.

Anthology Attempts

While Reed never attempted a "prestige" anthology series as other B TV producers had done, his company did make an episode of *Family Theatre* called "A Star Shall Rise." The drama, starring Raymond Burr, Richard Hale and Jay Novello, presented a traditional Christmas story told from the perspective of the Three Wise Men and their trek to

Bethlehem where they meet two shepherds, escape from Herod's soldiers and reach the stable to see Jesus.

Dramatizations of Bible stories were to be the focus of *His Way, His Word,* an anthology attempt by Reed in 1955. The first three episodes were to be filmed in color for syndication. The pilot, "The Fruitless Fig Tree," based on the parable, starred New York actress Peg LaCentra. *His Way, His Word* never became a series.

Men of Justice, a mystery anthology based on court cases, starred Gene Lockhart in the initial episode. M. Bernard (Ben) Fox, who had developed the series *Waterfront,* created *Men of Justice,* which also never resulted in a series.

Rocky Jones, Space Ranger

While Reed never made a Western series, he did launch a filmed science fiction series which, like a Western, pitted good guys against evildoers.

Rocky Jones, Space Ranger, Reed's 1954 sci-fi series for kids, featured Richard Crane as Space Ranger Jones and Scotty Beckett as his sidekick Winky. The team piloted the Orbit Jet XV2 spacecraft to various destinations in the solar system. The XV2, shaped like a missile, had a spacious interior. Rocky and Winky operated the craft sitting in front of a large console with a television monitor on top. Winky used expressions like "Conniving comets," "Galloping galaxies" and "Hoping Hercules" when remarking about the ongoing action. Vena Ray (Sally Mansfield), the ship's navigator, was the object of Rocky's sexist remarks. The series used rudimentary animation to depict the XV2 blasting off and traveling through space.

The series usually related a story over three episodes so that the episodes could be transformed into a feature-length movie to subsequently show on TV. In the first trilogy, "Beyond the Curtain of Space," Vena Ray arrives at Space Ranger headquarters to talk with Secretary Drake (Charles Meredith) about Professor Newton, who has apparently decided to stay on the hostile planet Ophiuchus to be with his young ward Bobby. Vena thinks the professor is being held against his will. Rocky and Winky decide to investigate.

Griff (Leonard Penn), part of Secretary Drake's staff, is in cahoots with the leaders of Ophiuchus and has the enemy attack the XV2 as it approaches that planet. Rocky and Winky destroy the enemy ship. Arriving on Ophiuchus, Bobby is being held captive to force the professor to work on a special project. Rocky lands on the planet under the pretext that his spaceship needs repairs. Brainwashed by the female leader of the hostile planet, Cleolanta (Patsy Parsons), Bobby and the professor do not want to leave. But Bobby recovers and explains what is really transpiring. Rocky also learns that Griff is a traitor. Rocky takes Bobby and the professor to the XV2, which returns to Earth. The Ophiucians attempt to crash the spacecraft into one of their moons but are not successful. However, they do tell Griff that Rocky is on to him.

From top to bottom, Tom Brown, Scotty Beckett, Richard Crane and Sally Mansfield appearing as their *Rocky Jones, Space Ranger* characters. Thirty-nine episodes were filmed.

When the XV2 lands on Earth, Griff and a confederate attempt to use it to escape and fly to Ophiuchus. Rocky learns that Griff has set explosives to demolish the headquarters of the Office of Space Affairs, and blows up the vehicle in which Griff is fleeing.

Reportedly, Guy Thayer convinced Roland Reed to produce *Rocky Jones, Space Ranger*. Abby Berlin directed the original, never-aired 1952 pilot, which featured Crystal Reeves as Vena Ray and Robert Carson as Secretary Drake. After recasting these roles, Hollingsworth Morse directed the second pilot.

Scotty Beckett was fired from the series in 1954 after being found guilty of illegally carrying a dagger when he was arrested in February of that year in the basement of a Los Angeles apartment hotel that had just been robbed. The actor subsequently skipped bail and fled to Mexico where he became involved in a wild gunfight with Mexican police who sought to arrest Beckett on bad check charges. Beckett's acting career never recovered from these incidents. James Lydon as "Biff" Cardoza replaced him on the series.

Waterfront and Adventure Series Attempts

Created by Ben Fox, *Waterfront,* a syndicated series which began in 1954, was a hybrid family melodrama and adventure show set in San Pedro Harbor. It featured Preston Foster as Captain John Herrick of the tugboat *Cheryl Ann*; Lois Moran as his wife May; Douglas Dick as son Carl, part of his father's crew; Harry Lauter as son Jim, a police detective; Billy Chapin as grandson Teddy, and Kathleen Crowley as Terry Van Buren, Carl's girlfriend. In addition to his tugboat business, John Herrick was also a Senior Harbor Pilot for the world's giant liners.

Some episodes dealt with the captain and his family becoming involved with crimes happening in and around the harbor, while others focused on human interest stories such as the captain helping a boy overcome his fear of the sea and aiding a runaway to reunite with his family. In the opener, "The Skipper's Day," Captain Jack learns that Carl, who is dating wealthy Terry Van Buren, wants to become a stockbroker like Terry's father instead of working on the tugboat. Meanwhile, son David (Carl Betz), a lawyer, is investigating the smuggling of radioactive cobalt. Jack and May visit the Van Burens to discuss Carl's career change. Before Jack can bring up the subject with Mr. Van Buren, he becomes concerned that David hasn't checked in with him. Jack, Carl and Terry locate the boat Dave is on, and Jack rescues him from the smugglers. After the incident, Terry changes her mind about Carl becoming a stockbroker.

The smugglers were played by two iconic character actors, Lee Van Cleef and Jack Elam, who usually appeared as bad guys on episodic television. After this episode, Harry Lauter replaced Carl Betz as son Jim Herrick.

African-American actor Willie Best played the role of Billy Slocum, the cook, on *Waterfront*. Often, when faced with a dangerous situation, the actor had lines like "Sure wish I was tucked into bed." Best had roles in several Roland Reed productions such as *My Little Margie*'s elevator operator and *The Stu Erwin Show*'s school janitor. It was rare to see people of color on '50s television, and when they did appear, they portrayed stereotypical characters carrying out menial jobs.

The career of the creator-producer of *Waterfront*, Ben Fox, illustrates how one successful series can serve as the launch pad for several "variations on a theme." Fox followed up *Waterfront* with a proposed series called *Harbor Inn*, an adventure show that would use seaside hotels and harbors as the basis for its stories. Then, in cooperation with the American Association of Railroads, Fox sought to launch the adventure series *Rails*, whose characters would be a railroad engineer and his family. Taking the family adventure series one step further, Fox also attempted *Charter Pilot*, an aviation adventure built around a family's airfield. The producer also sought to make a 90-minute movie or pre-pilot called *Isle of Anacapa* in cooperation with the U.S. Coast Guard, about the adventures of three Coast Guard cadets. None of these efforts became a series.

Guy V. Thayer Jr., vice-president in charge of production at Roland Reed, indicated how the firm saved money in making their shows:

> With less than an hour's work the sets of *My Little Margie* ... are converted into the sets for the syndicated *Rocky Jones, Space Ranger*. There is no change in lighting and thus electrical costs are cut. Likewise, the sets for *Trouble with Father* ... and the syndicated *Beulah* are interchangeable. We save the expense of bringing in crews to wreck sets and build new ones.
>
> The *My Little Margie* unit makes three or four pictures in succession. Then we give the players a needed rest and go ahead with three or four *Rocky Jones* films, using the same crew, changing only the director. Our crews develop such teamwork that if a new grip or sound man joins the unit it takes two or three days to regain its momentum.[5]

Alarm, another adventure project proposed by Reed, never resulted in a series. The 1954 pilot starred Richard Arlen as fire captain Ed London, along with Chick Chandler as Mack McCuen, Dick Simmons as Lt. Larry Jones and Howard Negley as Chief Reagan. The pilot told the story of an investigation into a serial arsonist. At the beginning, Keith E. Klinger, Chief Engineer Los Angeles County Fire Department, talks with Arlen about the concept of the series centering on the types of fires and rescues his department handles. The pilot uses stock footage of fires for many scenes.

Suspects in the arson investigation include young hood Ted Carn (Gene Reynolds), present at the first fire, and Brenon (Byron Foulger), a postman in the neighborhood in which the fires are occurring; his wife had died in a fire. The culprit turns out to be Mr. Lester (Fred Essler), a dry cleaner who sought revenge against the young toughs who had robbed his store.

Two years later, in 1956, Roland Reed Productions attempted to launch a revamped series, also called *Alarm*, based on the exploits of firefighters all over the country instead of just Los Angeles. The new format, that of an anthology series documenting major fires, had musician Fred Waring as host. The proposed show focused more on the stories behind a fire and not solely on the efforts of firemen.

The pilot concerned the November 28, 1942, Coconut Grove fire in Boston. At the beginning, Mr. Waring introduces the chief of the Boston Fire Department and presents him with a plaque in recognition of the efforts of his fire department. The story focuses on three sets of patrons at the overcrowded nightclub—actor Stuart Manning and his agent celebrating Manning's successful return to the stage after a long absence, a couple on the verge of divorce trying to rekindle their romance, and a Marine sergeant and his girlfriend out for a night before he has to return from leave. The fire is ignited by a patron using a lighted match to search on the floor for his girlfriend's lost lipstick tube. Panic ensues with people trying to leave through a revolving door that is stuck. With no fire exits, others escape through a small window in the back of the club with the help of the firefighters. Manning assists several patrons with their escape including the Marine's girlfriend. Manning and his agent also escape, but the husband of the couple contemplating divorce perishes. Roland Reed Productions had no more success with this version of *Alarm* becoming a series as it did with the original version.

Another of Reed's adventure projects, the syndicated series *Test Pilot,* starred Preston Foster and was to be made by Reed's production company along with Gross-Krasne Productions. This planned series concerned test pilots experimenting with new aircraft. While the pilot, produced in December 1955, did not result in a series, it appears to have inspired a 1957 Gross-Krasne movie, *Destination 60,000* with Foster as Ed Buckley, an aircraft company owner who has designed a supersonic fighter which his friend Jeff Connors (Pat Conway) wants to test.

A project envisioned by Reed, *Treasure Hunters,* concerned characters played by Roy Roberts, Britt Lomond and Nancy Hale seeking treasure on land and sea. The pilot, to be filmed on Catalina Island, was never made. The script titled "The Treasure of 'The Golden Scabbard'" featured three main characters who will take on a mission anywhere if they think it will lead them to some treasure. In addition to Captain Rutherford Light, presumably to be played by Roberts, and his daughter Genevieve (Hale), the script also delineated a Dan August character (to be portrayed by Britt Lomond) who supervised treasure hunting expeditions. The three had a boat named the *Lady Dowser.*

The story was supposedly based on fact augmented by legend of a treasure worth over $2 million in silver, gold and jewels that Spanish conquistadors had looted from South America. The ship carrying the treasure sank off the Mexican coast with most of the valuables now at the bottom of the sea except for one chest of gold and jewels that the ship captain saved and buried somewhere on an island. Arriving at the site where the ship went down, the divers find the water too deep for skin divers to recover the treasure. August suggests that they look instead for the hidden chest of gold. He deciphers a map left by the old captain and recovers the chest, which is taken unopened to their boat.

At night, two of the crew members decide to steal the chest and flee in a motor boat. Dan stops them, but in the course of a fight, the chest falls into the deep water and seems to be lost forever. With such a downbeat ending, it is probably not surprising that the pilot was never made.

Adventures of the Sea Hawk, another unsold pilot Reed made in 1956, featured movie actor George O'Brien as the captain of the ship the *Sea Hawk* and Douglas Dick as his son. A hurricane strikes the ship which is loaded with explosive cargo. O'Brien thinks his son is a coward, but the son redeems himself by saving the ship from exploding. In 1957, the pilot, written by David Dortort and Fenton Earnshaw, aired as an episode of the anthology *Studio 57*.

In association with MCA, producers Eugene Solow and Brewster Morgan launched a syndicated series in 1958 also titled *Adventures of the Sea Hawk*. This series, originally to be called *Caribbean Adventure*, dramatized the adventures of two electronic scientists played by John Howard and John Lee aboard a ship called the *Sea Hawk*.

One of Roland Reed Productions' final television projects was an unsuccessful attempt to produce a film series based on the private life of Abraham Lincoln. In the late 1950s and early 1960s, Reed devoted his time to producing commercials, industrial films and military training films as well as promoting the sale of reruns of his more popular series like *My Little Margie* and *Waterfront*. He passed away in Los Angeles on July 15, 1972, at age 78.

Jack Chertok

From Iconic Heroes to Fantasy Comedies

After graduating from preparatory school at age 16, Jack Chertok became a stage actor for two years before traveling to Los Angeles to work in the movies. He was hired by MGM as a laboratory technician to develop film. He progressed to several different positions at the studio including script clerk, assistant director and unit manager. In 1930, he became head of the music department after being involved with early musicals as a unit manager.

After five years in the music department, Chertok became a producer in MGM's short subject department, winning nine Academy Awards. In 1942, Chertok landed the position of feature film producer at Warner Brothers on movies like *Northern Pursuit* and *The Corn Is Green*. Two years later he became an independent producer making *The Strange Woman* and *Dishonored Lady*.

Aware that the new medium of television would demand filmed material, Chertok formed his own company in 1945 to make industrial films but was ready and willing to produce material for TV. He hired staff from the MGM short subject department, which was being disbanded, to fill positions in his new firm, Apex Film Corporation.

The Lone Ranger, Sky King and Other Western Projects

Chertok's first successful TV series was *The Lone Ranger* for ABC in 1949. It was produced in association with Lone Ranger, Inc., owned by George Trendle. *The Lone Ranger* had first aired on radio in 1933, starting on Detroit station WXYZ (owned by Trendle) with scripts by Fran Striker.

Sponsored by General Mills, Chertok shot the television series in batches of four to six episodes, filming several action scenes for different installments at the same time to save money. As the producer commented, "Anyone watching one of the shooting sequences would think we were wasting money by having actors mount and dismount from their horses time and time again. But each movement is planned for a certain week's film and combining them helps cut production costs."[1]

The debut, "Enter the Lone Ranger," revealed how the Lone Ranger came to be. Six Texas Rangers, tracking a group of outlaws known as the Cavendish gang, are led into an ambush by a man named Collins. The outlaws think that they have killed all the Rangers but one, John Reid, survives. Nursed back to health by a friendly Indian named Tonto, Reid vows to seek vengeance on the gang and preserve law and order. He tells Tonto that he will never shoot to kill anyone, only to wound. Reid dons a mask to protect his identity.

Before trying to find the Cavendish gang, the Lone Ranger and Tonto go to Wild Horse Valley where the Ranger finds a silver-white

stallion that becomes his steed, Silver. The two then visit Jim Blaine, a retired Texas Ranger. Blaine agrees to work an abandoned silver mine so that the Lone Ranger can obtain the needed mineral for his silver bullets. Tonto and the Lone Ranger eventually track down the Cavendish gang and capture them with the help of people from the town of Colby. This story played out over three episodes with subsequent installments having self-contained plots.

The Lone Ranger was different from other early television Westerns in that the Ranger was not a designated law

From TV's *The Lone Ranger,* **Clayton Moore and Jay Silverheels as the Ranger and Tonto. This Western series was the first adapted from radio specifically for TV.**

enforcement official but took on cases of injustice that he came upon or where the victim of the injustice requested his assistance. Wearing a mask, he was often mistaken for an outlaw. He also had a serious Native American companion portrayed by a real Native American, unlike other TV Westerns targeting a young audience where the sidekick's role was ordinarily one of comic relief.

A template for subsequent installments, the series' fourth episode "Legion of Old Timers" demonstrated how the Lone Ranger and Tonto helped others who had become victims of injustice. The Ranger and Tonto see that the Circle K Ranch is for sale. Outlaw Red Devers became foreman when the original owner's son, Bob Kittridge (DeForest Kelley), took over the ranch. When Devers framed Banty Bishop for stealing a payroll, Kittridge fired him and installed Devers in his place. Devers and his gang are holding Kittridge hostage until the ranch can be sold. Disguising himself as an old man (something very common in other episodes) to learn what is transpiring at the ranch, the Ranger pretends he is representing a buyer for the property. He later returns with Tonto and the former old timers who had been employed at the Circle K to take on Devers' gang and free Kittridge.

Clayton Moore played the Lone Ranger in every season of the series except for 52 episodes in 1952 when John Hart took over the role.

The Lone Ranger, Inc., and Chertok's Apex Films produced the series until 1954. In that year, Trendle sold all the rights to the series to Jack Wrather, whose company produced subsequent episodes of the show.

Chertok next produced a contemporary Western: *Sky King*, another TV series adapted from radio. It began on NBC in 1951. This Western concerned the adventures of airplane pilot–rancher Sky King (Kirby Grant) on the Flying Crown Ranch in Arizona and his favorite plane, the *Songbird*. Featured were Gloria Winters as his niece Penny and Ron Haggerty as his nephew Clipper. In its review of an episode, Leon Morse from *Billboard* wrote, "Kirby Grant was convincing here as Sky King, but he could take off a few pounds around thee waistline."[2]

This updated Western series replaced horses with airplanes and cars for the most part, but the stories still dealt with a hero, Sky King, and his "sidekicks," Penny and Clipper, taking care of bad guys. They became involved in situations involving gold smugglers, public corruption, murder, protection rackets, counterfeiters, blackmailers and spies. Chertok produced only the first season of *Sky King*, sponsored by Derby Foods (i.e., Peter Pan Peanut Butter). Later episodes were produced by Dorrell and Stuart McGowan.

Chertok also launched a more traditional Western series in 1951, the syndicated *Steve Donovan, Western Marshal* starring Douglas Kennedy in the title role and Eddy Waller as his older, grizzled sidekick, Rusty Lee. *Steve Donovan, Western Ranger* was the title of the series when first released for syndication. However, few TV stations aired the Western in the early '50s. The series was relaunched in 1955 with *Western Marshal* instead of *Western Ranger* in its title.

In the pilot, Donovan, always wearing a white hat, is assigned to capture an outlaw, the Comanche Kid, who, among other crimes, killed one of Donovan's friends. No one knows what the Kid looks like since he always wears a disguise when committing crimes. The Kid is attempting to gain the water rights on a ranch owned by John Hunter (Frank Fenton). Donovan, disguised as a regular cowboy, comes upon a wounded Hunter, who has been shot by one of the Kid's men. Hunter had returned fire and wounded his attacker. Donovan kills the Kid's accomplice. When he deduces that businessman Ben Morgan (Onslow Stevens) is really the Comanche Kid, he tells Morgan that Hunter has hired him to protect his ranch and that he will be out of town to round up more men to defend the ranch. That evening, Morgan as the Comanche Kid goes to Hunter's ranch where Donovan gets the drop on him.

David P. Sheppard, who wrote several *Lone Ranger* and *Sky King* episodes, penned the *Steve Donovan* pilot for Chertok. The series lasted for only a single season of 39 episodes.

In 1956, Chertok tried to sell a Western series starring Leon Ames. *Frontier Judge* concerned gunslinging circuit Judge John Cooper from the East, who falls in love with the West and plans to make the law as important to its people as their plows are.

A one-hour Western for NBC, *Trace Hunter* failed to find a spot on that network's 1959 fall schedule. To be filmed against a background of the Teton Mountains in Wyoming, the main character, Trace Hunter, was the sheriff of Green Hole, Wyoming, during the 1870s. Robert Reed (later of *Brady Bunch* fame) was reportedly in the running to play Hunter. Hunter's friend and spiritual adviser on the project was the Reverend Frank Olins, a former gunslinger who changed his calling when he became repulsed by his former, violent way of life. *Brady*, starring Mike Road, Frances Wong and Robert Gist, was a 1960 pilot for another Western series that Chertok attempted unsuccessfully to introduce.

One series Chertok sought to sell to CBS for the 1966–67 TV season was a one-hour Western called *The Iron Men* starring Mike Witney and Tom Simcox as railroad workers. This one also failed to become a series.

Anthologies

As with most producers profiled in this book, Chertok attempted several anthologies, a genre very popular in the 1950s. His first attempt with partner Tom Rockwell featured singer Jo Stafford in a 1950 anthology built around song stories. Stafford planned to sing and act on each episode. Actors would dramatize the story of a song. The pilot was filmed half in color and half in black and white. *Variety* indicated, "To date Miss Stafford's personal manager, Mike Nidorf, has not allowed thrush to make any tele appearances, fearing the flat lighting will not do her justice."[3]

Jack Chertok Television Inc. was a 1949 partnership deal between Chertok and Rockwell, president of General Artists Corporation. The new company was separate from Apex Films. General Artists planned to distribute films produced by Jack Chertok Television, and the latter would use GAC talent in its TV ventures.

Chertok's most successful foray in the anthology genre was in contributing over 30 episodes to DuPont's *Cavalcade of America* from 1953 to 1955. Dramatizing actual historical events was the series' original concept. One of Chertok's initial episodes, "Mightier Than the Sword," dealt with John Peter Zenger's defense of the freedom of the press. Zenger, who published the *New York Weekly Journal* in 1734, spoke out about the corruption of Sir William Cosby, the governor of both New York and New Jersey. The governor jailed Zenger but, from his prison cell, the journalist continued to write scathing editorials about the man. The executive charged Zenger with slander and libel. Philadelphia lawyer James Alexander defended Zenger and the result was a triumph for truth, Zenger and a free press.

Eventually, *Cavalcade of America* began featuring fictional contemporary stories. Chertok produced one of these in 1955, "Man on the Beat." Starring William Campbell and Constance Ford, the episode detailed a day in the life of a typical policeman, a member of a municipal police department. *Cavalcade of America* episodes were a step above the standard TV fare made by Chertok's company.

In the early '50s, the producer considered an anthology hosted by author Dale Carnegie, famous for the book *How to Win Friends and Influence People*. Carnegie would introduce each dramatization illustrating a theme from his work. Episodes would range from simulated Carnegie classroom presentations to portraying typical personal problems and the Carnegie solution for solving them. The never-realized series was alternately titled *How to Get the Most Out of Life* and *How to Stop Worrying and Start Living*.

The Family Tree, a 1956 anthology project that Chertok sought to produce, concerned an extended family that would highlight on each episode an individual on the family tree. Each installment would have featured a different cast in a story about a member of the large family.

Crime Dramas

Chertok made several crime drama pilots and was successful in launching two crime drama series.

Predating the 1960s ABC-TV series by several years, the 1951 *Green Hornet,* based on the radio series of the same name, starred Steve Dunne as Britt Reid aka the Green Hornet, Victor Sen Yung as Kato, and Trudy Marshall as Miss Cane, Reid's secretary. Like *The Lone Ranger,* this pilot was produced in cooperation with George Trendle, who had the rights to the *Green Hornet* radio show.

The pilot, "Waterfront Beat," focused on Jonathan, head of a crime syndicate, who has taken over control of a dock workers' union. Shipment of goods needed by the military has come to a stop. Britt Reid wants to demonstrate that Jonathan is supported by Communists. Two men who could testify as to Jonathan's activities won't talk for fear of death. The Green Hornet takes the men hostage. He pretends to contact his newspaper informing it that the two were not really kidnapped but left voluntarily to confess everything they know about the crime boss. Thinking they will be murdered by Jonathan's men, the two sell out Jonathan, leading to his arrest.

Challenge of the Yukon was based on the radio show of the same name, another George Trendle property. It predated the CBS series *Sergeant Preston of the Yukon* by three years. Paul Sutton appeared as Sergeant Preston on this 1952 pilot. Betting on the annual ice breakup, Clem Firsby (Byron Foulger) hides his ticket in a Chinese box. Stedman (Michael Whalen), a powerful man in his forties, and Monk (William Haade), rough and dull-witted, murder Clem and steal the ticket. Sgt. Preston discovers the truth, arrests the murderers and recovers the ticket for Clem's wife (Greta Granstedt).

While shooting the pilot, director Paul Landres had problems filming a scene with the character of Stedman fighting with the dog Yukon King. The dog refused to participate in the scene. Landres asked the dog's trainer what to do. The trainer replied, "Well, I could do it. I don't look like your man—he's white, I'm black—but I can get him to do it. He's six foot four up there and I'm down here at five foot six. I can get him to play with me and it will look like a fight."[4] Landres went on to say,

"So we put whiteface on the trainer and over his hands, and he and the dog enjoyed a beautiful romp in the snow. It worked out pretty well. You couldn't know how tall the man was because you didn't have any relationship to size at that point."[5]

The series *Sergeant Preston of the Yukon* was not produced by Chertok but by Trendle-Campbell-Meurer and Charles E. Skinner Productions.

Chertok produced *The Lawless Years* for NBC from 1959 to September 1961. Starring James Gregory and Robert Karnes and set in New York City during the 1920s, the show dealt with real-life police detective Barney Ruditsky (Gregory) fighting organized crime. The series was loosely based on cases worked by Ruditsky during his tenure on the New York police force. Because of the content of the episodes, NBC had difficulties finding a sponsor for the series.

Speaking about the series, Chertok commented that the 1920s were the most lawless decade of our history and added, "*The Lawless Years* will be different from the usual cops-and-robbers stories like *Dragnet, Line-up* and *Highway Patrol* because it deals with stories that happened 30 years ago. These aren't action pieces. They are studies of character."[6] Episodes featured well-known and not-so-well-known gangsters of the era.

The pilot chronicled the rise and fall of gangster Nick Joseph, played by Vic Morrow. After being released from prison for attempted murder, Joseph joins his cohorts in the protection racket. Impressed by his initiative, organized crime bigwigs recruit Joseph to take care of their opponents. After one gang member is arrested, he decides to inform on Joseph, and Joseph is arrested. Facing the death penalty, Joseph is killed trying to escape. The episode ends with a pronouncement, similar to *Dragnet*'s: "Although the actual names have been changed, the characters and places portrayed in this story are based on fact." Other episodes profiled the criminal activities of gangsters like Dutch Schultz and "Legs" Diamond.

In 1959, Chertok and actor Edmond O'Brien produced a private eye series starring O'Brien. The syndicated *Johnny Midnight* lasted for one year. O'Brien's brother Liam developed the concept for the series.

On the series, Edmond played a New York theatrical actor-producer who goes into detective work because he gets more kicks out of facing a gun than facing Broadway critics. Being a former actor gave Johnny a decided advantage in his work. He often wears disguises and his acting ability augments the characters he creates. But sometimes Midnight's disguises are so obvious, one wonders why the other characters do not instantly recognize him. Exteriors were shot in New York, interiors on the West Coast.

The theme song for the series was "The Lullaby of Broadway" with the storylines relevant to events in the theater. In "The Impresario," Johnny's friend Anthony King is rehearsing at Midnight's theater when sandbags fall on him from above. Johnny begins questioning the witnesses. Because King hinted that the producer, Michael Damon, may be behind the "accident," Midnight focuses on him. King mentions "da Vinci" to Midnight and then passes away. Midnight finds that "da Vinci" refers to a painting by the artist smuggled into America. Midnight comes up with a plan to show Damon that King is still alive by masquerading as the actor. He is able to entice Damon to confess that he smuggled the da Vinci painting into the States covered over by a painting of a woman, and that when King found out about Damon's operation, Damon engineered the sandbag incident.

Some *Johnny Midnight* episodes had comic overtones. In "The Whammy," Midnight flies to Hollywood to watch a movie being made from a play that he had produced and to see an actress, Nina Wylie, that he knows. Upon arrival, he finds that Nina is under arrest for the

Edmond O'Brien and Ann McCrea in a scene in *Johnny Midnight*. McCrea guest starred on two episodes of the series, "Mother's Boy," about the murder of the leading lady in a play, and "How Tight a Web," about an adulterous affair that turns deadly.

murder of the movie producer's son. Midnight believes that Nina has been framed. Disguising himself as an elderly police inspector, he calls all the suspects together: —Nina, the producer, the writer, the cameraman, and another actress. The supposedly dead son re-appears alive. The entire incident was simply a practical joke on Johnny.

In 1960, Chertok tried to launch a crime drama for NBC, *Port of Entry*. Paul Comi was to play as a U.S. Immigration Service operative working out of New York who becomes involved in stories about spies, drug smuggling, gunrunners, etc.

Female-Centric Pilots and Series

Jack Chertok produced several pilots and series with unmarried female characters as their focal point. His first attempt might have been the series *Claire Calls* starring Claire Trevor. This 1952 project was briefly mentioned in many newspapers at the time. Just what the planned series would have been about is unknown. No pilot appears to have been filmed.

The producer's first successful comedy featuring a female lead, *Private Secretary* with Ann Sothern, premiered on February 1, 1953. Sothern appeared as Susie McNamara, secretary to Peter Sands (Don Porter), a New York City talent agent. During most of its run, the comedy alternated with *The Jack Benny Program* on early Sunday evenings on CBS. Chertok talked about viewers' identification with the show: "Thousands of girls are private secretaries or want to be. Thousands of men have private secretaries. Thousands of families know private secretaries."[7]

The idea of Sothern playing Susie came about when her agent approached Chertok about making a comedy with the actress as a secretary. Chertok's secretary, Muriel McGinnis, may have been a model for the McNamara character. "She was Irish, saucy, at times flip, most efficient and a large contributor to the Chertok success," said a newspaper article. "Muriel McGinnis, in truth, is Susie, and Chertok is Peter Sands … to Muriel. Susie's last name was borrowed from Paul McNamara, Chertok Productions' vice-president in charge of sales."[8]

Buddy Rogers was considered for the role of Sothern's boss, but his salary demands were evidently too high because Don Porter landed the part. The comedy was built on the concept of "behind every successful man, there is a woman." A typical episode had Susie coming up with a plan to accomplish something her boss wanted but didn't know how to achieve. For example, on one episode, Sands seeks to interest a famous opera director, Mr. Hugo, in hiring two of his clients, Phyllis and Jeff, for roles in *Samson and Delilah*. Susie knows that the director's wife is really the one who makes most of his decisions. She meets with Mrs. Hugo and has her appoint Mr. Sands as the chairman of the upcoming Opera Association dinner. Susie arranges for her to meet Sands to discuss the menu. She then sets up a meeting with both Mr. and Mrs. Hugo at the same time that Phyllis and Jeff are auditioning in Mr. Sands' office so that Mr. Hugo can hear them sing. Hugo decides to hire both for his next opera.

Sothern eventually quit the comedy over a disagreement with Chertok. The producer sold the rights to the series and an option on a fifth season to Television Programs of America. As the actress explained to the media, "The thing that makes me angry is that I was unaware my option could be exercised by TPA should Chertok not exercise the fifth option of the five-year contract he had with me. Since Chertok's deal with TPA was misrepresented to me, I feel I have no moral or ethical obligation to TPA."[9]

Chertok attempted in 1954 to adapt Norman Reilly Raine's stories about an tugboat captain named Annie, into a comedy series in association with Television Programs of America. *The Adventures of Tugboat Annie* aired in syndication in 1957 with Leon Fromkess, instead of Chertok, producing for TPA. See Chapter 11 for additional *Tugboat Annie* details.

Calling Terry Conway, a 1954 pilot also known as *Las Vegas Woman* and *Las Vegas Belle*, starred Ann Sheridan as Terry, publicity and public relations director of the Paradise Hotel in Las Vegas, with Una Merkel as her secretary Pearl McCrath and Philip Ober as Harry Garvey, a member of the hotel's board of directors. Exteriors for the pilot were filmed at Las Vegas' Flamingo Hotel.

The proposed series, similar to *Private Secretary* in concept, had Harry Garvey interacting with Terry like Peter Sands did with Susie. The storyline of the pilot dealt with a prince and his mother from the Middle Eastern country of Karestan staying at the Paradise. Harry wants to impress the visitors so that they will permit his company to build a hotel in Karestan. Terry decides to hold a reception for the prince, but his mother refuses to attend. The mother hates antelope meat, a staple in Karestan, which Terry has ordered for the dinner. When Terry takes the mother out to sample American food, the mother confides that she is worried about her son being spoiled in America. Terry speaks with the prince about his mother's concerns. Bud, a hotel bellboy, punches the prince in the face for flirting with Bud's girlfriend and then saying that he is tired of the girl and prefers Terry. The prince's mother approves of what the bellboy did to her son and gives the go-ahead for construction of a hotel in Karestan. *Calling Terry Conway* never sold, perhaps because sponsors were touchy about being associated with a show indirectly related to gambling.

Again trying to repeat the success of *Private Secretary*, Chertok filmed *Publicity Girl* in 1956 for ABC. Episodes were to revolve around news items that Jan Sterling's title character attempts to have printed and those she wants to keep out of the papers. Subsequently, the producer made another attempt at a series with Sterling in the lead. This pilot had Sterling working at an orange juice company.

In 1958, the producer tried another female-centric comedy. Starring singer-violinist Gisele MacKenzie, the proposed series was originally titled *Bringing Up Katie* by its creator Everett Freeman before the character's name became Connie. Subsequent titles were *The Major and the Minor* and *The Miss and Missiles*—the title used when the pilot aired on *Lux Playhouse* on June 12, 1959. MacKenzie played Connie Marlowe, a magazine writer assigned to write a story about Air Force test pilot Bill Adams (John Forsythe). Her teenage brother Buzz (Gordon Gebert) complicates her interview with the pilot. If the test show had become a series, presumably Connie's budding romance with Bill would have been explored further.

An unsold 1960 pilot, *The Brown Horse*, starred Jan Clayton of *Lassie* fame. She played a widowed mother working at the Brown Horse restaurant in San Francisco to help fund her daughter's college education.

Male-Centered Sitcom Pilots

Chertok also tried, without success, to launch several comedies with male characters at the center. In 1957, he considered a comedy detective series starring Bobby Van called *The Reluctant Eye*. It was created by Phil Davis, who had authored scripts for *Private Secretary*. The series would have been for NBC. Co-starring on the planned series with Van was Douglas V. Fowley as Ben, the Van character's assistant. Van appeared as Sylvan van Brent III, whose deceased Uncle Carl bequeathed him $1,000,000 if he made his private investigator business work for at least five years, presumably the hoped-for run of the series. Sylvan, fundamentally a coward, only took on cases that seemingly wouldn't involve danger. Ben was to ensure that Sylvan kept his business running.

For his first case, Sylvan is hired by Sabra Morley, who wants the PI to find her Great Dane, Duke, who has run off. Oliver Harkness stops by Sylvan's office saying he owns Duke and that Sylvan should drop the case. A redhead named Dolores informs Sylvan of the whereabouts of the dog and then drugs the detective. Waking up in a funeral home, Sylvan finds the Great Dane but has to take the canine to a vet since the dog's paws are infected. The vet discovers pieces of glass in each paw which are really diamonds. The PI returns to his office to give the dog to Miss Morley, who is then arrested by the police as the smuggled diamonds are confiscated.

Chertok also made a "fish out of water" comedy pilot intended for the 1966–67 season, *The Man in the Square Suit*. Paul Dooley plays TV writer Frank Johnson who has misgivings about his new assignment, scripting a show for teenagers called *Teen Beat*. He initially says he will write only the presentation to the network for the show. When he is asked to write each weekly episode, he refuses. He goes to the show's production office to formally turn down the job, where he is informed that he is "too square" for the show's young image. He then has second thoughts and decides that it might be a challenge. When the producer visits Frank and pleads with him to do the show, Frank accepts. At a party for the series, Frank is the only one wearing a tuxedo. He does dance the frug but then throws his back out.

Gary Young (Michael Blodgett) is *Teen Beat's* young producer and Max (Astrid Warner) is Gary's blonde secretary. Jan Shutan co-starred as Frank's wife Marilyn, and Diane Sherry played the couple's daughter Nancy.

ABC aired the pilot as a one-time special on April 22, 1966. The planned series was created by writers John Aylesworth and Frank Peppiatt, who scripted variety shows in the 1950s, '60s and '70s. Among their shows was NBC's *Hullabaloo* (1965), a pop rock series aimed primarily at teenagers. Apparently, their experience scripting a show for teens gave rise to the idea for *The Man in the Square Suit*.

Fantasy Comedies

Chertok helped to launch one of CBS's few fantasy comedies during the 1960s, *My Favorite Martian* with Ray Walston as the Martian (Uncle Martin) and Bill Bixby as Tim O'Hara, a *Los Angeles Sun* reporter. Tim is assigned to cover a test flight of the X-15 at Edwards Air Force Base. However, he is late to view the flight. On the way back to his office, he sees a spaceship that crashes. Tim discovers a Martian in the ship and takes him to his apartment to recover. The Martian is a professor of anthropology who has visited Earth in the past but never crashed before. The Martian is marooned on Earth until he is able to repair his craft. Tim introduces the Martian to his landlady, Mrs. Brown, as his Uncle Martin. The Martian has small retractable antennae coming out of his head when he performs amazing feats like making himself invisible and telepathically moving objects.

Writer John L. Greene created the series. He sent the pilot script to his talent agency in 1960 but heard nothing. Chertok found the script at the bottom of a tall stack at the agency and said he liked the idea. A talent agent said, "It's the worst idea around here. It has been read by everyone and always winds up at the bottom of the stack."[10] Nevertheless, Chertok thought it would make a good series. Scheduled on early Sunday evenings, the series lasted three seasons.

CBS's president James T. Aubrey was so impressed with *My Favorite Martian* that he made Chertok executive producer of another fantasy launched in 1964. *My Living Doll* started out as another female-centric project initially called *Living Doll* about a female robot who is programmed to do anything she is told. The series was created to tell the story of a female android, but the title changed when Bob Cummings became part of the cast and the role of the robot's mentor expanded from that of a supporting character to a lead character. (Efrem Zimbalist Jr. was initially considered for the role of the robot's minder.) Two of Chertok's *My Favorite Martian* writers, Bill Kelsay and Al Martin, created *My Living Doll.*

On the premiere episode "Boy Meets Girl," project AF709 (Julie Newmar), wearing only a sheet, appears in Dr. Bob McDonald's (Cummings) office. Dr. Carl Miller had created AF709 for a complex outer space project. Miller asks McDonald to take the robot to his apartment. When Miller comes by McDonald's apartment, he wants to dissemble the robot to take her back to his lab. He shows Bob the controls on the robot's back disguised as beauty marks. Bob is not convinced that AF709 is indeed a robot. The robot thinks logically but shows no emotions. When Dr. Miller has to leave unexpectedly for a special mission, he asks Robert to look after his creation. McDonald names the robot Rhoda Miller and says she is Dr. Miller's niece. He invites his sister to move in to chaperone. Rhoda becomes McDonald's secretary, speaking in monotone to him but using a different enunciation with others when programmed by the doctor to take on alternative personalities.

McDonald would enlist Rhoda to carry out his various plans with unexpected results. In "Something Borrowed, Something Blew," Bob has Rhoda charm Mr. Armbruster to make a substantial contribution to a psychiatric institute. She does such a good job that Armbruster decides to marry her. When Bob objects, Armbruster wants to cancel his donation. Bob comes up with a plan to have Armbruster say he doesn't want to marry Rhoda by programming her to exhibit the worst characteristics of the benefactor's prior seven wives. The Julie Newmar character then plays a woman who won't listen to her husband, one that demands a pre-nuptial agreement, another that flirts with other men, etc. Armbruster decides against tying the knot. Evidently, during the filming of this episode, Cummings placed a sign up in front of the camera so that Newmar would have to do another take of the scene.[11]

The series premiered on September 27, 1964, at 9:00. Facing stiff competition from *Bonanza*, CBS moved the comedy to Wednesdays at 8:00 in December. Cummings left the series abruptly. Apparently there was friction between Cummings and producer Howard Leeds over the extent of his role on the series, given that he had been the lead character on his previous comedies (*My Hero, The Bob Cummings Show* and *The New Bob Cummings Show*). Leeds indicated that the title of the series was not "*My Living Doll's Keeper.*"

Cummings became upset when much of the series' publicity focused on the Newmar character instead of his. "I'm the central character," Cummings told the press. "Originally, the idea was to tell the series from the viewpoint of the robot, and I said I wouldn't be interested. Dramaturgically, that would have made me nothing but a custodian, somebody whose only purpose was to keep Rhoda from falling off a cliff."[12] The actor asked for and received his release from the series or, in some accounts, he was fired from the series after completing 21 of 26 episodes. Leeds later took the concept of a female robot and turned it into a syndicated comedy called *Small Wonder*, about a little girl robot that lives with the family of her inventor.

Something Different

In addition to his Westerns, anthologies, crime dramas, and sitcoms, Chertok attempted to launch a wholly new TV genre in the 1950s with a proposed daytime home shopping series, *What's New*, hosted by Jack Benny's announcer Don Wilson. The concept sought to bring to life advertisements from fashion magazines by modeling women's and children's apparel. Mannequins were presented against a plain background with Wilson describing the apparel features including colors, sizes and general price range. Interspersed during the pilot were vignettes about social behavior such as how a person can act gracefully while awaiting the arrival of another. Twenty-six half-hour episodes were planned over a year with the suggestion that the retailer sponsoring the series show the same episode on consecutive weeks. Retailers, of course, would sponsor only shows that featured merchandise they offered.

Chertok died on June 14, 1995, in Los Angeles.

CHAPTER 4

Jerry Fairbanks

The Art of Low-Cost Production

Born in 1904, Jerry Fairbanks produced many series of short subjects for movie theaters in the 1930s and 1940s. He acquired his interest in pictures from his father, whose hobby was photography. In 1930, Jerry started photographing the *Strange as It Seems* series distributed thorough Universal Pictures. He later made *Popular Science*, a short subject for movie theaters. Paramount, which owned the distribution rights to *Popular Science*, sold the shorts to distributors Toby Anguish and Elliott Hyman for them to edit the films and offer them as a quarter-hour series to local TV stations. Fairbanks would have shared in the revenue from this project with Anguish asking $5000 per week for first-run rights. But no television station or sponsor seems to have purchased the episodes.

Fairbanks made two other short subject series for Paramount, *Unusual Occupations* and *Speaking of Animals*. The latter series won him Academy Awards in 1942 and 1944.

In 1948, Fairbanks started providing NBC with film for its news broadcasts, and in 1949, he created *NBC Newsreel*. In the following year, the producer announced the development of a new way to film TV shows by using a three-camera system. Fairbanks' Multicam system was similar to that used later by Desi Arnaz for filming *I Love Lucy*. His system utilized three or more 16mm or 35mm cameras operating simultaneously to film three or more different angles of a scene, getting long, medium, and close-up shots at the same time. His system reduced the costs of filming a show by eliminating the need to do numerous takes of a scene to film it from different angles.

Fairbanks produced several different types of television series and pilots using his Multicam system.

Mini-Documentaries

In addition to *NBC Newsreel*, Fairbanks made *Television Close-ups* which premiered in syndication in late 1948 and aired through the mid–50s. Narrated by Van Des Autels, this series of 26 five-minute mini-documentaries was originally made for NBC. They were generally about historical subjects. The episodes were shot without sound; Des Autels' voiceover narration was added later. Several TV outlets showed this program at 6:55 p.m., others aired it in prime time.

Public Prosecutor, Front Page Detective and Proposed Crime Dramas

Public Prosecutor, another series that NBC had contracted with Fairbanks to produce starting in 1947, was supposed to have premiered in September 1948 on that network. The cast of characters included Steve Allen (John Howard) as the public prosecutor, Patricia Kelly (Anne Gwynne) as his secretary, and a police lieutenant (Walter Sande) who helped Allen. One newspaper described the series as "recounting the adventures of a modern Sherlock Holmes."[1] Howard had been an actor mainly in B movies with some exceptions such as *Lost Horizon* and *The Philadelphia Story*. Anne Gwynne had starred in several B features.

Public Prosecutor explored the workings of a district attorney who, speaking directly to the camera, would discuss the criminal case he is investigating. In the course of the investigation, he would interview likely suspects and at the end ask the viewers to decide who perpetrated the crime before revealing the true culprit.

In an initial episode, "The Case of the Missing Bullets," Allen interviews three suspects in the murder of a police officer. The gun has been found but not the spent cartridges. Witnesses say that three shots were fired in rapid succession. When Willy Spencer, a petty crook, is interrogated, he says that he was just taking a walk near the murder scene. Helen Ferris, whose brother had been sent to prison based on testimony from the murdered officer, says she was at the movies when the murder occurred but then admits that she was in the neighborhood around the time of the incident. Mike Costello, a gangster, admits he stole a car near where the cop was killed. Allen learns that Spencer's fingerprints were on the gun. Willy explains that indeed he and Mike Costello were planning to rob a jewelry store and that he fired warning shots when he saw the cop but says he used blanks in the gun. After a commercial, Allen reveals what actually happened. He points out that one cannot fire blanks rapidly, and thus Willy is the murderer.

Other episodes followed essentially the same format. In "The Case of the Dead Man's Voice," a murdered novelist, Clayton Kimball, left a message on his tape recorder naming three possible suspects: his literary agent, Kay Rodgers; ex-gangster Goofy Madden, who worked for Kimball; and Ron Lewis, Kimball's new publisher. The murderer turned out to be Kay Rodgers.

Producer Fairbanks filmed 26 episodes, each about 18 minutes in length. NBC sought to obtain a sponsor for the series in 1948, but the

Anne Gwynne and John Howard receive final instructions before shooting a *Public Prosecutor* scene. This was the first filmed television series.

network's asking price was deemed too high and so the producer shelved the series.[2] At one point in 1949, NBC and Motorola were in negotiations for the company to sponsor the program as a replacement for *Believe It or Not*, but those talks didn't lead to anything.

As columnist and TV host Ed Sullivan put it in his newspaper column:

> Hollywood continues to be bewildered by television. Most bewildered would be Jerry Fairbanks, producer of shorts, who plunged into the TV film production field as a pioneer.
>
> Fairbanks made 26 film shorts for TV. On the advice of someone at NBC-TV who persuaded Fairbanks that TV would split the hour into three sections of 20 minutes, he made 18-minute reels. These would be preceded and followed by one-minute commercials, accounting for 20 minutes in all.
>
> His adviser, of course, proved wrong. TV continued the radio pattern of splitting the hour into four 15-minute sections. So, Fairbanks has on his hands ... a whole flock of 18-minute shorts.[3]

Beginning in February 1951, episodes of *Public Prosecutor*, edited to 15 minutes in length, aired in syndication. Subsequently, the DuMont TV network showed the series starting on September 6, 1951, Thursdays at 9:30 p.m. under the title *Crawford Mystery Theater*. Crawford Clothes sponsored the show. To make each episode run 30 minutes, the format was changed to a type of quiz program with detective fiction writers and celebrities guessing the perpetrator, before revealing the actual culprit.

Warren Hull hosted the series. On the first episode aired, the panel included actress Glenda Farrell, ventriloquist Doug Anderson and actor John Derek.

Fairbanks' second successful crime series, *Front Page Detective*, a newspaper drama, starred Edmund Lowe as journalist David Chase and Paula Drew as his girlfriend, Sharon Richard. The drama was not only syndicated but also aired on the DuMont TV network in 1951 and again in 1953. Chase acted like a regular police detective in solving murder cases. The series, based on stories from *Front Page Detective* magazine, was filmed using Fairbanks' Multicam system.

As noted previously, one characteristic of B TV series is featuring aging movie actors who are no longer in demand. *Front Page Detective* is a classic example of this. Lowe began his career in silent films in 1915. He was in his sixties by the time he starred on this TV show. He commented on *Front Page Detective*: "I think we have the start of an exciting series in this new show. For one thing, it is being done on film which relieves the tension to which most television mysteries are subject, and the cast, all veterans of screen, stage or radio, seem to fit their parts perfectly."[4]

The scenes in *Front Page Detective* were limited to various soundstages with most exterior shots using stock film. An early episode, "Alibi for Suicide," focused on Don Lawton, who holds David Chase and his girlfriend at gunpoint for a night saying that he needs them as an alibi because his wife is going to kill herself but make it appear as if he murdered her. The next day, Lawton and Chase discover Mrs. Lawton dead and find the couple's friend Fran Bishop at the Lawton apartment. Initially, Chase thinks that Mr. Lawton and Fran Bishop murdered Mrs. Lawton since the husband was about to leave his wife and run off with Bishop. A letter written by Mrs. Lawton is discovered, saying that if she is found dead, it would be murder. But Chase changes his mind and believes that Mrs. Lawton did indeed commit suicide and the letter is to frame her husband. Chase points out that the woman's suicide note and the letter were written at the same time because each has a mark on them from her husband's cigarette butt.

Not all mysteries involved a murder. In "Seven Seas to Danger," Chase investigates a smuggling operation and wonders why Dutch Schmidt, the chief smuggler, is trying to return to the ship on which he had been a stowaway. Chase discovers that Schmidt left seashells on the vessel that contain diamonds and sees to it that the smugglers and their associates are arrested by a U.S. Treasury agent.

In 1951, Fairbanks piloted a crime drama called *Sheriff* based on files from the Los Angeles Sheriff's Office. This was another of many efforts by producers of B television to introduce "true" crime series to viewers. Detectives Joe King and Dan Cronin investigate the death of retired businessman Flint Matthews, shot with a .38 revolver. The police first suspect that a man Matthews treated like a son, Willis Jackson, shot him over an $800 loan that Matthews had second thoughts about giving to Jackson. When the detectives find a .38 in Jackson's possession, they take him in for questioning but find that the gun does not match the revolver that killed Matthews.

Suspicion then falls on Matthews' estranged wife and his daughter Janie, who is married to Dr. Fargo. Before his death, Matthews supposedly argued with Dr. Fargo and Janie about giving them half his property. King and Cronin subsequently discover another .38 near Mrs. Matthews' house. Finding that the gun is indeed the murder weapon, they take it back to where they discovered it and announce to the suspects that a search will be done at the property the next morning. The detectives hide out waiting for the real culprit to retrieve the gun. They find Mrs. Matthews looking for the gun and arrest her. She murdered her husband over his plan to give half his property to his daughter, not knowing that he had already done this. She is tried and convicted of first-degree murder.

Fairbanks sought to introduce another "true" crime drama in the late 1950s. *Roll Call* was a 1958 effort similar to police shows like *Dragnet*. *Roll Call*, whose stories would come from the files of the San Antonio, Texas, police department, focused on Patrol Sergeant Robert Easter. The pilot script, "No Ear to Hear," concerned two young toughs who visit the public library to discuss their plan to rob a loan company. Thinking they are alone in the reading room, the two talk about the heist. However, before leaving, they spy an elderly man in a corner of the facility who is about to leave. Not knowing that he is deaf without his hearing aid, the two beat him up, leaving him unconscious. After interviewing witnesses to the attack, Easter and his colleagues track down and arrest the boys. Easter tells them that the old man died and that, while he was in the library, his hearing aid was in his pocket.

Inexpensive Variety Shows

Fairbanks' *Paradise Island* premiered in April 1949 on 22 TV stations and ran for 26 weeks. Hosted by singer Danny O'Neil and featuring singer Anne Sterling and the Everett Hoagland Orchestra, the episodes were 15 minutes in length. Set on a fictional South Seas island, the show was filmed in Mexico City to reduce costs.

On the premiere, O'Neil sings an original song, "Paradise Island" (written as the program's theme) along with other compositions like "There'll Be Some Changes Made." Sterling vocalizes "Hokus Pokus" and guest Tony Larue plays Brahms' "Fifth Hungarian Rhapsody" on the xylophone. Hoagland performs "Cuanto Le Gusto."

The series made frequent use of original songs to minimize the costs for using already published music. In addition to singers, the show included specialty acts like banjo players, pianists, accordionists, mimics and a variety of dancers. Perhaps the show's most noteworthy aspect was the buxom Ms. Sterling. Fairbanks ordered a flock of dresses with an "overflowing" look to highlight Sterling's anatomy. He told the singer to squeeze into them and turned her loose in front of the camera. The successful syndication of this series led producer Fairbanks to consider a syndicated sequel with a Western setting, but that effort never materialized.

Fairbanks also attempted to launch a half-hour series of book musicals starring Tom Drake and Trudy Marshall in 1951. Initially titled *Make Mine Manhattan* and then *Meet Me in Manhattan*, the series never got off the ground.

Children's Shows

Syndicated to local stations between 1949 and 1955, *Going Places with Uncle George* featured Dick Elliott as the host and narrator. Aimed at juvenile viewers, the series presented unusual people, places and things. Each episode was ten minutes in length, but with commercials, TV stations could fill 15 minutes of airtime. While many stations aired this series outside of prime time, usually between 5:00 and 6:59 p.m., others did broadcast the show in prime time between 7:00 and 8:00 p.m., often coupled with Fairbanks' *Paradise Island.*

Advertisements for the show described it as "[a] fascinating adventure-education program with 'Uncle George' taking his audience into the world of sports ... fantasy ... curious pursuits ... strange people."

Sitting in a rocking chair and smoking a pipe, friendly, gray-haired

Uncle George would narrate stories about various subjects. On one episode, he relates the tale of "The Master Cat," otherwise known as "Puss 'n' Boots." George begins narrating the story and showing illustrations from the book. The remainder of the episode, with Uncle George's voiceover, uses animated puppets to dramatize the tale. Character actor Dick Elliott, who played Uncle George, is best remembered for his role as Mayor Pike on early episodes of *The Andy Griffith Show*.

Beginning in 1950, Fairbanks syndicated *Crusader Rabbit*, the first animated series produced especially for television. The cartoon, featuring Crusader Rabbit along with his sidekick Ragland T. Tiger, had been created by Alex Anderson and Jay Ward, who later developed *Rocky and Bullwinkle*. Through their Television Arts Productions, the partners tried to sell the series to NBC. NBC did not air the series but, through the network's association with Fairbanks, they permitted him to produce and sell the series in syndication. NBC, however, evidently retained title to the series. *Crusader Rabbit* initially ran from 1950 to 1952. One hundred ninety-five episodes were made with each in movie serial form, ending in a cliffhanger until the particular "crusade" story ended.

The first crusade was "Crusader vs. the State of Texas." Crusader listens to a radio report that Texans are chasing jack rabbits out of the state. He wants to help his cousins, all named "Jack." After freeing Ragland T. Tiger from a circus, the two go to Texas to begin their crusade.

In February 1952, NBC sold *Crusader Rabbit* back to Fairbanks along with *Public Prosecutor, Paradise Island, Jackson and Jill, Going Places with Uncle George* and *Ringside with the Wrestlers*. Fairbanks then defaulted on the payments, and the network obtained a court order to dispose of the series by public sale. Consolidated Television Sales, which had been distributing these series, entered into an agreement with NBC to resume making payments to the network for the shows.

In 1953, Television Arts Productions filed a breach of contract suit against Jerry Fairbanks, NBC and Consolidated Television Sales, contending it was due 50 percent of the net profits from the sale of *Crusader Rabbit*. The defendants denied the claim, alleging that they were sole owners of the series.

Jackson and Jill and Other Comedy Efforts

Fairbanks' company syndicated a sitcom, *Jackson and Jill*, which aired at various times on different stations. In New York, the series premiered on WNBT (now WNBC) on June 23, 1949, at 8:00 p.m. and ran for 13 episodes. The cast of characters included Jackson Jones (Todd Karns), a salesman newly married to Jill (Helen Chapman), a stereotypical scatterbrained blonde, and Mr. Gimmling (Russell Hicks), Jackson's boss.

Originally ordered by NBC and filmed between April and August 1949, this comedy series presented the story of a young couple who had been married for six years and lived in an apartment. Each episode began with Jill writing in her diary about their latest misadventures.

When NBC failed to find a sponsor for the series, the network made it available to its affiliates. It premiered in summer 1949 on most of those stations. The network decided to air a preview of the series nationally on November 24, 1949 (Thanksgiving), at 8:00 p.m. but the preview apparently sparked no interest from potential national sponsors.

In the November 1949 preview, episode 6, "Model Mix-Up" by D.H. Johnson, Jackson learns that a big sugar plantation owner, Jose Alvarado (Fritz Feld), is in town. Jackson wants to try to sell him tractors for his plantation. Meanwhile, Jill has her heart set on a necklace of cultured pearls and is hoping that her husband will receive a $200 bonus from the sale. Jackson finds that Alvarado is more interested in wine, women and song than in purchasing tractors. When Jill learns this, she goes to see the plantation owner at his hotel. In the meantime, Alvarado has contacted a "modeling" agency to interview a female for possible marriage. When Jill arrives at his hotel room, Alvarado thinks she is the representative from the agency. She tells him about "models," and he thinks she is referring to women although she is really talking about tractors. But, as usual, in the end, things are resolved with Alvarado purchasing the tractors and Jill getting her necklace.

Most of the episodes dealt with contrived situations arising from misunderstandings and mistaken identities. The storylines of other episodes included Jill talking Jackson into reliving their first date when they were college students, resulting in a dance party at their apartment with neighbors complaining about the noise ("It's Ridiculous"); a marital spat turning into a split as Jill decides to move out of their apartment ("A Man's House Is Her Castle"); Jackson becoming jealous when Jill goes out with another man, prompting Jackson trying to make Jill jealous ("Parting Is Such Sweet Sorrow"); and mistaken identities when Jackson confuses a house painter with an artist and when Jill confuses the painter for her friend's husband ("Who's Whose").

In the episode with the most intriguing title, "The Grand Lama Laughed," Jackson and Jill prepare for a two-week vacation at a mountain resort. Their apartment's handyman convinces Jill that she needs a camera in order to take photos of their adventures. At a camera shop, the clerk convinces her to not only purchase a camera but all the equipment that goes with it including a camera case. She spends over $120, meaning the couple will not have much money left for the vacation. Subsequently, a photographer enters the camera shop looking for his camera case, which contains the negative of a photo he took in Tibet of the Grand Lama, laughing. The clerk realizes he sold the case to Jill. The clerk goes to the Joneses' apartment to retrieve the item and return the money Jill paid him. However, Jill already had taken the negative out of the case and can't locate it. The photographer then appears at the apartment as Jill finds the negative in another bag she packed. The photographer gives her a $500 reward which means the Joneses can extend their vacation.

A script for at least one episode was written but never filmed. Like the installments that were made, this script by producer-writer David Victor sets up a contrived situation: Jill befriends the eccentric J. Lexington Nasby, a millionaire business owner. Since he likes to feed the pigeons in the park (as does Jill), she comes up with a scheme to have Nasby hire Jackson at a substantial salary. Jill invites Nasby to dinner to meet Jackson.

While at work, Jackson is offered a promotion with a salary increase, but Jill tells him to think about the offer for a day. Jackson invites his boss Mr. Gimmling to dinner as well. Nasby decides to hire Jackson as a junior partner in his company provided that he quit Gimmling's employ. Before Jackson has a chance to accept, Nasby's lawyer, who takes care of the elderly gentleman, comes by to advise Jill that Nasby's sons actually run his company since Nasby is senile. When Gimmling learns that Nasby's job offer was not for real, he wants to fire Jackson, but then Jill informs him that Nasby's sons appreciated how she befriended their father and so are giving Jackson exclusive rights to handle their new line of electric irons. Wanting the Nasby business, Gimmling retracts his threat to terminate Jackson.

The role of Jackson Jones was originally to be filled by young actor Jack Laird. Laird went on to write, direct and produce episodes of series like *Ben Casey*, *Night Gallery* and *Kojak*. The actor who did land the role of Jackson Jones, Todd Karns, was the son of actor Roscoe Karns.

After *Jackson and Jill*, Fairbanks tried to introduce several comedies, mostly warm-hearted in nature. He had no luck.

The producer sought to purchase the television rights to a book by Clinton "Buddy" Twiss, *The Long, Long Trailer*, and turn it into a TV comedy. The novel focused on a couple who buy a new travel trailer and tour the United States. While this project never happened, the book did serve as the basis for a 1954 motion picture starring Desi Arnaz and Lucille Ball.

In 1954, Fairbanks attempted negotiations with author H. Allen Smith to turn his novel *Low Man on the Totem Pole* into a 30-minute comedy series. The title of the book came from comedian Fred Allen's comment about Smith's small stature, saying that if the author were an Indian, he would be the low man on any totem pole. The novel recounted Smith's encounters with the famous (e.g., Jimmy Durante, Herbert Hoover) and the not-so-famous (e.g., the man who sold refrigerators to Eskimos).

In association with Norman Taurog, Fairbanks tried to launch a comedy series focused on the adventures of two 12-year-old boys. *Skinny and Me* would have starred Steve Winter and Charlie Herbert. The unrealized series was to go into production beginning in March 1959.

The pilot script, written by Ben Park, focuses on Paul "Dunk" Pattersall, the *Me* in the title of the proposed series. His best friend is Erskine "Skinny" Kimball. Dunk takes money that his mother had given him to purchase a new baseball glove. His father wanted him to save his own money before buying the glove. Dunk promises to reimburse his mother the $10 and looks for ways to raise the money. He and Skinny decide to sell flowers by picking them from neighbors' gardens and then convincing people to buy them at 50 cents a bunch. Dunk finally shows his dad the baseball glove after he reveals how he is raising money to repay his mother. His dad gives him $10 to give to his mother after Dunk promises to reimburse the neighbors for the money they spent on the flowers.

Fairbanks also tried to introduce a comedy by Adele Comandini, *The D.D.'s Daughters,* about a widowed minister, Angus Dean, raising five daughters: Angela, Eleanor, Jocelyn and twins Jess and Tess, both of whom are still in school. The pilot script, "Thanks for Everything," took place a week before Thanksgiving with the Drew house cold because the furnace is not working. The reverend, who is also the chairman of the city council, is on the outs with Mr. Ballard, who installs furnaces, after accusing him of taking a kickback from the town's paving fund. The girls try various ways to raise money for a new furnace including selling the family's piano and betting on a dog race with hopes that the winner will earn them $200. In the end, Mr. Ballard agrees to repay the paving fund and to install a furnace as a donation because his wife convinces him to do so after the Drew twins saw Ballard at the dog races with a beautiful younger woman. Ballard reveals this fact to his spouse after she mentions she saw Jess and Tess at the drug store with Ballard, and he assumed that the twins had already mentioned seeing him with the young woman.

Silver Theatre, Bigelow Theatre and Other Anthology Projects

Jerry Fairbanks successfully launched two syndicated series in 1950, the anthologies *Silver Theatre* and *Bigelow Theatre* (aka *Hollywood Half Hour*). Reportedly, one episode per day was filmed using Fairbanks' Multicam process.

Silver Theatre started out as a live half-hour anthology on CBS. In April 1950, Fairbanks introduced a filmed version made in Hollywood. The initial filmed installment, "Coals of Fire," concerned the efforts of a young girl to get her miserly father to become a more generous individual. Most of the episodes were melodramatic in nature.

In "Closeup," Albert Clayson (John Gallaudet) needs money to send his little girl to Arizona for her health. He finds a lost wallet with cash inside. Richard King (Donald Woods) lost the wallet, which has a letter inside from his estranged wife notifying him that if he wants to reconcile with her, he should meet her that evening at a certain address. King remembers the time for the meeting but not the address and so is desperate to retrieve the billfold. Clayson uses the money inside to purchase a train ticket for his daughter. But, after persuasion from his wife, he decides to return the wallet to King. King greatly appreciates the gesture and allows Clayson to keep the train ticket and the remaining money as his reward.

Many *Silver Theatre* episodes were later rerun on *Bigelow Theatre*, sponsored by Bigelow-Sanford Carpet Company. The series included both melodramas and crime dramas. At least one installment was a pilot for a new series: "Agent from Scotland Yard" starring Lynn Bari, Patric Knowles and Alan Mowbray concerned a British agent in Los Angeles who seeks to solve the disappearance of a senior code clerk in order to avert international complications.

In 1950, Fairbanks produced a TV version of the radio series *Satan's Waitin'*. It starred Jeanne Cagney and Pierre Watkin. The pilot, which aired June 25, 1950, on *Colgate Theatre*, was made in conjunction with Joel Malone, who wrote episodes of the radio series in which the Devil makes people do dastardly things. In the test show, a woman who has married for money falls in love with a young executive at her husband's company. The two decide to murder the husband, but their plans are foiled when the husband learns of their plot.

Malone, without Fairbanks, tried again in 1964 to launch a TV version of his radio show. In this version of *Satan's Waitin'*, Ray Walston played "The Stranger," who was actually the Devil.

In 1951, Fairbanks, in conjunction with Father Patrick Peyton of the Family Rosary Crusade, began filming periodic TV specials with an all-star cast syndicated to local television stations. They were titled *Family Theatre* and one of the earliest installments, "Hill Number One," aired March 3, 1951. It related the story of what might have happened among Jesus' followers in the three days before the Crucifixion. The story was told in the context of a U.S. Army company stationed in Korea during the Korean Action. Among the actors were Ruth Hussey, Joan Leslie, Gene Lockhart, Roddy McDowall and Todd Karns.

Other *Family Theatre* specials produced by Fairbanks included "That I May See," relating the miracle of Bartimeus, a blind beggar whose sight was restored by Jesus Christ. It featured Don Ameche, Gail Russell and Pat O'Brien. "The Triumphant Hour," dramatizing Christ's resurrection and ascension, featured Raymond Burr and Jeanne Bates.

Family Theatre had been originally developed as a Mutual Broadcasting System weekly radio series.

In 1958, Fairbanks—in association with writer Arch Oboler— filmed the pilot "Hi, Grandma!" for an anthology, *Arch Oboler's Plays*, to be narrated by Oboler. The episodes would range from mystery and suspense to science fiction. The unsold pilot dealt with a young mechanical genius who resurrects the voice of his dead grandmother. As Oboler put it, "Officials at one network expressed real interest in the project, but they didn't think it was 'in trend' for 1958–59. I don't know how they figure out such things, but they said my series would be very good for 1959–60." Lamenting the plethora of Westerns on TV at the time, he added, "Maybe I should have written a ghost story about a six-shooter."[5]

Fairbanks' TV Western Attempt

Almost every early producer of B TV series sought to launch a Western in the '50s. Fairbanks was no exception. In 1951, his production company made the pilot *The Buckskin Rangers*, starring Ray "Crash" Corrigan, Bill Hale as Buckskin Brown, and Max Terhune as Alibi Terhune.

In the color pilot "Lady Tenderfoot," Rangers Corrigan, Hale and Terhune (who besides being a Ranger was also a ventriloquist) come to the aid of Carol Webster (Virginia Herrick), whose Uncle Jess has just died. Carol and her brother Tommy (Bob O'Dwyer) arrive in Loganville to visit her uncle's ranch. The executor of the uncle's will, Victor Gerard (Dick Powers), tries to persuade her not to go to the ranch. Gerard has his men attempt to scare her away from the place, but the three Rangers fend off the men. Carol is under the impression that her uncle committed suicide. However, since the uncle, although left-handed, was shot in the right temple, "Crash" concludes that he didn't take his own life but was murdered—presumably by Gerard who found the body. Tommy finds oil on the ranch. The next day, Gerard and one of his men, posing as a buyer, come to the ranch to convince Carol to sell at a low price. "Crash" confronts them and accuses Gerard of murder. A fight ensues. "Crash" takes care of Gerard while the other Rangers handle Gerard's men.

The pilot did not become a series.

Fairbanks' Other Entertainment Projects

In the late 1940s, Fairbanks attempted to launch a 30-minute quiz show called *Quizology.* It was scheduled for 16 weekly episodes.

In 1948, Fairbanks tried to introduce a series called *States of the Union* which would document the cities and landmarks of the then 48 states. The planned series would use documentary film and a narrator describing historical sites in each state along with the state's natural attractions. The show would open presenting a map of the U.S. with a narrator announcing,

> What you see here is not merely a map. It is one of the most unusual phenomena in all the history of the world—48 individual, self-governing states, each with its own laws, banded together in a single, indivisible nation, with liberty and justice for all. A nation composed of many people, whose ancestors came from many different lands.[6]

The concept never became a series.

Two years later, the producer sought to make a series called *What Ever Happened to—*, profiling once-famous personalities. Fairbanks Productions acquired films from newsreels and old motion pictures to show former celebrities and other headliners at the height of their success. New footage would show the same personalities currently, with radio news analyst Harry W. Flannery acting as narrator and interviewer.

Fairbanks also completed arrangements to bring professional wrestling to television in a syndicated weekly series on film called *Ringside with Rasslers,* filmed at American Legion Stadium in Hollywood.

Keeping with the sports theme, Fairbanks contemplated a unique show, *Sports Fictional Theatre,* which would have been a series of sporting events between champions of different eras. The unsold concept would, for instance, pit tennis players Pancho Gonzales against Bill

Tilden, Babe Ruth and his baseball team against Bob Feller and his team, and Ty Cobb's team vs. Dizzy Dean's team. As the script, written by John J. Simmons, explains: "For centuries, second guessers and armchair philosophers have argued who was the best in sports ... the question is, who would have won if athletes of different eras could have been matched in their prime. Well, now you, the television audience, are about to break through the barriers of time and see the impossible...."[7] The planned pilot depicted a boxing match between Jack Dempsey and John L. Sullivan, with Dempsey being declared the winner in the eighth round. Dempsey wins on a foul because he fell to the canvas and Sullivan did not go to a neutral corner but instead trampled Dempsey.

Turning to variety series, in 1950, Fairbanks made a pilot for *The Edgar Bergen and Charlie McCarthy Show* with Bergen, Jim Backus, Pat Patrick and Bill Baldwin as the announcer. This comedy-variety project, which aired on November 23, 1950, brought radio's Bergen and his ventriloquist dummies to TV in what was planned to be a series of intermittent specials. The show, similar in format to Jack Benny's, combined situation comedy with variety.

Bergen begins the show with a visit to Charlie McCarthy's bedroom where Charlie is taking a bubble bath. They talk about doing a show for charity that night and perform a routine about Miles Standish (the pilot aired on Thanksgiving Day).

During the charity performance, Bergen introduces a new marionette, life-sized Podine Puffington, with whom he dances. She talks about her life as a Southern belle from Alabama. Diana Lynn performs a piano composition. In the dressing room, Edgar and Mortimer Snerd do a routine preparing for their onstage appearance and the after party. Pat Patrick, dressed as a Pilgrim, introduces a sketch about witches in Massachusetts with Charlie and Bergen accused of witchcraft since ventriloquism was considered a black art. The two are found guilty and due to be burned at the stake with Charlie as kindling wood, but an Indian maiden frees them and the townspeople agree to let them go in the spirit of Thanksgiving.

During the 1950s, Fairbanks contracted with several corporations to produce films that advertised their products. One such endeavor in 1950, *Rocket to the Stars,* advertised the Oldsmobile Rocket 8 sedan. Two episodes were made for the series intended to be syndicated across the country. Each installment featured Johnny (Hal Hedland) and Lucille (Kay Westfall) visiting the homes of stars in their Rocket 8 Oldsmobile.

The first episode had Johnny and Lucille visiting David Niven and his wife at their Pacific Palisades, California, home. The show included performances from Veloz & Yolanda and the Modernaires. The second installment featured Charles Laughton and his spouse Elsa Lanchester with Laughton showing Johnny his collection of statues and Lanchester performing songs from a play in which she starred. Laughton also reads a scene from *A Midsummer Night's Dream* and promotes his latest movie, *The Man on the Eiffel Tower*.

During both episodes, Johnny and Lucille drive their new Oldsmobile around Los Angeles and sing the Oldsmobile theme song, highlighting the features of the Rocket 8.

Other such productions made by Fairbanks included *The Story of a Star*, showing the history of the Texas Company, i.e., Texaco, and *With This Ring*, about Miller High Life and the German Brewing Company. He also produced films for AT&T, Metropolitan Life, Greyhound, New York Life and Boeing.

Fairbanks partnered with Harry Wayne McMahan in the late '50s to make a daytime panel show, *Love Is the Problem*, hosted by Barbara Dean. Produced by Cupid, Inc., the company formed by Fairbanks and McMahan, two pilots were made. Columnist and counselor Dean asked a panel of so-called experts on problems of love and romance to comment on letters sent in by viewers. The panelists included lawyer Helen Sherry, psychologist Dr. Eleanor Metheny, and actor Freeman Lusk. A fourth guest panelist would also appear on each episode. The first episode had actress Vanessa Brown as the guest; the second featured actor Jacques Bergerac. Fairbanks' Multicam system filmed the show.

One of Fairbanks final television series attempts was 1961's *The Outdoorsman*, a proposed show made in conjunction with *Outdoorsman* magazine. Richard Stokes starred in the pilot "Bear for Honey," about a magazine writer and his veterinarian friend who travel to the Sierra Nevada mountains to trap a wild bear.

Reportedly, in 1963, Fairbanks wanted to turn away from TV production and devote his time to making movies to combat perceived Communist subversion. He created Jerry Fairbanks and Associates, a subsidiary of his production company, that would take over his TV and commercial production and allow him to make features. The projects he contemplated were *World Medicine for World Peace*, showing what American medicine and drugs distributed by the U.S. Air Force will mean to countries around the world, *The Miracle of Guadalupe*, and a feature on the life of Dr. Tom Dooley.

In 1966, Fairbanks produced a B movie, *The Bamboo Saucer*, about Americans and Russians finding an unidentified flying object in Communist China. The film marked the last appearance of actor Dan Duryea.

Jerry Fairbanks passed away on June 21, 1995, at the age of 90.

CHAPTER 5

Bernard J. Prockter

Turning Real-Life Stories into TV Series

Born in 1908 in Chicago, Bernard Jay Prockter worked at CBS in various capacities from 1929 until 1940. He then joined the Biow Company as radio director in 1941. While at that advertising agency, he was in charge of producing shows including *Take It or Leave It, What's My Name?* and *Philip Morris Playhouse.* In 1944, he became an independent packager of radio programs such as *Quick as a Flash* and *The Big Story.* He expanded into the field of television in the late 1940s; in 1953 he formed Prockter Television Enterprises. The following year, he claimed that his firm was the only TV operation that produced live shows, made filmed shows, and owned its own studios.

The True Story Crime Dramas

Developing series based on real-life stories related by journalists or from law enforcement files became Prockter's forte.

His first major TV success, *The Big Story,* premiered September 16, 1949, on NBC Friday at 9:30 p.m. and ran until June 28, 1957, with an additional season in syndication. Bob Sloane narrated each episode from 1949 to 1954; other narrators took over in succeeding seasons. Pall Mall cigarettes sponsored the series for most of its run.

This docudrama anthology, based on actual stories of reporters who solved crimes or rendered significant public service, originally combined live drama with filmed segments.

The first episode, written by Arnold Perl and directed by Charles E. Skinner, featured the story of Frank Shenkel of the *Pittsburgh Sun Telegraph.* Shenkel investigated the murder of a woman shot in her sleep. The reporter broke open the case by tracking down a witness willing to testify against a powerful racketeer.

About the making of *The Big Story*, columnist John Crosby wrote:

Prockter, the producer, now has a seven-man crew which travels all over the country in a station wagon equipped with motion picture cameras, shooting platforms and recording equipment. *Big Story* is a combination of live and filmed drama, the proportion of film ranging from five to 75 percent, depending on the story. Prockter insists on authenticity of background. He'll send his crew to Detroit to film the street where the crime took place, though he could find a similar street in Long Island City.[1]

Prockter followed up *The Big Story* with several series based on the same concept: taking actual events surrounding types of criminal activity and turning them into a TV show. *Treasury Men in Action* in 1950, based on case files from the Treasury Department, involved counterfeiters, tax evaders, gunrunners and other crimes under the purview of that department with each story focused on the criminal perpetrators. Walter Greaza played "The Chief"—the head of whatever division was associated with the case of the week.

Walter Greaza as the Chief of the Bureau in *Treasury Men in Action*. Greaza played roles in feature films and on TV, radio and Broadway.

In a typical episode, "The Case of the Buried Treasure," Paul and Marie LaCosta bury in their backyard $200,000 the couple got from a numbers operation to avoid income taxes. After five years, the couple digs up the money only to find it covered with mold and holes in each disintegrating bill. They dry out the money and attempt to purchase items with it. But the damaged bills end up with the U.S. Treasury; they identify the mold and locate the LaCostas. In the meantime, Marie has approached a former associate to launder the money at 20 cents on the dollar. Treasury agents close in and arrest Mrs. LaCosta and the associate. Paul LaCosta is sent to a mental institution after having a nervous breakdown over the money.

The series ran on ABC until December 1950, then NBC until 1954, and switched back to ABC for its final season. Prockter contemplated producing a feature-length film based on *Treasury Men in Action* in early 1955, but those plans never materialized.

With producer Jerome Robinson, Prockter launched *Police Story* in 1952. The CBS series, narrated by Norman Rare, was based on the files from various police departments across the U.S. The opener, set in Nashville, was about a baffling murder mystery. The episodes were done live. The show concentrated on police solving various street crimes like robbery, arson, drug dealing and homicides. The series ended after 24 installments.

In the fall of 1953, Prockter premiered a similar series told in semi-documentary style and based on case files from all types of law enforcement agencies—not just police departments. *The Man Behind the Badge*, produced with Jerome Robinson, debuted on CBS and ran for one season. It featured tales of police officers, park rangers, military police, public defenders, postal inspectors and fire chiefs. After ending its run on CBS, the series ran in syndication with new episodes.

The initial *Man Behind the Badge* installment focused on a Las Vegas probation officer who takes a juvenile delinquent under his wing to try to rehabilitate him. A review of this episode indicated, "The acting was so transparent you could see the eggs through the ham. For economic or other reasons, narration was frequently employed over the dramatics. This is an acceptable technique but not when thespians gesture like they did in the old silent movie days."[2]

A later episode chronicled a murder that occurred in Chittenden County, Vermont. A harness maker loans money to people at exorbitant interest rates. A businessman turns up dead. Lawrence Deslaw (Wendell Holmes), the state's attorney, finds that one of the man's clients, Carl Wingate (Gene Reynolds), beat him to death after Wingate asked for an extension on his loan payments and the harness maker refused.

A syndicated series produced by Prockter, *International Police* (aka *Police Call*) debuted in 1954. Instead of stories based on the files of police departments as in *Police Story* or on any law enforcement agency such as *The Man Behind the Badge*, *International Police* dramatized police cases from around the world with each episode taking place in a different country.

Episodes dealt with topics like an Italian juvenile delinquent and his attempts to escape from a life of crime, the wife of a man framed for a crime aiding Havana police in trapping the real culprit, and a jewel smuggler operating across the Swiss-Franco border.

Prockter produced *The Mail Story* (also known as *Postal Inspector*) for ABC in 1954. This anthology used case histories from the U.S. Postal Service. Some episodes dealt with the services provided by the Postal Service while others concerned individuals seeking to misuse the postal system. Examples of the latter included a story about a psychopath telephoning a doctor day and night and then sending anonymous threatening postcards to the doctor, which prompted an investigation from postal inspectors. Another episode related the tale of an elevator operator for a building housing a daily newspaper; he obtains a part-time job in the post office to work a scheme to win the paper's "Pick a Winner" contest. He overworks his scheme, bringing postal inspectors into the case. The series, which premiered in October 1954, was canceled in December of that year.

Game Shows

In the early '50s, Prockter adapted his radio game show *Quick as a Flash* for ABC-TV. It was initially hosted by Bobby Sherwood. Premiering March 12, 1953, the show tested a team's speed in guessing a person, place, thing or event based on viewing a short presentation containing clues. Each team consisted of a celebrity and a regular contestant.

The *Quick as a Flash* pilot, made in 1952, had Bill Cullen as host and Boris Karloff and Wendy Barrie as the celebrities. Subjects included "Storks Delivering the Dionne Quintuplets" with clues from a presentation showing military officers discussing "D-Day," "5 in the echelon," "delivering babies" and "emergency operation." Another subject was "Louis Pasteur" dramatized with a man being interrogated by a committee with clues like "enemy of the killers," "pack of wild dogs" and "boiling point."

Another game show produced by Prockter in 1953 was *Anyone Can Win,* hosted by cartoonist Al Capp of "Li'l Abner" fame. A panel of four celebrities competed in a general quiz. Three of the four were visible to the audience while the fourth wore the mask of "Hairless Joe," a comic strip character created by Capp. Before the quiz began, the studio audience would choose the celebrity they thought would answer the most questions correctly. The audience members who picked the right celebrity divided $2000. The game show ran on CBS during the summer of 1953.

Prockter's Fictional Anthology Series

Prockter launched an NBC anthology series titled *Short, Short Dramas*. Premiering September 30, 1952, it aired twice weekly, presenting 15-minute programs. Commenting on the shows, Prockter indicated, "Whether it be a mystery, a love story or a comedy, our *Short, Short Dramas* will strike a familiar chord to each listener."[3]

Departing from Prockter's "true story" franchise, the first melodrama concerned a little boy who is told that his mother will soon die. He writes a letter to God describing his mother's illness and asking that God save her. Not knowing what to do with the letter, a mail clerk puts it in a post office drawer. Miraculously, the letter disappears, and the boy's mother recovers as the letter reaches its destination.

Other episodes dealt with a waitress befriending a hungry man with unexpected results, the disappearance of an atomic scientist, and a would-be robbery by telephone with threats against the victim's family forcing the man to do the thief's bidding.

Model Ruth Woods hosted the series, introducing the star of each episode who would provide background information to set the scene for the play. *Short, Short Dramas* ran until early 1953. It was subsequently syndicated under the title *Playhouse 15*. Not to be outdone by NBC, ABC also premiered a series in the early evening hours called *Little Theater* which presented two complete stories in 15 minutes.

A Comedy Attempt
Starring Walter Brennan

Turning away from dramas and game shows, Prockter Television Enterprises tried to launch a Walter Brennan comedy called *Hickory Hill*, set in 1910 New England. Brennan was to play a dual role: Samuel Clayton Cooper, a postmaster and veterinarian, and his father, a man-about-town.

The initial effort was made in mid–1953 with old man Cooper playing only a small role. The story focused on Sam trying to resolve problems between two of Hickory Hill's prominent families, the Cassidys (the father is the town's mayor and druggist with two sons, Clay and Blake) and the Jordans (the father is the town's banker and he has a daughter named Anne). Clay seeks to keep a dog he has been given, but it bites his dad, who insists that he get rid of it.

When Sam's father visits Hickory Hill, Sam decides to throw a party at his home for his dad, the Cassidys and the Jordans. After a delicious supper prepared by Sam's housekeeper, everyone relaxes and the two families begin to get along. Mayor Cassidy likes the dog staying with Sam, not realizing it is the same canine that bit him.

After *Hickory Hill* failed to become a series, a second attempt, made in fall 1953, used essentially the same characters. The series title became *My Boy Sam*, with Sam's father, now named Caleb, taking a more prominent role and narrating the story, oftentimes speaking directly to viewers. Caleb, an irascible character, was just passing through Hickory Hill, really didn't like the town, and didn't have a high opinion of his son Sam, saying at one point that his son had a head full of jelly and a spine like a wet noodle.

In *My Boy Sam*, Sam is still a postmaster but also the new chief of Hickory Hill's volunteer fire department. He plans a drill by setting the town's bandstand on fire so his men can practice putting it out. The practice doesn't work as planned with the bandstand burning to the ground. Meanwhile, one of the two churches in Hickory Hill needs a new bell for its steeple. Caleb gives the church the fire bell. When the other church in town catches fire, there is no alarm and that church burns down. Come Sunday, Sam persuades the one remaining church to hold services for both congregations at the same time with one congregation sitting on the right side of the building and the other on the left. Although both congregations try to sing different hymns simultaneously, the two ministers alternate delivering their sermons. In the end, both congregations come together.

In another script written for the series, the town's spinster wants a willow grove near her property cut down because young couples use the place on Saturday nights to fool around. Sam thinks that the town council should vote on the matter. He has an idea to purchase a movie projector for Hickory Hill to show films on Saturday nights to keep the young people occupied. The council, made up of Sam, Ed Cassidy and Bill Jordan, can't agree on the proposal with Ed voting no, Bill abstaining, and Sam voting yes. Under the by-laws, a new temporary member of the council may be appointed to break the deadlock, and Sam appoints an inmate from the local jail who votes yes. Sam purchases a projector and orders the silent movie *The Count of Monte Cristo*. Unbeknownst to Sam, his father changes the order to *Flames of Passion*, about a female trying to resist sin. The townspeople are not scandalized by the film, instead liking its ending where the young girl, having drunk alcohol and smoked cigarettes, returns to her father. The audience consisted primarily of older people. The young ones were still at the grove on a Saturday night.

Soap Opera Attempts

Prockter was among a group of businessmen who had purchased Eagle Lion Studio in 1953 to make TV films. The new company was called American National. Among the group that bought the studio was comedian Bob Hope. Ziv Television Programs Inc. purchased the studio in 1955. Prockter said at the time Ziv bought the studio that his primary reason for disposing of his stock in American National was so he could devote his time to his TV properties.

The Family Next Door was to be a syndicated, 15-minute, five-days-a-week soap opera; 260 episodes were contemplated. The concept, differing from other such series, focused on the trials and tribulations of one family for a week with a complete story relayed in five episodes. The following week, the story of another family would be told. The actors would change each week as well.

"We feel that this type of property is a natural for the little guy around the country," Prockter told *Variety*. "It will cost a local or regional sponsor less money for this series each week than if he had one half-hour show at night."[4]

Prockter came up with a story for a soap opera called "Mrs. Murphy's Boarding House." An initial script was written by Jameson Brewer in August 1953. It is not known if the story was intended for *The Family Next Door* or for another standalone soap opera.

Mrs. Murphy, owner of a boarding house and a dressmaker, is a widow whose 35-year-old son Michael and his wife Kathy live in the house along with other boarders: Mrs. Leighton, a young widow whose husband died in the war, and Colonel Gladd, an elderly author. Michael is starting his own real estate business and is living at his mother's house to save money. Kathy would like to move into their own place with her husband since she has little to do living with her mother-in-law. Also, she is somewhat jealous of Mrs. Leighton, who wants Michael to find her a home of her own so she can leave the boarding house. Michael and Mrs. Leighton, who is about the same age as he, seem to develop a relationship that might be more than just friends. At the end of the story, Mrs. Leighton receives a phone call supposedly from her deceased husband Herb, much to Kathy's delight.

The script is only 16 pages in length, so apparently it was intended as an episode of a 15-minute soap opera.

In 1953, Prockter and Ed Conne sought to launch another 15-minute daytime drama, *My Sister and I*, starring Robert Hutton, Adele Mara and June Kenney. Lack of sponsor interest led to it not being produced.

Prockter's Work at CBS

In May 1955, Prockter sold all the series produced by his company to Pyramid Productions, owned by two former PTE executives, Everett Rosenthal and Leonard Lowenthan. In June of that year, he became a producer for CBS.

For CBS, Prockter attempted to adapt, in 1957, another radio series that he had produced: *21st Precinct*. Edmon Ryan would have starred each week as the precinct captain, with Franchot Tone featured as the guest star in the pilot. The series was to be filmed in New York City.

21st Precinct had debuted in July 1953 on CBS Radio and ran until 1956 with Everett Sloane as Captain Frank Kennedy in a police drama similar to *Dragnet* but set in New York instead of Los Angeles. The precinct was described as "just lines on a map of the city of New York. Most of the 173,000 people wedged into the nine-tenths of a square mile between Fifth Avenue and the East River wouldn't know if you asked them that they lived or worked in the 21st."[5]

Prockter also sought to adapt the 1930s *Nancy Drew* films which featured Bonita Granville in the lead role as a series for CBS in 1957. The Drew character, a teenage amateur detective, was played by Roberta Shore, her father, Carson Drew, by Frankie Thomas (a veteran of the old movie series) and her boyfriend Ted Nickerson by Tim Considine.

Bernard Prockter died in 1986 at the age of 77.

Prockter Television and Conne-Stephens Productions

Mention should be made of Conne-Stephens, which began as the physical production outfit filming TV shows for Prockter Television Enterprises. Founded by William Stephens and Ed Conne in the early '50s, the company shot such series as *International Police* and *TV Reader's Digest*.

In the 1950s, Conne-Stephens decided to produce their own TV series but without much luck. Among their series attempts were:

Arabian Nights: The pilot for this anthology, "The Princess and the Beggar," starred Marla English as an Arabian princess named Zumurrud, and John Barrymore Jr. as the beggar Ali Shar. Tommy Kirk had a featured role as Habib, Ali Shar's servant. In the opening, a turbaned Genie rubs a magic lantern, laughing wickedly. A cloud of smoke rises from the lantern and the tale begins.

A slave auction is being held. Zumurrud is among the women being auctioned. She demands that Ali Shar exercise the right of challenge for her by engaging in a sword fight with the highest bidder. Ali wins the duel. Zumurrud informs him that she is a princess who has been kidnapped. Men ride into the town square and seize the princess after clubbing Ali. Habib arrives and declares that Fu Shen (Aaron Spelling) will know where the men took the kidnapped princess. Fu Shen says that Zumurrud is in Samara and being forced to marry Rachid Al Din (Dan Seymour). Ali and Habib rush to rescue her. Ali engages in a duel with bow and arrow and kills Rachid. Zumurrud becomes queen, while Ali is made king of Samara.

The narrator states: "Ali ruled wisely with the help of Zumurrud to the contentment of all of the people of Samara." He laughs and declares that his tales have just begun. To save Scheherazade, a thousand more must be spun. No further stories ever resulted from this project.

Big Foot Wallace: Starring a pre–*Rifleman* Chuck Connors in the lead role and Chubby Johnson as his sidekick, the pilot (filmed in December 1955) had Wallace, a frontiersman who supported Texas' claim for independence from Mexico, on a mission to blow up a Mexican ammunition stockpile in order to impede the Mexican war effort. Big Foot and two helpers are captured before they can complete their task and imprisoned with other Texans. With his men facing a firing squad, Big Foot punches the captain in charge of the prison. He and the other prisoners escape, blow up the ammunition dump and return to Texas.

My Most Exciting Moment: Based on real-life stories, this planned anthology centered on dramatic events in people's lives. The pilot "Ring of Steel" starred Margaret O'Brien in a tale about a small-town circus going broke. In order to save his business, O'Brien's father, the circus owner, hires a knife-throwing act. Guess who becomes the assistant in the act on the receiving end of the knives? The pilot, made in late 1955, aired in syndication in 1960.

Sheriffs of the U.S.A.: Originally titled *The Sheriff*, the pilot starred Keith Andes. Called "The Dandy Man," Andes played a lawman who saves his money for a fancy pair of boots and ends up tracking down some train robbers with one-of-a-kind boot markings. Narration for the anthology would be provided by Rex Bell.

Boys' Town: Conne-Stephens also attempted to make a pilot dramatizing true stories from the files of Father Flanagan's youth center.

Mammon: Considered by CBS as a series, the anthology would depict the effects of money and greed on people.

After making four pilots in 1955 (*Big Foot Wallace, Arabian Nights,*

My Most Exciting Moment and *Sheriffs of the U.S.A.*), Conne-Stephens indicated in 1956 that it had no plans to resume production unless at least one of the pilots became a series. William Stephens said, "We may write the whole thing off as a bad investment, start all over again or we may decide to call it a day."[6] Apparently, they called it a day.

CHAPTER 6

Martin Stone

From Series Featuring Critics to Kids' Shows

Martin Stone, a successful New York City lawyer, quit the law profession in 1947 to become an independent TV producer. Born in New York City on May 26, 1915, Stone graduated from Bard College of Columbia University in 1935 and from Yale Law School in 1938.

Describing Stone's physical appearance, veteran TV writer Jerome Coopersmith indicated that the producer was "tall (at least 6 feet), had dark hair, and somewhat resembled Cary Grant, though not quite as handsome. He never wore a hat, even in the coldest weather."[1]

Stone's Initial TV Series

Author Meets the Critics was producer Stone's first TV show. The series began on radio in 1946 with Stone a part-time producer while practicing law. Barry Gray moderated the radio series. Subsequently adapted for television, it premiered on April 4, 1948, on NBC Sunday 8:00 p.m. Its initial run lasted until September 1950. John K.M. McCaffery hosted.

The premise of the show had an author appearing with two critics of his or her recent work. Stone had been asked to do a book review program on the radio in New York and thought a face-to-face encounter between authors and critics would be more interesting.

On the TV series, one critic liked the book, another did not. Before being aired by the network, the series had been on the local New York station WNBT as early as July 1947. For TV, the producers opened up the format to include authors of ideas such as fashion design, movies and sculpting as well as writers. For instance, an April 24, 1949, edition of the series presented actors David Wayne and Lillian Gish performing scenes from the motion picture *Portrait of Jennie*.

Author Meets the Critics went from NBC to ABC on October 3, 1949. Stone then launched a series called *Americana* which premiered

December 8, 1947, on NBC and ran until July 4, 1949. The series had several hosts: John Mason Brown (1947–48), Deems Taylor, who emceed for two episodes, January 21 and 28, 1948, and finally Ben Grauer (1948–49). Vivian Ferrer joined Grauer as co-host in 1949.

"Your program about your country" was the opening slogan for the show. Contestants answered viewer-submitted questions about American history. A panel of four or five adults, known as the Board of Experts, was involved with the initial shows.

On the first show, the panel included Millicent Fenwick, then part of *Vogue*'s editorial staff and later a New York Congresswoman, Bennett Cerf, publisher and long-time panelist on *What's My Line?*, *New York Herald Tribune* book critic Lewis Gannett and 11-year-old Linda Nissen. In the initial segment, three items from Colonial days were presented to the panel to guess what they were. They turned out to be a foot warmer, a candle mold and a sugar-loaf cutter. In another segment, Brown performed a series of charades for the panel to guess the title of a play, book or poem. Viewers who sent in a question that stumped the panel won prizes including a set of encyclopedias, luggage and $50 worth of books of their choice. However, the viewer had to identify the baby picture of a prominent American to win everything.

In 1948, the format changed to a panel of five high school students answering questions sent in by viewers. On June 6, 1949, another format modification had three students playing against three celebrities in a Q&A on American history. Three actors performed short skits acting out the question, after which the contestants attempted to answer.

Recalling this series on which he first worked as writer and assistant producer, Jerome Coopersmith indicated that the questions sent in by the audience were mostly useless,

> so I had to invent them myself. If a question stumped the teenage panel, you may wonder who would receive the encyclopedias. They were sent to me, using phony names. As a result, the floor of my bachelor apartment on West 68th Street was littered with encyclopedia volumes. Martin Stone didn't care what I did with them. They made marvelous gifts for newlyweds, children's birthdays and bar mitzvahs.[2]

Such a practice would not be permitted today under current television standards and practices.

Howdy Doody and Bob Smith

While Stone's initial series would not be considered B television, the next show he helped launch, *The Howdy Doody Show*, started as basically a variety series for kids.

The iconic star of *The Howdy Doody Show*, which ran from 1947 to 1960. It was the first nationally broadcast children's TV show.

In late 1947, Stone began producing the beloved children's show with the freckle-faced puppet Howdy Doody along with Buffalo Bob Smith, Clarabelle the Clown and many other characters. As Smith recalled in his autobiography, "Marty had great connections for opening doors in television.... He asked me, 'Hey, what about putting Howdy Doody on television?'"[3]

The show actually began as a one-hour series titled *Puppet Playhouse* that featured puppets, vaudeville acts and old movie shorts. The original Howdy Doody puppet looked like a country bumpkin with a pinched face and wild hair. Thanks to Stone, Smith owned the Howdy Doody name and character. When stores wanted to merchandise the puppet, Frank Paris, who constructed the marionette, thought he should receive royalties. When NBC indicated that Paris had accepted $500 for the puppet's construction, he left the network, and so a new Howdy Doody was created with a freckle-faced countenance and a more boyish appearance. Smith shared the royalties from merchandising the Doodyville characters with NBC as well as with Stone. As Smith pointed out, "[I]f a manufacturer paid me $100,000 to put Howdy's picture on a wristwatch or shirt or toy, Marty got $50,000, NBC $25,000, and Buffalo Bob $25,000."[4] In 1948, Stone formed Martin Stone Associates which, in addition to licensing merchandising for the *Howdy Doody* characters, also arranged licensing contracts for celebrities such as Jackie Gleason, Gabby Hayes and Lassie.

Illustrative of the series' early episodes is one from March 8, 1949, where Howdy Doody presents a segment called "Ask Howdy Doody" in which he answers letters from viewers. One submission asks Howdy to sing "Start Your Day with a Song." After the number, Howdy responds to a request from a little girl for advice on how to get into the movies. This results in Buffalo Bob directing a scene from *Romeo and Juliet* with the puppet as the former and a girl from the Peanut Gallery playing Juliet. During the segment, the premiere of *Portrait of Jennie* with Jennifer Jones is plugged, apparently for any parents watching the show. Finally, Howdy and Buffalo Bob present an old-time Howdy Doody movie about flying machines narrated by Smith.

In 1950, Smith sold the rights to the Doodyville characters to Kagran Corporation, headed by Stone. Kagran produced live and filmed TV series and also merchandised. Stone had a 40 percent interest in Kagran with 30 percent owned by NBC and 30 percent by Lehman Brothers. While Stone had the majority interest, Smith received $250,000 in bonds as part of his reimbursement. Howdy Doody writer Edward Kean was in charge of programming for the company. In 1955, he sold his interest in Kagran to NBC.

The Gulf Road Show Starring Bob Smith, which premiered September 2, 1948, on NBC Thursdays at 9:00 p.m. and ran until June 30, 1949, was the next TV series Stone produced. Smith hosted this prime-time variety half-hour that experimented with different formats over its run.

The first episode had Smith leading the studio audience in a community sing-along, engaging in an audience participation stunt by having four females compete in a screaming contest, reminiscing at the piano about the year 1922 while showing some newsreel clips from that year, playing accordion with the Enoch Light orchestra, having bandleaders Fred Waring, Vincent Lopez and Blue Barron perform with him in a "kitchenware" band, and doing commercials for Gulf Oil. Segments changed in later shows with Smith interviewing persons of note like the author of *Sorry, Wrong Number* and then showing clips from the Barbara Stanwyck film, doing other features on new inventions, books and movies, and holding talent contests and musical quizzes. Howdy Doody appeared on the Christmas show singing "All I Want for Christmas Is My Two Front Teeth."

The Quaker Oats Show and *Johnny Jupiter*

Stone next produced *The Quaker Oats Show*, an entertainment and educational series for children in which Gabby Hayes related stories about American history, dramatized by actors. Jane and Buck, two children representative of the show's target audience, listened to Hayes' tales. The series, which began in the fall of 1950, was a step above the ordinary fare aimed at kids in its emphasis on educating children about the country's history. It received an Emmy nomination for Best Children's Program in 1953.

The show would begin with Hayes singing about Quaker Oats cereal followed by a playlet on the topic of the day. On the premiere, Gabby relates the story of Lewis and Clark and their exploration of the land bought by President Thomas Jefferson under the Louisiana Purchase. Various drafts of the script are available in the Vincent J. Donehue Papers at the New York Public Library. Donehue directed the episode, which was written by Jerome Coopersmith and Ray Wilson.

Actors played Lewis and Clark and the Native Americans they encounter. The Indians believe that the explorers are invaders who did not come in peace. The tribe's chief challenges one of them to wrestle an Indian brave with the understanding that if the brave wins, it will be evidence that the adventurers are not telling the truth about their mission. Clark wrestles the Indian and wins, meaning that the pair will become tribe members and be set free to continue their exploration.

In some versions of the script, Lewis and Clark's female Indian guide helps Clark win the match by firing a gun to distract the brave. In other versions of the script, Gabby Hayes' great, great grandfather, Cannonball Hayes, creates the distraction.

At the end of the playlet, Hayes introduces Roy Rogers, Dale Evans, Trigger and Bullet. Roy plugs Quaker Oats which, in a bit of cross promotion, also sponsored Rogers' radio show. Bullet, Roy's dog, and Trigger, his horse, each perform tricks, and Dale Evans sings "Don't Ever Fall in Love with a Cowboy."

Later scripts for the show, each based on historical fact, were written by Coopersmith and Horton Foote. Coopersmith wrote the first draft of each script with Foote then making changes. Foote is probably best known for writing *The Trip to Bountiful*. Fred Rogers of *Mister Rogers' Neighborhood* fame was the show's floor manager.

Other *Quaker Oats Show* episodes focused on historical personages and events such as the story of Iwo Jima, a dramatization of amity between Union and Confederate soldiers, a chronicle of the fall of the Alamo, and a portrait of crusading newspaperman James King of William.

Stone kept a record of the ongoing costs of producing each show to determine if an episode was over-budget or under. If a particular installment came in over budget, the next episode would have to cost less. If a show was heavy on scenery and props, on-air talent would be cut back. If an episode was heavy on talent, sets would be simplified.

In 1952, Stone attempted to launch a show starring Tony Rivers as Choctow Indian, Silver Cloud, in a program aimed at children, but the proposal never turned into a series. The following year, Stone created and produced a children's show called *Johnny Jupiter*. The show first aired on the DuMont TV network with character actor Vaughn Taylor playing Ernest Duckweather, who worked as a janitor at a TV station and was able to communicate with beings on the planet Jupiter.

The series, offering satirical takes on American culture, was entertainment for both adults and children. Adults would understand the satirical elements, kids would like the puppets from Jupiter. The DuMont series featured puppets Johnny Jupiter and B-12 along with Duckweather and his boss at the TV station, Mr. Preel.

Duckweather yearns to be more than just a janitor. He also wants to be a television engineer or an actor. In the station's control room, he contacts Johnny Jupiter and Jupiter's sardonic friend B-12. On the second episode, written and produced by Jerome Coopersmith, Duckweather gets into a discussion of television programming trying to describe Westerns to Johnny and B-12. In turn, Johnny talks about a Jupiterian TV show called 3DX and Her Famous Wiggle, an educational series. Sexy 3DX, a puppet, sings a song about mathematics called "If I Were a Line and You Were a Circle, I'd Want to Be Tangent to You" while wiggling one ear, slinking around and warbling like a torch singer.

After she completes the song, an announcer says that the next episode will be about space navigation and feature the song "When We Lost Our Heated Suits in Outer Space, Why Did You Seem Cold to Me."

B-12 then informs Duckweather that Jupiterian television used to be excellent but, after years of research, it is now simply mediocre. The medium performs a community service on Jupiter as a convenient, harmless outlet for Jupiterians' frustrations. The most creative minds on the planet are devising ways to make TV even worse.

Satirizing B television, the puppet B-12 takes Duckweather inside the building housing the Jupiterian Broadcasting System, where viewers observe a producer criticizing a writer for providing fresh material instead of trite situations, stale dialogue and corny endings that the producer requested. Both the producer and writer were also puppets. The producer tells his writer that yesterday's story was the worst ever and tells him, "Just change the names, and no one'll know the difference."[5]

The writer asks Duckweather to describe American television. The janitor proceeds to recite lines from *Romeo and Juliet* as an example of Shakespeare on American TV. The Jupiterian writer and producer appreciate the selection but abhor Duckweather's acting. They want to hire him for a series on Jupiter to be slotted following the 3DX show, believing the janitor's acting will make the citizens of Jupiter forget their other troubles. Duckweather agrees even though it means turning over all his household possessions to the Jupiterian network. However, B-12 advises Duckweather that his appearing on Jupiter television means that B-12 will have to end his relationship with Duckweather since no one on the planet ever talks to television people. But as a consolation, and perhaps as a nod to Stone's TV merchandising expertise, B-12 tells Duckweather that he will see his name on lots of merchandise promoting the new show.

After he signs off with his friends from Jupiter, his boss, Mr. Preel, notes that Duckweather is probably the world's worst actor. The janitor replies, "I'm delightfully artificial, refreshingly unconvincing. That's why I'm going to be a television star."[6]

Wright King as Ernest P. Duckweather, with Johnny Jupiter on the left and the robot Major Domo on the right. This Martin Stone–produced children's series was not as successful as *The Howdy Doody Show*.

The series transferred to ABC with actor Wright King playing Duckweather who, in this version, worked as a store clerk in a business owned by Horatio Frisby (Cliff Hall). Frisby's daughter Katherine (Pat Peardon) also had a job in the store and became Duckweather's girlfriend. Duckweather communicated with Johnny Jupiter and robot Major Domo through a special TV set in the store. Johnny Jupiter was reminiscent of the hand puppet, Kukla, from *Kukla, Fran, and Ollie*. Major Domo with a gruff voice liked single-breasted steel jackets and conservative politics but disliked intellectuals and classical music.

One episode, "Lecture," guest starred Ross Martin (later of *Wild Wild West* fame) as the Professor, a radio lecturer on the subject of "money isn't everything." Duckweather is tasked with having the Professor fill in for an ailing presenter at the town's lecture hall. But when the Professor asks for a $1000 fee to present a lecture, Duckweather attempts to impersonate the Professor to give the talk. Ernest enlists the help of Johnny and Major Domo. They transport a robot named Reject to Earth, but Reject messes up the slides for the presentation. Reject, a pathetic character, appeared to have been constructed of spare parts. Kathy comes to the rescue by convincing the Professor to give the lecture.

Johnny Jupiter and Major Domo were puppet-size when they appeared on Duckweather's TV screen but became life-size when they came to Earth.

And so, *Johnny Jupiter* evolved from a satire to a B grade situation comedy. According to Coopersmith, in the early days of television, power was in the hands of advertising agencies. He elaborated:

> If I criticized TV in one of my scripts, the ad agent representing the sponsor might think that was funny and laugh loudly, and the owners of the TV station would be afraid to say "boo." But as time went on, that changed as TV stations began to affiliate with one another. Networks were beginning to form and the power passed on to them because they now controlled the geographic extent of a program's exposure to the public. The ad agencies were not unhappy about this because it increased the scope of their ability to advertise their clients' products. None of those in power wanted anything too controversial on the air because they knew their programs would not be received in places where liberal or progressive views were not admired. I believe this will explain why *Johnny Jupiter* changed from satire to sitcom, much to my sadness.[7]

NBC bought out Stone's interest in Kagran in 1955 in order to launch their own licensing corporation, California National Productions, to license all of the network's properties.

Stone's Other TV Projects

Stone produced a new version of *Super Circus* beginning on ABC in 1955. Jerry Colonna, the ringmaster, appeared with Sandra Wirth (Miss Florida of 1955) and Jerry Bergen.

In 1956, the producer developed the summer replacement for *Super Circus*: *Going Places,* hosted by Jack Gregson. The show aired live from Miami featuring variety acts performing in various Florida locations like the Seaquarium, Hialeah Park and the Parrot Jungle.

In that same year, Stone launched another circus-themed series, *Circus Time.* "This will be a true variety show—more like the indoor circus of Europe than the American outdoor show," he said. "In fact, we hope to introduce many fine and unusual European performers in the course of the season. ...The setting will represent a tent, with five rows of spectators and one ring. Paul Winchell and Mahoney will be the ringmasters and will also contribute to the entertainment."[8]

Departing from shows aimed at children, Stone sought to do *Prowl Car,* a series based on the files of the Miami city police department in 1957. He did not find a network or syndicator.

Also in that year, Stone tried to make a 90-minute kids' show for National Telefilm Associates. It would have starred Red Buttons along with Gabby Hayes, Roger Price, Jerry Colonna and Billy Gilbert. The unrealized series would have been written by two of Jackie Gleason's writers, Coleman Jacoby and Arnie Rosen.

During the summer of 1958, Stone produced a game show, *Lucky Partners,* for NBC daytime involving studio audience contestants attempting to match serial numbers on dollar bills with players on stage. Five panelists on stage answered questions to determine which number on a large board was to be put into play. Viewers used Bingo-type cards with dollar serial numbers on them to complete the required patterns and become eligible for prizes. Carl Cordell was the host. Stone produced the show with his brother Allen.

The Stone brothers also syndicated *Bingo-at-Home* which had begun on a New York station. The show had viewers creating for themselves a Bingo card. At the top of the card, the viewer writes five digits of their phone number. Then the viewer goes down each column numbering in sequence based on the number in that column at the top. As the numbers are drawn randomly on TV, the viewer checks each off until they get Bingo. The card is sent in and is eligible for prizes. The Stones provided TV stations with the materials to present the program with each outlet providing their own announcer.

One of Stone's final television projects, *Let's Make a Hit,* a 1959 pilot, broadcast from a recording studio and focused on a top talent making an album. The pilot did not become a series.

Stone left TV production in the late 1950s and became president of the Herald-Tribune Radio network. He passed away in 1998 at the age of 83.

CHAPTER 7

William F. Broidy

One Hit, Several Misses

William F. Broidy came to California in 1946 after being an interior decorator. He spent the next three plus years learning motion picture production at Monogram, where his brother Steve was president. He formed William F. Broidy Productions in 1950.

Broidy began producing the game show *Pantomime Quiz* for CBS in 1950. Hosted by Mike Stokey, the show took place on a living room set involving two celebrity teams of four members each trying to guess phrases, quotes, song titles, etc., through pantomime. The series initially debuted in Los Angeles in 1947 and then was picked up by Chevrolet dealers and shown in New York City on WCBS beginning in October 1949. Subsequently the CBS network broadcast the program during the summers of 1950 and 1951.

The Adventures of Wild Bill Hickok

The producer's most successful TV series was *The Adventures of Wild Bill Hickok* starring Guy Madison and Andy Devine, which aired in first-run syndication from 1951 to 1958. Sponsored by Kellogg's cereal, the show also aired on radio during most of its TV run. Madison played U.S. Marshal James Butler "Wild Bill" Hickok with Devine as his comical sidekick Jingles B. Jones. Wild Bill's horse was called Buckshot; Jingles' horse was Joker.

Martin Levy and Maurice Tombragel wrote the series' initial episode "Behind Southern Lines." Individually, each writer had scripted several B Western movies such as *Calamity Jane and Sam Bass* (1949), *The Daltons' Women* (1950) and *Marshal of Heldorado* (1950). They were adept at devising fictional stories centered on actual Western figures.

In "Behind Southern Lines," Bill Hickok, a Union Army officer during the Civil War, meets Jingles while on a spying mission. Other episodes generally dealt with the marshal and his deputy Jingles ferreting out bad guys and saving honest citizens from evildoers. According to Broidy, there were only so many basic plots for Westerns. The only storyline he indicated he would not use "is the one which shows a woman as the 'heavy.' The reason for that being, of course, that the sponsor doesn't want any child who watches this program thinking that his mother is a potential 'heavy.'"[1]

Andy Devine and Guy Madison in character from *The Adventures of Wild Bill Hickok.* Devine began appearing in movies in the late 1920s; Madison's first movie was *Since You Went Away* in 1944.

Many episodes mixed comedy with drama. For example, in "Papa Antonelli," a first season installment, Wild Bill and Jingles investigate a robbery from the Wells Fargo office witnessed by Mama and Papa Antonelli, itinerant peddlers. Bill thinks that a man named Cody (Francis McDonald) is involved with the robbers. He arrests Cody for killing one of the bandits, thinking that Cody did it to prevent the man from betraying him. Cody's niece wants to spring him from jail. When two men attempt to break Cody out of jail, Jingles hides in the peddlers' wagon and dresses as a woman to disguise himself from the outlaws. Bill then wants Jingles to continue the masquerade so he can spy on Cody's niece, who lives in a "ladies only" boarding house. While Jingles is sleeping, the niece breaks into Jingles' room and sees his gun. The robbers go after Jingles but are subdued. In the end, Jingles still has to wear women's clothes because someone stole his pants.

How this Western series came to be was unique at the time. Clothing and toy manufacturers often sign contracts with production companies and/or movie stars to make and market merchandise based on a well-known character in a popular radio, movie or television series. The *Wild Bill Hickok* series reversed this idea: A group of companies wanting to participate in the lucrative merchandising market for radio and TV characters formed a company to create a new radio and TV hero for the express purpose of promoting sales of their products tagged to their new creation. The companies (Robert Bruce Knitwear, Irvin B. Foster Sportswear, DeLuxe Wash Suit, Variety Manufacturing, Western Junior Manufacturing and George Schmidt Manufacturing) created Delira Corporation in 1950 to implement their idea of developing both a radio and a TV show around a new Western hero who would catch on with the public. The corporation employed David Hire, a motion picture producer, to develop the series. He suggested "Wild Bill Hickok" as the hero.

Delira would finance a series of 52 TV episodes (and 39 15-minute daily radio episodes) starring Madison and Devine, with both stars having stock in the corporation. As radio and TV columnist Lou Larkin put it, "The companies plan to promote and exploit Madison as Wild Bill. In return they'll have exclusive rights to produce cowboy suits, cap pistols, spurs, hats and other gimmicks associated with a big-time cowboy."[2]

The companies behind the Delira Corporation were not interested in sponsoring the *Wild Bill* series—only in selling products based on their new TV hero. As noted above, Kellogg's cereal sponsored the TV show. Evidently, producing both a TV series and a radio show were too much for David Hire. He brought in William Broidy to make the TV series, while Hire made the radio series. Broidy sold the rights to *Wild Bill Hickok* to Screen Gems in 1957. Screen Gems produced the final season of the series in 1958.

Broidy's only other attempt at a Western series, *Ride the Bugle*, was earmarked for the 1956–57 season. The series was to star Dennis O'Keefe as a cavalry officer.

Broidy's Attempts at Launching an Adventure Series

Broidy sought to follow up the *Wild Bill Hickok* series with other projects that would appeal mainly to young audiences. Broidy tried to introduce a series, *The Phantom Pirate,* starring Robert Stack in the main role. Stack's crew consisted of Dave Sharpe as Dandy, Frank Gerstle as Squint, Frank Richards as Francois, Bobby Jefferson as Bowknot, David DuVal as David and Henry Marreo as Toby.

The series would depict the adventures of the Phantom Pirate, who fought for justice and thwarted criminals on the high seas. The crew of the Phantom's ship, the *Avenger*, consisted of Dandy, Squint and Francois. The unaired pilot was made during the spring of 1952.

The pilot begins with the Phantom retrieving Master David from the British ship *Isabell* along with David's less-than-effective guardian Bowknot and David's friend Toby. David is the young son of the governor (Roy Gordon), a good friend of the Phantom's. The Phantom wants to save David from becoming a hostage of men who want to take over the governorship. Wearing a disguise, the Phantom visits the governor to warn him about the usurpers and asks the governor to leave his house. The usurpers find out about the warning and capture both the Phantom and the governor. The Phantom escapes and frees the governor from incarceration with the help of his shipmates. Before he dies, the governor advises his son to follow the dictates of the Phantom. David, Toby and Bowknot then become members of the Phantom's crew.

Trail Blazers, starring Alan Hale Jr. as Roger Stone, the director of a Boys' Club, was a 1953 pilot produced by Broidy's company. Other actors in the pilot were Dick Taylor as Ben, Henry Blair as Spike, Bobby Hyatt as Jim, Barney McCormick as Feathers, Jim Flowers as Pudge and Duke York as Angus.

Titled "The Fugitive," the pilot involved an escaped convict seeking the money that he and a partner had stolen. Stone, camping with a group of boys, comes upon the convict's dead partner, who had been killed by his fellow escapee. After speaking with a deputy sheriff (Lyle Talbot), Stone decides to take the boys back to the lake thinking that would be safer, but the escapee, wearing the deputy's coat, comes upon the group. Stone and the boys pretend they don't know that the man is the fugitive. Stone fights with the convict and is knocked unconscious. The convict then takes one of the boys, Spike, hostage. When Stone regains consciousness, he goes after the fugitive with the other boys. Thanks to trail markings left by Spike, Stone locates and captures the convict and frees the boy.

If the pilot had become a series, apparently future episodes would have also placed different members of the Boys' Club in dangerous situations. When the pilot didn't sell, a second pilot was made which apparently dealt with juvenile delinquency, focusing on two Boys' Club members involved in an illegal trapping venture. When there were no buyers for that one, the two pilots were released as a motion picture titled *Trail Blazers* in 1953 through Allied Artists.

Drama, Variety and Comedy Series Projects

In 1951, Broidy sought to adapt for TV a religious radio series, *The Hour of St. Francis*. The TV version, to be known as *Trinity Theatre*, was made in cooperation with the Third Order of St. Francis. The planned anthology would use stories from the radio series which dealt with spiritual subjects but not specifically religious ones. The Franciscans were to retain 76 percent of the profits from the series with Broidy receiving the other 24 percent. Thirty-nine episodes were contemplated with each to be shot over a five-day period. There is no record of this series ever premiering on television.

In the fall of 1951, Broidy attempted to launch a situation comedy, *Heavens to Betsy,* starring Alan Mowbray and ZaSu Pitts and written by the husband-and-wife team of Agnes Christine Johnston and Frank Dazey. Presumably Pitts would have appeared as Mowbray's scatterbrained spouse.

In 1952, Broidy tried to syndicate a music-travelogue series filmed in Hawaii, *Hawaiian Paradise.* Twenty-six half-hours were made in color by producer John Jay Franklin, who sold the series to Broidy. John M. Kennedy narrated.

Also in that year, Broidy Productions made a pilot for a medical series called *Case History* starring Regis Toomey and Sara Haden. This potential series featuring melodramatic medical stories, based on the experiences of Dr. Frederick Loomis, was initially titled *Consultation Room* with Ray Collins, who later played Police Lt. Tragg on *Perry Mason,* cast in the lead as a doctor. Toomey took over the main role as Dr. Garret Thompson, and the title became *Case History.* Haden played Hennessey, the doctor's main assistant.

The pilot script involved Dr. Thompson treating two victims of a car accident at his clinic. Kathy Hamilton, the driver, has a broken ankle. Her passenger, George Baldwin, is in more serious condition with a head injury. Kathy is Baldwin's sales associate and wants to marry him. Mrs. Baldwin is informed of the accident and flies from San Diego to Los Angeles to visit her spouse. Semi-conscious, Baldwin talks about Hamilton, saying he loves his wife and doesn't want to divorce her. Upon realizing the true relationship between her husband and Kathy, Mrs. Baldwin decides to fly back to San Diego. Once fully conscious, Baldwin tells Kathy he doesn't want to marry her. She leaves the clinic alone. Baldwin then has a setback in his recovery. Dr. Thompson has to operate to correct a subdural hematoma and needs Mrs. Baldwin's authorization. He contacts her just as she is about to depart. After the successful surgery, Mr. and Mrs. Baldwin reconcile.

Frank McDonald, who had helmed several *Wild Bill Hickok* episodes, wrote and directed the pilot. Thirty-nine episodes were initially planned. Based on the pilot script, the series would have been more like a soap opera dealing with each patient's personal issues instead of a "disease of the week"–type show.

U.S. Secret Service Agent, a proposed 1954 series starring Broderick Crawford as John Bronson and based on Secret Service case files, would detail the exploits of that government agency, focusing on presidential security and counterfeiting of U.S. currency. The pilot looked behind the scenes of the Secret Service, emphasizing the authenticity of the planned series and showcased Broderick Crawford on a trip to Washington, D.C., touring Secret Service headquarters and meeting with the head of the agency.

Written by Al Martin and Vernon Delston, the script for the regular pilot, "Mr. Jade," dealt with the counterfeiting of French francs by an older man posing as a Spanish prince, a French industrialist and a Greek importer. Since the man likes to collect jade, Bronson and another agent visit various firms that handle jade. From a driver's license number found on a note pad, the agents identify Carl Langford, an importer of Oriental art. Langford says that his driver's license was stolen by a customer who recently purchased some jade from him. However, Langford's description of the man does not fit that of the counterfeiter. The agents ask Langford to run a newspaper ad indicating that he has received a new shipment of jade. The agents stake out the store to see who responds to the ad. Jose Hermande visits the store in response to the advertisement only to be told that the shipment has not yet arrived. The agents shadow Hermande to his apartment where they find him posing as a South American movie producer. They discover that he has been using theatrical makeup to disguise himself as an older man when passing counterfeit money. "Mr. Jade" is arrested when he is about to board a plane to Havana. Hermande tells the agents that, in addition to purchasing jade, he needed money to help pay off his mother's gambling debts. He also wanted to join the Cuban air force, where pilots have to buy their own airplanes.

Throughout his years producing television shows, Broidy also made several B movies, mainly Westerns. One of his last films, *Bullwhip* (1958), starred Wild Bill Hickok himself, Guy Madison, along with Rhonda Fleming in a story about a man about to be hanged for killing someone in self-defense. A crooked judge offers to free him if he agrees to marry a woman so she can receive an inheritance.

Broidy passed away at age 44 on July 14, 1959, after a long illness.

CHAPTER 8

Frederick W. Ziv

Mastering the Art of Location Filming

With a law degree from the University of Michigan, Frederick W. Ziv formed his own advertising agency in September 1930 in Cincinnati, Ohio, his birthplace. The agency began advertising on radio for its clients in the late 1930s. From those beginnings, Ziv expanded into producing and syndicating his own radio shows and eventually television series.

He entered the field of TV production and syndication in 1948 when he bought the General Film Library, which was used in the production of several 15-minute highlights programs.

Ziv's First Series

Ziv's first ventures into television were series based on repackaged newsreel clips.

Yesterday's Newsreel, which premiered in syndication December 1948 at different times on various TV stations, ran for 139 episodes and was the first series Ziv offered for syndication. For some nostalgia, for others a history lesson, this quarter-hour series repackaged theatrical newsreels and sold them to local stations. The first episode featured clips from 1928 about the presidential election, the Byrd expedition, the Olympics and Johnny Weissmuller's swimming record.

Other episodes chronicled such events as Lindbergh's flight across the Atlantic, the abdication of Britain's Edward VIII, the assassination of Alexander I of Yugoslavia, and the surrender of Germany at the end of World War I.

Sports Album premiered in syndication in 1948 and ran until 1949. Dennis James and Bill Slater narrated the newsreel clips. This package of old sports newsreels was often aired by TV stations right before and/

or right after live sporting events like baseball and football games. An episode consisted of three newsreels running five minutes each. Some stations would air just one newsreel for five minutes; others would air the full 15-minute program.

The featured newsreels most often dealt with baseball and football. One program showed footage of famous opening days in baseball, the New York Giants in spring training, and the legendary baseball player Ty Cobb. A football-themed show consisted of Southern California Rose Bowl classics, Army-Navy games and Yale-Harvard games.

Easy Aces premiered on December 14, 1949, on the DuMont network Wednesday at 7:45 p.m. and aired until June 14, 1950. It featured Goodman Ace as himself, and his wife Jane Ace. Dorothy (Betty Garde) played Jane's friend. The filmed 15-minute series featured Goodman and Jane Ace commenting on film clips. Jane was a little eccentric or, to put it another way, somewhat confused in her thinking. The series opened with Jane reading a book titled *Brain Surgery—Self-Taught*. Ziv had produced and syndicated the *Easy Aces* radio program beginning in 1945.

Goodman Ace had a unique approach to TV, believing that he and his wife should not appear on the screen all that much. With his career as a writer, he preferred words to pictures and so developed the idea of showing old films while he and his wife provided audio commentary.

Goodman was the straight man, while his wife was like Gracie Allen, usually misunderstanding or misusing a word or phrase (for instance, "Time wounds all heels").

On the premiere episode, in a facsimile of their living room, the Aces view and talk about a film of New York City in the 1900s showing fashions, places and people.

The Cisco Kid and Other Westerns

The Cisco Kid, one of Ziv's first hits in syndication, starred Duncan Renaldo as Cisco and Leo Carrillo as his sidekick Pancho. Beginning in 1950, the series ran for 156 episodes—all of them in color, although most TV stations at the time aired them in black and white.

The Cisco Kid character was first introduced in a 1907 story by William Sydney Porter (aka O. Henry) called "The Caballero's Way." Originally, the character was a gunslinger who liked killing for sport. But the character's image changed in a 1928 film adaptation titled *In Old Arizona* where the Kid became a likable and charming bandit. In 1943, Ziv optioned the character. A live radio series featuring Cisco premiered on a Los Angeles radio station in 1946 with Ziv recording the presentations for syndication across the country.

Each TV episode began with a narrator announcing, "Here's adventure, here's romance, here's O. Henry's Robin Hood of the West, the Cisco Kid." Duncan Renaldo first appeared as the Cisco Kid in the 1945 movie *The Cisco Kid Returns.*

As with other Westerns for kids, the horses ridden by Cisco and Pancho each had a name. Cisco called his horse Diablo; Pancho named his steed Loco.

In the premiere episode "Boomerang," Cisco and Pancho are wanted men after two men impersonating them robbed a bank. Real estate agent Jim Brent is behind the ruse. He is plotting to take over the bank and next wants to rob a banker bringing money from another establishment to replace the stolen money. Cisco and Pancho want to protect the banker, but the sheriff arrests them before their doubles have a chance to steal the money. Cisco and Pancho break out of jail with Cisco capturing one of the masqueraders and making him confess who hired him. After Cisco takes care of Brent, he and Pancho return the stolen funds to the bank.

As fighters against injustice, Cisco and Pancho were either attempting to help an innocent person accused of a crime or, as in the foregoing episode, bring to justice those who had framed the duo for a crime they didn't commit.

While the heroes of B television Westerns are immune from serious injury or death, the actors who play them are not. During *The Cisco Kid*'s fourth season, an on-set accident sidelined Renaldo from appearing as the Kid on a number of episodes. In "Battle of Red Rock Pass," the Cisco Kid is after an escaped convict. While helping the sheriff find the escapee, Cisco goes off alone. The convict and his gang lob a fake boulder to prevent Cisco from coming for them. Instead of the boulder bouncing away from Renaldo, it knocked him unconscious and broke two vertebrae in his neck. He was placed in traction for a number of weeks. To cover his absence, a stunt double was used in many scenes with Renaldo recording his dialogue from his hospital bed.

The episode following the one on which the accident occurred, "The Death of the Cisco Kid," had a storyline about a dynamite explosion that supposedly killed Cisco. On the installment, the guy who planted the explosion is actually killed. Cisco tells the doctor attending him to list his name on the perpetrator's death certificate, while Cisco assumes the identity of the villain in order to determine who his boss is. Cisco wears a bandage completely covering his head so that Renaldo's stuntman could play the character with Renaldo dubbing his lines. The producers took other measures such as the Cisco Kid turning his back to the camera in several scenes or being filmed in the shadows until Renaldo was able to return to work.

In 1955, Ziv sought to launch a comedic Western created by Steve Fisher, *Luke and the Tenderfoot*, starring Edgar Buchanan and Carleton Carpenter. The Buchanan character, an iterant peddler–con man named Luke Herkimer, befriends tenderfoot Pete Quinn (Carpenter). Quinn is out West looking for a job. Since he is from Boston, Herkimer nicknames him "the Boston Kid." To protect him from bullies played (Michael Landon, Leonard Nimoy, Richard Bakalyan), Luke tells everyone that Quinn is a professional boxer. Gunslinger Johnny Dent (Lee Van Cleef) challenges the Kid to a boxing match with each of the town bullies taking him on in turn. All the townspeople including Dent bet that the Kid will win; Luke bets against him. Miraculously the kid wins the first two bouts but loses the last one. For winning his bet, Herkimer is challenged to a gunfight by Dent. The kid steps in and dares Dent to shoot him. Dent decides to abandon the fight. Luke buys the kid a horse and saddle with his winnings, and the two leave town.

Ziv made a second pilot of the planned series. In "John Wesley Hardin," Luke informs Pete that he once saved the life of the gunslinger. Hardin arrives in town to see his wife Stella. He clears out the local saloon, leaving only him and his partner, Sandy Burke. Despite this, Luke and Peter enter the saloon, where Hardin says he doesn't know Herkimer and that he hates braggarts. A woman who looks like Stella enters the saloon, forced there by the townspeople. In the process, Hardin shoots two bounty hunters. He wants to know why his wife hasn't shown up.

Luke has a plan to allow Hardin to escape. For $500, Luke informs Hardin he can smuggle him out of town in the back of his wagon. Since there is only room for one person in the wagon, Hardin shoots his partner Burke. Pete and Luke then leave town with Hardin in the wagon. Luke tells the gunslinger that he gave the $500 to Hardin's wife as Hardin escapes into the woods.

Mixing comedy with the Western genre is difficult to pull off. Viewers were used to having their Western heroes fight injustice. The character of Luke Herkimer as a grifter did not fit the stereotype of the typical Western lead character, nor did the naïve Tenderfoot character, which is probably why the show did not become a series.

Ziv premiered a more adult Western on ABC on October 16, 1957. Running for a season and a half. *Tombstone Territory* starred Pat Conway as Sheriff Clay Hollister and Richard Eastham as Harris Claibourne, editor of the newspaper *The Epitaph*. In the late '50s, Ziv turned to Westerns loosely based on historical documents and books instead of child-friendly characters like the Cisco Kid and Pancho. Producers Frank Pittman and Andy White used articles from the real-life *Tombstone Epitaph* as the basis for stories on *Tombstone Territory*. ABC dropped the series after its first season but brought it back as a midseason replacement in 1959. The network then canceled the Western for good after airing 12 more episodes. Ziv Television self-financed an additional 26 episodes for syndication.

The Claibourne character narrated each episode while Hollister handled the action. The main plot of most stories had an outsider coming to Tombstone and creating trouble that Hollister had to resolve. In the opener, "Gunslinger for Galeyville," the sheriff attempts to collect taxes from the residents of Galeyville, who are mostly outlaws. Hollister enlists the help of gang leader Curley Bill Brocius to assist in the collection by making him a deputy. The two are successful, but Bill warns him about Monk, a member of Bill's gang, who swore vengeance on Hollister when the sheriff ordered him out of Tombstone for running roughshod in the local saloon. Monk won't permit Hollister to return to Tombstone with the tax money. In the showdown, Hollister wounds Monk, but then Monk draws his other gun and the sheriff has to kill him.

Bat Masterson, debuting on October 8, 1958, was a different type of Western hero. Unlike the typical cowboy lead, Masterson (Gene Barry) wore a derby hat, had a gold-topped cane, and dressed in attire more suitable for large Eastern cities at the time than for Western towns. *Bat Masterson* ran for three seasons on NBC.

According to Barry, the series was "based on the book by Richard O'Connor, which is thoroughly documented by old-time newspapermen who worked with Bat when he left lawman work in the West to work on a New York newspaper."[1] Bat Masterson had been the sidekick of Wyatt Earp when he was a U.S. marshal. He got the nickname "Bat" from the cane he carried. He had been wounded in the hip during a gunfight and needed the cane for his bad leg. Masterson sometimes used the cane, instead of a gun, when facing an opponent. He always wore his best clothes, suitable for burial, because he never knew when he might die.

The pilot "Double Showdown" had Masterson coming to the aid of friend Shorty Keenan, the owner of a gambling house, the Alhambra, that is being forced out of business by Keel Roberts, owner of the competing Oriental gambling establishment. After the story ends with the villain being pumped full of lead, Barry himself appears on screen stating that history is in doubt as to the way this incident actually ended. While most authorities agree that the ending was the one that had just been shown, others say it concluded differently. With Barry back in character as Masterson, the episode proceeds to relate an alternate ending in which the villain is punished but not killed.

Instead of a Western with one hero, why not make a series with three? Apparently, that was the thinking of Ziv in 1958 when the company launched *The Rough Riders*, which dealt with three Civil War veterans who unite to start a new life out West. Capt. Jim Flagg (Kent Taylor, formerly Ziv's Boston Blackie), Lt. Cullen Kirby (Jan Merlin) and Sgt. Buck Sinclair (Peter Whitney) comprised the Rough Riders. Flagg and Sinclair were in the Union Army; Kirby had fought for the South. The series aired for one season on ABC.

The three former military men fought against evildoers as they traveled across the country during the period of Reconstruction. Episodes involved the three heroes aiding farmers harassed by land raiders, rescuing a family held captive by renegade Indians, settling a feud between two warring clans, and taking on law enforcement duties in a town whose marshal had been killed.

The idea for the series stemmed from a Ziv executive interested in the post–Civil War era. Ziv's researchers spent months reviewing newspaper reports and other periodicals about that time in history and found enough material for a series. They uncovered the fact that the term "Rough Riders" came into widespread use during that era, and so the phrase was adopted for the series' title. The opening episode had the three Rough Riders pursuing "The Murderous Sutton Gang," who had kidnapped a farmer's daughter. The outlaws, headed by Wes Sutton (John Doucette), got theirs in the end.

Another adult Western that the company premiered in 1958, *Mackenzie's Raiders* featured Richard Carlson, who had previously starred on Ziv's *I Led 3 Lives*. The actor played Colonel Ranald S. Mackenzie who, under secret orders from President Grant, attempted to stop Mexican marauders terrorizing Texas settlers. Mackenzie would pursue the marauders across the Rio Grande River into Mexico if necessary.

The series was based on Russell P. Reeder's book *Mackenzie's Raid* which described the raid led by Mackenzie and his 550 cavalrymen to destroy a Mexican village 60 miles south of the border, inhabited by bandits burning ranches in Texas and running off cattle as well as kidnapping children and selling them into slavery in Mexico.

One reporter writing about the syndicated series asked, "How do you take a punitive raid into Mexico which lasted 32 hours and make it a 39-week series of half-hour filmed dramas?"[2] The article doesn't really answer the question. The answer seems to be that the TV series dealt with a whole passel of problems affecting the Southwest beyond just marauding bandits. Episodes concerned young Indian braves on a robbery and killing spree, renegades (the series term for Mexican bandits) ambushing wagons carrying guns and ammunition, Americans trying to invade and conquer Mexico, and a gambler murdering townspeople and acquiring their property on the cheap.

The opener related the story of how Mackenzie received secret orders to invade Mexico if necessary. Mackenzie's lead scout, Trooper John Ryan, is captured by Mexican renegades after they slaughtered an American family. The renegades flee across the Rio Grande with Mackenzie unable to follow. The Secretary of War visits Fort Clark and informs the colonel that the president will permit Mackenzie and his raiders to cross into Mexican to stop violence in the Southwest part of the U.S. but the orders must remain secret. That night, Mackenzie organizes his first raid and rescues Ryan.

In 1959, Ziv considered several concepts for new Western series. One, *The Bravo Duke*, set in Mexico, featured a man named Duke who owns a cantiña and helps people in distress. One day a rebel leader and his wife come to the cantina looking for Duke, hoping he can get them out of the country. Mr. Ortegas, the rebel, is wounded in combat with men who want the $80,000 he has raised for his cause. Ortegas escapes, but his wife is kidnapped. In return for a percentage of Ortegas' money, Duke goes looking for his wife. After Duke rescues her, she turns out to be in league with her captors greedy for the $80,000.

The unsold *Bravo Duke* pilot aired on *Vacation Playhouse* in July 1965. Gerald Mohr starred as the Duke with Jay Novello playing the revolutionary leader and Kathleen Crowley as his wife.

Another 1959 Western project featured a character by the name of Noah Jones, who works as a detective for a Cattleman's Association. In the pilot script, Jones is asked to determine who stole 400 head of cattle. Two men implicated in the theft have already been jailed. Jones frees them with hopes they will lead him to the mastermind of the rustling. The men take him to see a man named Bleek. A buyer for the cattle arrives at the encampment wanting to purchase the herd to feed his Chinese workers, who are building a railroad. Noah ends up arresting Bleek, collecting $10,000 from the railroad builder for the cattle, and giving the money to the Cattleman's Association.

A third project contemplated by Ziv was somewhat different from the typical Western. *Ranchero* was the proposed name for a Western focusing on James Spencer Stanton and his family as he settles in Corona County, New Mexico, in the 1800s. Tom Blackburn wrote the treatment for the planned series. Stanton, a former Army officer, had been dishonorably discharged for not following orders. He takes up residence in Corona County, marries and has a son. The series would have chronicled the Stanton family as it built a cattle empire, dealt with Mexican landowners as well as tribes of Native Americans and squatters on their property. New characters would have been introduced during the series run, such as a man who becomes the local doctor and a railroad builder.

Boston Blackie, Highway Patrol and Other Ziv Crime Dramas

In 1951, Ziv launched several syndicated crime drama series including *Boston Blackie* starring Kent Taylor in the lead role. Blackie, a reformed crook, often solved crimes ahead of the police. The series was adapted from the radio program, movies and short stories featuring the Blackie character. Ziv began syndicating the *Boston Blackie* radio series in the mid–1940s.

On the TV show, Lois Collier portrayed Mary Wesley, Blackie's girlfriend, and Frank Orth appeared as Faraday, the typical not-so-bright police detective often found on private detective shows. The series ran for two seasons.

Street-smart Blackie was called "enemy of those who make him an enemy, friend to those who have no friend." He is often called to investigate by a friend or acquaintance who is the victim of a crime, the presumed suspect of a crime, or a person acquainted with a crime suspect.

In "Blonde," a typical episode from 1952, Blackie is asked by a young lawyer to investigate a hit-and-run accident involving the lawyer's first client. The client, George, says that he picked up a woman at a café because he was too tired to drive and that the woman was driving the car when the accident occurred. He remembers the woman wearing a special sequined dress.

Blackie and Mary find the designer who made the dress for a movie company. At the studio, Blackie meets the actress for whom the costume was designed. Initially, she claims she was filming when the accident occurred but later shows up at the police station saying she was driving the car when it hit and killed a man. George, upon seeing the actress, says that she is not the woman he picked up. Examining the dress more closely, Blackie discovers a bullet hole. Turns out that the actress and the dress designer murdered the actress' husband and tried to make it appear a suicide. The model, whom George picked up, had taken the dress from the wardrobe department at the studio to wear at a party. After the hit-and-run, the actress killed the model who had been aware of the murder committed by the actress and the designer.

In most of the episodes, Blackie solves murder cases. A few dealt with other crimes like robbery. In "False Face," a banker friend of Blackie's is kidnapped, drugged and then let go after an impersonator steals $500,000 from the bank. No one believes the banker's story. Blackie sets out to prove that his friend is not guilty.

Unlike most crime dramas at the time, this series was not bound to a soundstage but had a lot of outdoor location scenes, many involving car chases. Blackie drove a futuristic, customized two-door sports car that may have been a version of the Muntz Jet. Stunts on the series reminded one of those seen in cowboy series. For example, in "The Motorcycle Kid," Blackie jumps on the top of a bus being driven by a robber, similar to Western heroes who leap on top of a stagecoach being driven by bandits.

Reportedly, in 1953, Ziv wanted to sign actor Dick Powell to star in a series similar to *Boston Blackie*.[3] One of the properties under consideration was *The Falcon*, based on the novels, films and radio series of the same name. Although Powell was then part-owner of Four Star Productions, apparently he wanted to keep his options open for other projects. However, a deal with Ziv never materialized.

The production company adapted another of its radio dramas for television in 1954. *Mister District Attorney* starred David Brian as D.A. Paul Garrett with Jackie Loughery as his girl Friday. CBS had previously aired a live version of the series in the early 1950s with Jay Jostyn in the lead role.

As with other B television series featuring lawyers as the main character, *Mister District Attorney* downplayed courtroom drama and focused on the attorney as investigator, acting much like a police detective in solving crimes and ferreting out criminals.

Mister District Attorney opened with the statement: "Champion of the people, defender of truth, guardian of our fundamental rights of life, liberty and the pursuit of happiness." A typical episode showed Garrett and other law enforcement officers investigate a crime. In "Hit and Run," Garrett and the police probe the death of a collector for a bookie syndicate, mowed down by a car. Witness Joe Coogan says that the vehicle intentionally hit the victim. Another witness, Mr. Thompson, a respectable businessman, tells authorities that the incident was an accident. Investigators find that the car swerved out of its lane to kill the man. However, Coogan is known by the police for prior instances where he didn't tell the truth. The investigators subsequently discover that Thompson is having financial troubles and recently had $5000 deposited into his bank account. The District Attorney uses Coogan as a ploy to trap Thompson and learn who bribed Thompson to lie about the incident. Thompson and the gangster who gave him money are arrested.

Highway Patrol, starring Broderick Crawford as Chief Dan Matthews, presented stories about the police unit investigating crimes occurring in an unspecified Western state. It ran for 156 episodes between 1955 and 1959. A typical episode was filmed in two days with a lot of outdoor locations. Each episode moved fast with plenty of quick cuts to the next scene mirroring Crawford's rapid-fire acting style. A hallmark of the series was the two-way radio used to communicate among patrol cars

Broderick Crawford (left) as Chief Dan Matthews and an unidentified player in a scene from *Highway Patrol.* The series is still rerun on "nostalgia" TV channels.

as well as to headquarters. The police code "10–4" (meaning "acknowledged") was used by the characters throughout each episode. This led to *Ten-4* sometimes being the title of the series in reruns.

The debut episode, "Prison Break," centered on escapee Ralph Neal, who steals a car and knocks out a mechanic who had changed a flat tire for him. These incidents give Chief Matthews clues to Neal's whereabouts. Neal abandons his car, which is found by a Highway Patrol officer. Hitting the officer on the head with a tire jack, Neal takes the policeman's vehicle, his gun and his uniform. Masquerading as a Highway Patrol officer, Neal hijacks a school bus (with two children aboard) hoping to avoid police roadblocks. When the bus does not drop her children off at home, the mother contacts the Highway Patrol. As Matthews tracks down the escapee, Neal knocks the bus driver unconscious and allows the kids to depart. In a restaurant parking lot, the convict is shot by the chief.

Stuart Jerome scripted the debut episode. He had written the *Mister*

District Attorney "Hit and Run" installment described above, as well as several other scripts for Ziv series. The California Highway Patrol provided technical advice and assistance to the show to make it appear that the series was based on real-life incidents. Broderick Crawford put in long hours making a typical episode as chronicled in a 1955 news article:

> 4:15 a.m.—The studio telephones and wakes the actor so that he will be ready when the studio driver arrives.
> 4:45 a.m.—The studio car arrives to drive Crawford to the filming location. The actor goes over the script for the day.
> 6:15 a.m.—Crawford arrives on location but there is too much fog to begin filming.
> 7:00 a.m.—Fog begins to lift and the makeup man begins his work.
> 7:18 a.m.—Fog comes in again and so Crawford rests in the car.
> 7:45 a.m.—Since weather is too bad for outdoor filming, the cast and crew travel to Ziv studios.
> 9:00 a.m.—Rush hour traffic in Los Angeles delays trip to the studio but everyone eventually arrives.
> 10:05 a.m.—Everybody is called to positions for first scene but there is too much glare on the walls and so a painter corrects the situation.
> 10:24 a.m.—Scene of a raid on a gambling hall is filmed but an actor, playing a police officer, trips on the rug and so scene is ruined.
> 10:32 a.m.—Scene redone, but Crawford accidentally drops the handcuffs and so scene done once more.
> 10:40 to 12:12 p.m.—Filming goes smoothly except for an interruption by the noise of low-flying aircraft.
> 12:14 p.m.—Photographers take publicity pictures.
> 12:30 p.m.—Quick lunch with newspaper columnists.
> 1:15 to 5:15 p.m.—Shooting resumes and goes smoothly except the technical advisor objects to two scenes as inaccurate. Scenes have to be rewritten.
> 6:00 p.m.—Consultation with director and producer about the next day's schedule.
> 7:05 p.m.—Car picks Crawford up and takes him home.[4]

The series episodes focused mainly on street crimes and criminals such as robbers, murderers, con men and kidnappers. Even while on vacation, Chief Matthews could not avoid crime. Checking into a resort, Dan encounters bad guys running a drug smuggling operation.

After United Artists purchased Ziv, Crawford tried a comeback to syndicated television in a Ziv–UA series, *King of Diamonds*, in the early

1960s. Reportedly, Ziv held Crawford's ten percent share of *Highway Patrol*'s gross (about $2 million) until the actor signed a contract for the new series.

On *King of Diamonds*, the actor played John King, a troubleshooter for the International Diamond Industry, pitted against illicit diamond buyers. The series lasted only one season since it was expensive to make for a non-network program.

In 1957, Ziv resurrected another early radio and TV series focusing on the adventures of detective Martin Kane. William Gargan played the lead character in *The New Adventures of Martin Kane*, filmed in London, Paris and elsewhere in Europe. Gargan had originated the role on radio and, during the series' first season, on TV. In the new syndicated adventures, Kane was an international investigator. Ziv produced the series in conjunction with Harry Alan Towers, who also made *Dial 999* with Ziv. Two episodes a week of *The New Adventures of Martin Kane* were shot at Associated British Studios.

The reboot was on film instead of done live like the original TV detective drama. The Kane character on the new series became involved in cases such as probing the theft of a $50,000 violin from a famous French musician. Virtuoso Claude Chagal asks Kane to recover his stolen violin before his next concert. However, before Kane can cut through the red tape of the Paris police, he finds that Chagal has followed the thief and is now in mortal danger. The PI commandeers a police car and drives furiously to overtake and save the musician and his violin.

Other cases had Kane joining forces with the Copenhagen police to thwart a greedy nephew who is trying to drive his wealthy aunt insane, and the detective taking the case of a British prizefighter who is told to throw a big fight if he wants his kidnapped wife returned safely.

As a follow-up to the success of *Highway Patrol*, Ziv introduced another police drama, this one set in the harbor of a large city. The series could have been called *Waterways Patrol* but instead was titled *Harbor Command*. The show, syndicated for one season beginning in 1957, starred Wendell Corey as Captain Ralph Baxter, head of the Harbor Command.

Like other Ziv crime dramas at the time, *Harbor Command* dealt with the usual cases of murder, theft, smuggling, counterfeiters, etc. One episode concerned a theft occurring at a yacht club where the two thieves take an eyewitness as hostage, leaving his blind daughter to contact Harbor Command. Baxter joins in the effort to locate the thieves and hostage before the hostage, who has diabetes, dies from lack of insulin. Not all of the action took place on the water; Baxter spent most of the episode traveling in his police car, tracking down the suspects.

Rising production costs for syndicated series prevented *Harbor Command* from being renewed beyond its initial run of 39 episodes.

Since the production company had successfully launched a series, *Mister District Attorney*, about a lawyer investigating crime, why not attempt one involving a physician becoming involved in police matters? In 1957, Ziv considered a crime series revolving around police doctor Robert Marriat. The pilot begins with a voiceover: "In our story that follows, there is danger, violence, the sound of the ambulance siren, and there is a gun, but this time the gun is pointed at me, the Police Doctor."

While being treated by Dr. Marriat, Joe Burns, the victim of a construction accident, experiences symptoms of post-traumatic stress disorder and gets hold of the gun of the police officer who escorted him to the hospital. The police give Marriat one hour to resolve the situation before storming the treatment room. Marriat contacts one of Burns' fellow construction workers, a man who served in Korea with him. Learning of Joe's experience in trying to fight off the enemy and hold a hill during the war, Marriat pretends he is a medic and is able to retrieve the gun. The pilot, *Police Doctor*, aired as an episode of the Ziv anthology *Target* in March 1958. Gene Barry starred as the doctor with Leo Gordon appearing as Joe Burns.

Dial 999 was another one-season wonder syndicated by Ziv in 1958. Shot in England in conjunction with Towers of London Productions, the drama starred Robert Beatty as Inspector Michael Maguire, a Canadian police detective sent to London to learn about English police methods. The series, produced by Harry Alan Towers, was labeled the "British Highway Patrol," in that it featured plenty of location shooting.

In one installment, Maguire is assigned to the Scotland Yard branch dealing with national security. Enemy agents seek to capture an American scientist, Dr. Stafford, flying into London. The agents take over a taxi business to use the cabs to surveil the scientist upon his arrival as well as to use the company's communication system. A cab driver overhears their plans and calls the police before he is killed by the agents. Maguire and his colleagues use various ruses to confuse the enemy agents as to which vehicle the scientist is taking from the airport. The police close in on the taxi company's headquarters to disrupt the agents' communications. Scotland Yard rounds up and arrests the enemy agents. The police had Dr. Stafford arrive in London dressed as the plane's pilot and he was safely escorted to his destination.

The character of Michael Maguire also narrated. Each installment was shot over a period of five days, slower than most syndicated series at the time. "999" is the UK equivalent of America's "911."

Perhaps foreshadowing NBC's *CHiPs*, in 1958, Ziv attempted a series called *Motor Cycle Cop.* The project seems to have been another attempt by the company to parlay the success of *Highway Patrol* into a similar series with motorcycles substituting for police cars. The never-realized series' pilot, "Man on a Bike," appears to have aired on the anthology *Target.* Starring Paul Burke as a veteran motorcycle cop, the episode concerned the Burke character seeing his rookie partner shot by two thugs. He leads a city-wide search for his partner's killers.

Macdonald Carey starred as attorney Herbert L. Maris in *Lock Up,* which ran in syndication for two years beginning in 1959. Olive Carey, no relation to Macdonald, played Casey, Maris' secretary. Maris, a real-life Philadelphia lawyer, took the cases of those he believed had been unjustly convicted. Maris' police contact, Lieutenant Weston (John Doucette), was a tough Broderick Crawford–like character.

The *Lock Up* pilot aired on *Target* as "Shadow of a Doubt" (aka "Unreasonable Doubt") and concerned a man framed for the murder of his ex-boss. Maris realizes that the man is innocent and ends up facing the actual murderer. Audience reaction and survey data on that episode convinced the production company to launch *Lock Up.*

In the premiere episode, "Stake Out," Maris takes the case of Robert Arnold, a former convict, who drove another ex-con, George Gult, and his girlfriend Margie to a drugstore where Gult robbed the business and shot a police officer. The police arrest Arnold but are still looking for Gult. Maris locates Margie and follows her to Gult's hiding place. Gult is shot by the police. Margie then states that Arnold didn't know that Gult was going to rob the store.

Ziv syndicated still another crime series, *This Man Dawson* (1959-60), starring Keith Andes as former Marine Colonel Frank Dawson. Dawson takes over a big-city police force to fight crime. William Conrad co-produced and narrated each episode. The series dealt with the usual crime stories such as a serial killer on the loose, corrupt boxing syndicates, narcotics organizations, and blackmail. In one particularly graphic episode, a young blind woman is kidnapped and her seeing-eye dog shot by the perpetrators. The kidnappers demand $250,000 in ransom which Dawson delivers. Dawson throws phosphorous on the car's roof as the man picking up the ransom leaves so that a police helicopter can track the vehicle. In the end, one of the kidnappers is shot as the woman is rescued.

Andes played the lead as a very terse, almost robotic character. To show his human side in the above episode, he gives the blind woman a new seeing-eye dog in the final scene.

Writers Mort Fine and David Friedkin developed a script for an untitled Ziv detective drama featuring the characters of Sergeant Jess

Bailey and his young partner Adam. Adam, new to the police force, is assigned to investigate a potential suicide. Before he receives his assignment, the audience learns at the beginning what really happened before Walter Blair, the victim, fell out of his apartment window to his death. This proposed crime series is different from other such Ziv dramas in that it is not a "whodunit" where the detective attempts to determine who committed a crime. Rather, this would have been a *"Columbo*-like" drama where viewers know at the beginning who the perpetrator is and the mystery is how the culprit will be discovered.

Blair, a former acrobat, part of the Three Dervishes, hadn't performed in years but had just won $2100 on a daily double. Adam learns that another member of the acrobatic troupe has also died by apparent suicide after he had appeared on a TV show in a comeback attempt. Only Tom Gage, the third member of the troupe, is still alive. Gage tells the detective that he has been lying low since he is scared that he might be next. The police arrange for Gage to win $100 as the millionth visitor to an amusement park, thinking that the resulting publicity will draw out the person who staged the two "suicides." Adam and Jess stake out Gage's house, but no one comes around. Gage's wife divulges that her husband killed the other two acrobats. He was jealous of their prior involvement with his wife.

Anthologies, Melodramas and Mysteries

The Living Book was the first TV anthology series that Ziv syndicated beginning in 1951. Produced by the non-profit Crusader Films, the series dramatized stories from the Bible, including "Exile from Eden" about the Creation, "Noah and His Family" and "The Story of Joseph." Sixteen episodes were filmed in color.

In 1952, the production company syndicated a 30-minute suspense anthology, *The Unexpected*, hosted by actor Herbert Marshall. The series told stories with twists at the end. Many episodes were scripted by Jerome Lawrence and Robert E. Lee, who later wrote the plays *Inherit the Wind* and *Auntie Mame*, among others.

"Calculated Risk," also known as "With Malice Toward One," was the first episode of the series written by Lawrence and Lee. In San Francisco, Richard Sutherland, contemplating suicide because of financial reverses, meets Diana Marlowe in a hotel elevator. Richard bears a striking resemblance to Diana's husband Gordon, from whom she has been estranged for three years. Gordon recently got in touch with Diana, who is wealthy, to ask her for money. Richard comes up with an idea to kill

Gordon but pretend that Gordon is Richard. He suggests that he could eliminate her husband and then assume Gordon's identity since he looks so much like her husband.

Richard places a newspaper ad advertising the sale of his mountain retreat. Diana informs Gordon that she intends to purchase the property and that he should fly with Richard, posing as the real estate agent, to see the retreat. Richard breaks into Gordon's hotel room to wipe it clean of Gordon's fingerprints and place his own there. In addition, Richard goes to a dentist pretending to be Gordon to have a special bridge made. Richard, a pilot who owns a light aircraft, packs a parachute for himself. Gordon is somewhat late for the flight. When he arrives, the two take off. Richard knocks Gordon unconscious and parachutes out of the plane. The aircraft crashes, bursting into flames. Richard lands near the crash site and throws the special dental bridge into the fire. He takes a bus back to the city.

Richard goes to Gordon's room and discovers a plainclothes detective waiting for Gordon. Richard, whom the detective believes is Gordon Melville, is arrested for murdering Diana with a knife in her back. Melville murdered his wife before going up in the plane with Richard. Richard attempts to explain whom he really is, but the police do not believe him. With the evidence Richard planted before killing Gordon, no one buys his story that he is not Diana's estranged husband.

"High Adventure" was typical of the series attempts at maintaining suspense throughout the half-hour. Elaine Barlow, her son Tommy, and Tommy's nurse, Miss Ryan, drive to a mountain retreat in Crest Line for Tommy's health. After they arrive, Miss Ryan takes the suitcases upstairs. When Elaine goes to find her, she discovers that the nurse has been strangled. The mother and son flee to a neighbor's home. They hear footsteps behind them and become lost in the woods. Eventually, the mother and her son end up back at the house. When Mrs. Barlow calls the police, she hears someone breathing through the upstairs phone. The police tell her that they cannot come until the following morning because of flooding in the area. Viewers see a newspaper headline on the police officer's desk about a "cat and mouse" killer in the area. Mrs. Barlow finds a pair of scissors and goes upstairs to get Tommy's medicine. After she gives her son the medicine, the electricity goes out. In the dark, the police arrive and capture the homicidal maniac, who is never seen throughout the episode. The officer informs Elaine that, knowing someone else was on the phone line when she called, they made up the story about coming the next day.

The Unexpected, also titled *Times Square Playhouse*, lasted for 39 episodes.

Ziv launched a more successful anthology the following year, *Your Favorite Story* hosted by actor Adolphe Menjou. Menjou and his wife, Verree Teasdale, had hosted a radio talk show for Ziv called *Meet the Menjous* in 1949. The syndicated TV series, based on a radio show, presented short stories adapted by Ziv's writers from the works of authors such as Tolstoy, Chekhov and Edgar Allan Poe. Menjou introduced each story and then showed up again in the middle of the episode dressed as one the characters from the story to present a commercial. At the end, the actor again appeared, dressed splendidly with an ascot tie, and say something like, "Well! That was something, wasn't it?"[5] The series lasted until 1955.

In the original concept of the radio version of *Favorite Story*, prominent personalities presented their favorite tales. The creators of the radio series were the above-referenced Jerome Lawrence and Robert Lee and the host was actor Ronald Colman. While the radio program may have been considered prestige drama, the TV adaptation was less than such. Most of the episodes presented were either melodramas or mystery-suspense dramas. As an example of how the works of famous authors were turned into dramas for syndicated television, veteran Ziv writer Stuart Jerome took a Robert Louis Stevenson poem, "The Vagabond," and scripted a story titled "Sword of the Vagabond" starring Robert Clarke in the lead role as poet and swordsman Francois Villon. In Paris in the 1500s, during a snowstorm, Villon seeks shelter at the Blue Goose Tavern, offering to pay for his room with an original poem. At the behest of a soldier who promises him money in return for a poem about the soldier, Villon makes up a rhyme insulting the military man. The two then engage in a swordfight with Villon winning the match. The following day, the soldier is found murdered. Apparently, the soldier had been cheating at cards. Aware that the police will accuse him of the murder, Villon flees with a barmaid. When they ask a stranger to give them shelter, he turns out to be the head of the Paris police. After describing what happened at the Blue Goose, the police chief places Villon under house arrest. He attempts to escape but is stopped by a guard. The police chief reveals that the soldier's murderer has already been captured; the chief simply wanted to hear the vagabond's poetry. The chief warns Villon to change his lifestyle but, as Villon departs with the maiden, he steals a valuable plate from the chief's house.

With Paul Kelly as host and sometimes star, Ziv made a 1955 pilot for a proposed syndicated anthology to be called *I Love a Mystery*, directed by Ida Lupino and starring her husband Howard Duff and Maria Riva (Marlene Dietrich's daughter). Kelly was set to host each episode and star in six of them. The pilot never sold, reportedly because Screen Gems already had a mystery series in production.

Dr. Christian, a medical melodrama adapted from a radio series and several films, concerned a small-town physician, Dr. Mark Christian, played by Macdonald Carey before he starred as an attorney in Ziv's *Lock Up*. Mark was the nephew of Dr. Paul Christian, portrayed by actor Jean Hersholt, star of the *Dr. Christian* movies and radio series. Ziv syndicated the series for one season beginning in 1956.

Hersholt appeared as the original Dr. Christian in the first two episodes of the new series to anoint his fictional nephew as the new doctor carrying on his tradition. Similar to other B-TV medical shows, the stories dealt more with the human interest aspect of medicine rather than the "disease of the week." For instance, in one installment, Dr. Christian treats a gunman with a heart condition. When the man escapes from under police guard at the hospital, Dr. Christian follows him into the hills outside of the city. To bring the man in, the doctor has to go up against him with the knowledge that exertion on the criminal's part could be fatal.

Speaking about the series to journalists before it premiered, Carey stated, "The fast-moving scripts sold the series to me. I was leery about doing the series at first. But I have a director I can talk to, and the writers are as good as you can find."[6]

Also, in 1956, Ziv launched *The West Point Story*, a military anthology on CBS. The series dramatized incidents and people based on the files at the Army academy. Donald May appeared as Cadet Charles C. Thompson during its initial episodes. ABC picked up the show for the 1957 TV season.

Stories dealt with the lives of cadets, with episodes such as two cadets falling in love with the same girl; a cadet seeing his roommate cheat on an exam and being torn between friendship and his duty, under West Point's honor code, to report the incident; and the mother of a society girl disapproving of her relationship with a cadet.

A nine-man board of officers at the academy reviewed the outline for each episode and then went over the final script line by line to check authenticity. Exterior filming was done at West Point, interiors at Ziv studios in Hollywood.

In 1957, the company premiered a companion series to *The West Point Story* called *Men of Annapolis*. Location filming was done at the U.S. Naval Academy in Maryland for this syndicated anthology that each week profiled the story of a different midshipman. One episode, "The Look Alike," concerned George "Tecumsah" McGuire (Carleton Carpenter) who, since a young kid, has had a broken nose with a deviated septum. Self-conscious about his nose, he reluctantly dates an attractive girl named Madge (Audrey Dalton) who liked him but suggests to him that he is afraid of his nose. He sees a doctor who straightens his nose. When George becomes overconfident, Madge breaks up with him. After his new nose is broken during football practice, he decides to leave it crooked similar to his old nose.

Ziv also contemplated a series based on the U.S. Air Force, but such a series never came to fruition.

Still another anthology launched by Ziv in 1958, *Target*, was hosted by *Your Favorite Story*'s Adolphe Menjou. Each episode opened with the image of whirling concentric white circles against a black background. Like a missile, the word "target" is shot into the black bullseye. Menjou is then faded into the image in silhouette.

Menjou indicated that each installment would be characterized by "a lot of emotion and action, whether the theme is a Western, law enforcement, crime, drama or comedy. Who is the target? It varies each week. Sometimes the villain. Sometimes the hero. As with life, it changes all the time."[7] In addition to hosting, Menjou also acted in about a third of the 39 episodes.

Most installments fell into the category of mystery and suspense. In one, a woman is taunted to her breaking point by a stranger and her own husband. In another, a detective kills a murderous thief. The detective's girlfriend convinces him to assume the thief's identity to commit more crimes and then blame them on the dead man.

According to Hal Erickson's book on syndicated television series, *Target* was not renewed because of a rumor about the future of the series. "An unconfirmed report came out that Ziv would film only 38 episodes of the series, whether it was successful or not. By the time Ziv was able to issue a statement, *Target* had been dropped by one of the largest East Coast sponsors in favor of new syndies.... Thanks to hearsay, Ziv couldn't have gotten sponsor support for a second season of *Target* even if it had tried."[8]

One of Ziv's final melodramatic series concepts, written by Roland Drake in January 1960, dealt with the life of a Broadway producer, David Temple. He is in the process of producing a musical starring the Kingston Trio and actress Jane Marvin. Jane's boyfriend, Vinny Draco, a former hood now trying to become respectable, meets with Temple to have Jane dropped from the show since he feels they are growing apart. Later, Jane informs Temple that she wants to leave the show after Draco physically abuses her. Temple decides to have a dinner party inviting Jane, Vinny and Wilma Pearce, a friend of his, whom he hopes will lure Draco away from Jane. The plan works with Wilma and Vinny wanting to marry. But Wilma has told Draco how Temple planned for them to meet. Upset, Draco threatens to harm Temple and Jane. To defuse the situation, Temple shows him a news article about how Draco took Wilma away from Temple.

This untitled project never became a series.

Meet Corliss Archer, The Eddie Cantor Comedy Theatre and Other Comedies

In 1949, Ziv produced three installments of a try-out series, *Vic and Sade* (aka *The Gook Family*), based on the radio program, which were aired in the time slot for *Colgate Video Theatre* on July 11 through July 25, 1949. Written by Paul Rhymer, the episodes featured married couple Vic (Frank Dane), an accountant, and his wife Sade (Bernadette Flynn), a homemaker, and their son Rush (Dick Conan). The storylines of *Vic and Sade* included Vic being sent out of town on a business trip on the same day that Sade is planning a big supper party and Vic and his archrival Ike Kneesuffer competing to have their respective streets paved to prove their importance to their boss, a city official. Vic wants the city to pave two blocks of Virginia Avenue where he and his family live, while Kneesuffer seeks to have two blocks of his street, University Avenue, paved.

Billboard, in reviewing the program, indicated that Rhymer was better at writing for radio than for television since the latter requires comical action and not just funny dialogue.[9] The try-out was not successful enough for Colgate Palmolive to pick the series up as a regular feature for fall 1949.

In 1954, Ziv syndicated a new version of the radio and early TV series *Meet Corliss Archer*. CBS first introduced the Corliss Archer character to TV in a live 1951 show. Corliss, a 1940s-1950s stereotypical high school student, got into various comical situations with her boyfriend and her parents. She was played by Lugene Sanders on the CBS show; the Ziv series starred Ann Baker and ran for a single season.

The Corliss Archer character, created by F. Hugh Herbert, first appeared in magazine articles, then the Broadway play *Kiss and Tell*, before becoming a feature film and then a weekly radio series and finally a TV series.

The series, narrated by Hy Averback, used cartoons to illustrate different situations. In the opener, "No Clothes for the Party," Corliss wants a new wrap to wear to a dance and her boyfriend Dexter needs to borrow a tuxedo. Corliss suggests that Dexter borrow his dad's tux while Corliss wants to wear her mother's mink. However, they are both hesitant to request the items from her parents. Dexter ends up asking

Mr. Archer to request that his wife allow Corliss to wear her wrap. Corliss seeks help from her mother to request that her father permit Dexter to use his tux. Corliss then decides that she and Dexter should rent their outfits. Dexter sells his carburetor to rent a tux but ends up spilling an ice cream sundae on it. Corliss doesn't like the wrap she rented. When she dons her mother's coat, Dexter accidentally rips off a sleeve. Dexter gives his mother's wrap to Corliss to wear. Dexter wears Mr. Archer's tux to the dance.

In 1955, Ziv syndicated a comedy anthology series, *The Eddie Cantor Comedy Theatre*, hosted by the legendary entertainer. The series included half-hour sitcoms as well as variety shows. Ziv began selling the series to New York stations for $5000 a week but soon dropped the price to $3500. This anthology was the production company's costliest series to produce, at $53,000 per episode. Ziv produced 38 episodes instead of the usual 39 for a season since it offered the series to two sponsors with each having an equal number of installments for advertising.

Cantor had signed a contract with Ziv for a reported $9 million to do radio and TV shows for seven years. The radio show, a half-hour in length, ran five days a week. On the television anthology, he would star in certain episodes, singing and acting in comedy sketches. On other episodes, he would simply introduce a comedy that starred a special guest (Vincent Price, Basil Rathbone, Joan Blondell, Joe E. Brown, etc.). As host, Cantor would appear at the beginning of an episode normally involved in some type of comedy subplot and then allow the story with the guest star to play out. For example, in the Vincent Price installment "How Much for Van Such," Cantor talked with Price about wanting to do Shakespeare and, in the middle of the episode, Cantor appeared in a Shakespearean costume to introduce a commercial. At the end, he simply sang his theme song "I Love to Spend These Moments with You."

The Vincent Price story concerned a penny-pinching multi-millionaire who is kidnapped but refuses to pay the $1 million ransom. He is finally released by the kidnappers when he agrees to at least cover their expenses for renting a costly hotel room where he was kept.

By August 1955, Cantor was indicating that the work on both the radio and TV series was too much for him. After suffering a heart attack in 1952, he was not in the best of health. His contract with Ziv was canceled. Commenting on the series, Cantor bemoaned the "assembly line" process of making a TV series that Ziv, and other B TV producers had introduced. He wrote, "For once in my life I allowed my better judgment to be swayed by the money involved. I'd give all the money back if I could take back the shows...."[10]

Ziv made a final attempt in 1960 to launch a comedy called *Time Out for Ginger* starring Candy Moore as Ginger Carol, a rambunctious teenager who easily manipulated her father into doing what she wants. Also starring in the pilot were Karl Swenson as Ginger's dad Howard, a research physicist; Maggie Hayes as Agnes, Ginger's mother; Roberta Shore as Joan, Ginger's older sister; and Margaret Hamilton as the Carols' maid Lizzie. In the pilot, Ginger tries to find a car so that Joan and her boyfriend Eddie can go to a dance. Ginger's dad needs their vehicle to take his wife and others to a party. Eddie's father's car is in the garage for repairs. Ginger first attempts to have Joan ask her father for her own car thinking that, as an alternative, the father will permit her to use his car. When that doesn't work, Ginger goes to a dealership intending to convince the salesperson that her father is interested in buying a new car and wants to test-drive it that evening. Failing at that plan, she next attempts to rent a car but doesn't have enough money. Ginger subsequently talks with Eddie's father about asking the garage mechanic to fix his car more quickly. When all her plans fail, she says to her dad that she is a failure, but he replies that only people that never try anything are failures. In the end, the new car dealer comes by the Carol house to offer a test drive, the rental car agent finds a vehicle that Ginger can afford, Lizzie's friend offers his truck to Joan and Eddie, and Eddie's father's car is repaired in time for the couple to go to the dance.

I Led 3 Lives, Sea Hunt and Other Adventure Series

The production company's adventure series included spy dramas as well as sea adventures and something different—a scientific adventure series.

Ziv hit the jackpot in 1953 with the syndicated spy drama *I Led 3 Lives* starring Richard Carlson as Herbert Philbrick. The Philbrick character became an everyday hero in the U.S. government's fight against Communist infiltration in this country after World War II. Each episode opened with this description: "This is the fantastically true story of Herbert A. Philbrick, who for nine frightening years did lead three lives: average citizen, member of the Communist Party, and counterspy for the FBI. For obvious reasons, the names, dates and places have been changed, but the story is based on fact."

For three years, the series was very popular in syndication based on the idea that Communists were everywhere, sabotaging and otherwise threatening the American way of life. Ziv had hoped to adapt its syndicated radio show, *I Was a Communist for the FBI*, which had begun in 1952, for television but legal complications made that impossible.

In the first episode, Philbrick attends an emergency meeting of his Communist cell. A female member confesses that she has deviated from Party policy concerning the overthrow of the U.S. government. The next day, FBI agent James Adams presents Philbrick with photos taken by the FBI of participants in the meeting. The Bureau has identified all of the individuals except one, whom Philbrick recognizes as Leroy Wilkerson. The FBI is then able to complete its file on Wilkerson.

Other episodes dealt with Communists infiltrating labor unions, performing industrial and government espionage, raising money and distributing their propaganda about the deficiencies of the capitalist system. The episode "Child Commie" illustrates how the Communist Party supposedly attempted to spread propaganda to American young people: Philbrick is asked by a Party member to take care of his daughter, Beth Dixon, for the weekend. The father asks his daughter to spy on Philbrick to determine his loyalty to the Party. Philbrick wants to get information on the "Commie Youth Program" and turn it over to the FBI. As he says, "Never underestimate a Commie, even a baby one."

Beth befriends Connie, one of Herb's daughters, telling her that George Washington and Thomas Jefferson didn't really care about starting a new country, they just wanted to become wealthy. Beth questions Herb's loyalty after he chastises the girl for her opinion of America's forefathers. Later, the girl finds Herb's report on the youth program which he intends to give her father (but also furnish to the FBI).

In her father's presence, Beth accuses Philbrick of being a spy since he made a copy of the report he presented to her dad. In response, Philbrick accuses Beth of making wild, unfounded accusations. Mr. Dixon drops the matter and gives Herb a copy of details on publishing Communist propaganda for American children, which Philbrick turns over to the FBI.

Although often under suspicion by various Party members of being a spy, the Philbrick character was never outed during the series' three season run.

I Led 3 Lives set the pattern for other Ziv "continuing character" dramas. Find a former movie star, tailor a series to his needs, give the actor an ownership interest in the series to make him want to work at it, and then stick to an action-adventure format. In 1955, Carlson indicated, "Over a five-year period, I will receive $1,700,000 as my share of *Lives*. This includes $2000 I draw for each episode plus my percentage. We will have 117 pictures canned by February when we finish the series. And Ziv estimates our gross per picture will eventually total $100,000."[11]

In 1956, Ziv debuted another series based on a radio program. *The Man Called X* starred Barry Sullivan as Ken Thurston, a U.S. intelligence agent whose code name is "X." *The Man Called X* had aired on radio from 1944 to 1952 with Herbert Marshall in the main role.

Thurston used various aliases as he worked undercover to protect American interests from hostile foreign threats. Like Hal Roach Jr.'s *Passport to Danger*, each *Man Called X* episode took place in a different country. As might be expected from the production company that made *I Led 3 Lives*, about Communist influence in America, many of Thurston's undercover activities involved the USSR and its satellite countries.

"Simulated Attack" had Thurston on a mission to obtain Communist naval war game plans involving an attack on America. He enlists the help of Yurick, a Russian naval officer who has hated his government since it killed his parents. Before Yurick can provide the information, his superiors become suspicious of his activities. For Yurick's protection, Thurston devises a plan for the naval officer to escape with him to the U.S. but also give the Russian military the impression that both have been killed during the escape.

The syndicated series ran for 39 episodes. All of the stories were based on material from the files of one of America's foremost intelligence experts.

Ziv premiered *Harbourmaster* in 1957, first on CBS and then at midseason switching to ABC where its title changed to *Adventures of Scott Island*. Barry Sullivan appeared as Capt. David Scott, the harbormaster of a small island off the New England coast. Also on the series were Paul Burke as Jeff Kittridge, Scott's assistant, and Nina Wilcox as Anna Morrison, who ran the island's Dolphin Restaurant.

Harbourmaster dealt mainly with stories about crime in and around Scott Island as well as emergencies such as hurricanes and the dumping of dangerous waste in the area. In "The Wreckers," a crime episode, a freighter runs aground on Dead Man's Reef. Jorgensin (Bruce Gordon), the ship's officer, claims that a buoy light was not in the right position causing the accident. Scott and Jeff find that the light was not working. When the ship captain is found dead, Jorgensin is suspected of grounding the ship in order to salvage its cargo for money. However, the cargo on the vessel, originally thought to be expensive machine tools, is really coal. Scott finds that a local salvage operator and her partner sabotaged the buoy to force the ship aground and then murdered the captain. They wanted to salvage what they thought was its machine tool cargo.

The sponsor of *Harbourmaster*, R.J. Reynolds Tobacco, was behind the series' move from CBS to ABC.

Probably the most popular of Ziv's adventure series, *Sea Hunt* with Lloyd Bridges as scuba diver Mike Nelson, was syndicated by the company for four seasons beginning in 1958. Produced by Ivan Tors, the pilot for the series, "60 Feet Below," opened with Nelson working at Marineland of the Pacific, force-feeding a blue shark in captivity when he hears a sonic boom from a jet overhead. The jet nosedives into the ocean with the pilot unable to bail out. Nelson is called in to mark the location of the downed jet before the weather turns bad. He locates the craft and finds that the pilot is still alive, breathing the last of the oxygen inside the cockpit. Mike tries various means to free the man. Finally, he is told to cut the metal under the canopy, which will force the canopy to release. The procedure works and the pilot is rescued.

Frederick Ziv stated that before *Sea Hunt* was syndicated, it was offered to all three networks, and they all turned it down as a series. "They liked the pilot, but they figured—and each one seemed to be of the same opinion—'Well, what do you do the second week and what do you do the third week—you've done it all the first week.'"[12]

Ziv added that he emphasized action in most of the series he produced. "[T]he chase is a technique that was particularly desired at the time. *Cisco Kid* was a chase on horseback; *Highway Patrol* was a chase on the highway; *Sea Hunt* was a chase underwater. We were particularly effective in 'the chase.'"[13]

In late 1958, the production company contemplated launching a series similar to *Sea Hunt*, focusing on adventurers on land instead of under the sea. The characters in the untitled effort were Scott Warner, a soldier-scientist-explorer, and his partner Sandy Harrison, a New Zealander. Warner worked for the International Geophysical Year, mainly in Antarctica.

In the planned opener, Warner and Harrison have to return to the frozen continent after staying there for six months on a scientific expedition. They are given the mission of escorting a scientist, Dr. Staples, from Ellsworth to Shackleton in time to catch the last ship out of Antarctica before the winter closes everything down. Dr. Staples doesn't want to leave until he verifies a colleague's seismic soundings. He goes out alone to obtain his readings despite Warner's objections. Warner and Harrison find Dr. Staples lodged in a crevasse and must rescue him.

Ziv sold a different kind of adventure series to NBC for its 1959–60 season. Produced by Ivan Tors, *Man and the Challenge* starred George Nader as Dr. Glenn Barton, a scientist working for the Human Factor

Institute helping others test the limits of their endurance. In one episode, he is asked to help a test pilot, Dan Wright (Jack Ging), who suffers from PTSD after crashing an aircraft into the ocean. Wright has confined himself to his bed, saying he cannot walk even though there is nothing physically wrong with him. Through hypnosis, Barton gets Wright to walk again and then, with further hypnotic treatments, he lessens Wright's fear of heights and speed until he is well enough to resume flying.

Other episodes dealt with how to improve the potential of Olympic skiers, an investigation of high-altitude existence and the phenomenon of humans disassociating themselves mentally and physically from the earth at such altitudes, and how long men, unaccustomed to living on a submarine, could survive on such a vessel in the event of a nuclear war.

Commenting on the development of *The Man and the Challenge*, Richard Dorso, Ziv's Director of New Program Development, stated:

> The show collects a number of areas of action which in themselves couldn't be handled as a series, such things as auto racing, mountain climbing, bullfighting, skiing and the like. All good for one or maybe two episodes. In television we hate to waste any material, so we came up with the idea of combining. Our biggest problem was to create a believable running character. Ivan Tors, the producer, came up with the idea which was refined into *Challenge*. ...[W]e created a scientist attached to the Department of Defense whose job it was to examine people under uncontrollable conditions to determine endurance and how people react under pressure.[14]

One installment, written by actor Richard Carlson and titled "Man Without Fear," grew out of Tors' experience as a research subject at the UCLA Research Clinic to determine the effects of a new chemical which psychiatrists thought could help them unlock the mysteries of the human mind. The chemical, derived from fungus, produces hallucinations. Tors reported his experiences to Carlson, who wrote the script for the episode in which Barton uses a supposedly courage-instilling chemical (lysergic acid) on a firefighter to show that in a burning forest fire, fear is a part of courage.

Bold Venture, syndicated in 1959, was a TV adaptation of a Ziv radio show that had begun in 1951 with Humphrey Bogart and Lauren Bacall as the leads. The television version had Dane Clark and Joan Marshall replacing Bogart and Bacall. The series, set in Trinidad in the Caribbean, concerned the adventures of Slate Shannon (Clark), owner of a hotel and the 60-foot boat *Bold Venture*. Sailor Duval (Marshall) accompanied Shannon in his exploits.

Talking to reporters about his upcoming series, Clark remarked,

We feel that this is the year when ... viewers will still be looking for escape
programming, outdoors action-adventure shows—but also escape from
Westerns and police dramas. ...The stories are told to a calypso beat. Ber-
nie Gozier plays the role of calypso singer King Moses whose bits of chant
punctuate the story from time to time and, in the background, there's the
beat of bongo drums and the strum of guitars.[15]

Slate Shannon seemed to always become involved in some type of
dangerous situation. In "Back from the Dead," Wit, a man from Slate's
past, accuses Shannon of failing to save him from an ambush during the
Korean conflict. Shannon tells Sailor that he had to make a decision to
either save two men or numerous others. Wit is looking for vengeance.
He puts a poisonous snake in Sailor's room, beats up King Moses, and
shoots at Slate's car. The police pick up Wit, but his girlfriend gives him
an alibi. Slate sets up a trap for Wit; Wit falls into it and starts shooting.
Slate fires back, killing him.

In 1959, Roy Huggins, who created the classic series *Cheyenne*,
Maverick and *The Fugitive*, developed a treatment for a Ziv adventure
series set on the French Riviera. Andrew Gorman and Matt Comerford
were the lead characters in the proposal. Gorman, newly arrived in Port
d'Or, begins working for Comerford, who runs a travel service. Mrs.
Huston and her daughter are among their clients. Smugglers plant diamonds in Mrs. Huston's car, thinking she will be traveling to Marseilles.
However, as a thank you to Andy and Matt for showing her the French
Riviera, Mrs. Huston gifts them her vehicle and takes the train to Marseilles. When the car is stolen by the smugglers, Andy and Matt follow
them and find the diamonds. The police, who had the smugglers under
surveillance, intervene and confiscate the jewels. It is not known what
the title of the planned series would have been.

Science Fiction Series for Adults

Produced by Ivan Tors and predating his involvement with *Sea
Hunt* and *Man and the Challenge*, *Science Fiction Theatre,* an anthology,
dealt with subjects like UFOs, robots, mental telepathy and space flight.
Seventy-eight episodes were made between 1955 and 1957. Unlike *Rocky
Jones, Space Ranger* which was aimed at juveniles, *Science Fiction Theatre* was chiefly for adult viewers. Each episode was based on some scientific fact. Truman Bradley hosted and narrated.

As a Ziv executive remarked at the time, "We aren't trying to look
into the future 2000 or 200 years from now. Our science fiction is based

on science that's on the threshold of reality. We're dealing with facts and fictionalizing a relation to those facts. In no sense will the series be fantasy. The stories we use may well happen during our lifetime."[16]

The episodes had stories dealing with topics like a scientist seeking to produce synthetic oil from a 50,000,000-year-old piece of amber containing a spider; photographers taking pictures of a mysterious flying object and finding a dead alien; a man claiming to be over 200 years old who had learned a secret youth formula from the medicine man who raised him; and a former teacher with a bad heart who wants his former student, a doctor, to implant an artificial heart in his chest.

The premiere episode, "Beyond," starred William Lundigan as test pilot Fred Gunderman, who flies the FA962 with an experimental fuel designed to boost speeds. During the test flight, he indicates to ground control that he sees an object shaped like a missile and flying faster than his aircraft. Thinking the object will crash into his jet, he ejects. Later, in the hospital, he is questioned about what he experienced and insists he saw a UFO. The test center scientists contend that Gunderman saw a fountain pen in his cabin that floated into his field of vision when he was weightless during the flight. Gunderman accepts this explanation, but additional reports subsequently show that the pilot may have indeed experienced a UFO. A story by Tors served as the basis for this installment.

In some respects, Tors' *Science Fiction Theatre* was an outgrowth of a pilot that the producer had made a few years earlier for A-Men Productions. That company was formed in 1952 by Tors, actor Richard Carlson and writer Curt Siomak to produce science fiction–adventure series. Their first project, *Office of Scientific Investigation* starring Richard Carlson, started out as a 1953 film called *The Magnetic Monster*.

The movie was the first in a trilogy about the Office of Scientific Investigation, whose staffers are called "A-Men"—"A" for atom. Carlson played Dr. Jeff Stewart who, along with Dr. Dan Forbes (King Donovan), is tasked with finding out what is causing an extreme magnetic force in a hardware store. They think that an unknown radioactive element is causing the magnetism. The scientists identify a physicist named Howard Denker who was experimenting with a new element called serranium in a room above the store. Denker had bombarded the serranium with alpha particles for 200 hours and now the isotope must absorb energy to expand. If it is not continuously electrified, it will seek to expand by causing implosions to absorb matter. Stewart is concerned that the element could grow large enough to throw the Earth out of its orbit. The scientists use a Deltatrom located in Canada to overfeed the element with enough electricity to destroy it.

The 75-minute movie was edited down to 30 minutes as a TV pilot titled *O.S.I.* which never turned into a series. Tors subsequently signed Herbert Marshall to appear in two more Office of Scientific Investigation movies. The second film was originally labeled *The Meteor Hunters* and then called *Riders to the Stars*; the third movie was to be called *Space Station, U.S.A.* but then titled *Gog*. Both were released in 1954. Marshall was also to star in another attempt at a television series called *Office of Scientific Investigation*, as the head of that agency.

One of Ziv's most fantastic series was the brainchild of Ziv programming chief Richard Dorso: *World of Giants* (aka *WOG*), starred Marshall Thompson as Mel Hunter, a six-inch-tall secret agent, who usually traveled sitting on a chair inside a briefcase carried by his full-size partner, Bill Winters (Arthur Franz). Hunter was reduced in size after being exposed to a mysterious rocket fuel during an explosion behind the Iron Curtain. CBS considered scheduling the series on Wednesday nights in October 1958. One of Ziv's production executives, Jay Sheridan, told columnist Hal Humphrey, "I just dare the critics to look at this one, then say there's nothing new on TV this fall."[17] However, critics didn't have a chance to review the series, at least not on CBS in fall 1958. The network, through its syndication arm, decided to sell the series to local stations in 1959.

The opening episode of *WOG*, "Special Agent," took place six months after the accident that reduced Hunter in size. He lives with Winters—something like an odd couple arrangement, but, of course, Hunter didn't take up much space. Winters and Hunter are assigned to go to a warehouse, avoiding the guard, to find a list of enemy agents. Bill leaves Mel in the warehouse office thinking he can't be detected by the guard. The documents are found in a safe behind a fuse box. Bill is discovered by the watchman, who shoots him. Injured, Bill fires back and kills the guard. Mel has to phone headquarters on a telephone 29 times his size. But before he can reach the phone, he has to scare away a cat that wants to attack him. Using a fire extinguisher, he sprays the cat, who scats. Mel then climbs up the phone cord, takes the phone off the hook and, using every muscle in his body, dials the number for help.

The original title of the series was *The Little Man*. Only 13 episodes of *WOG* were made.

Tors, as executive producer, was also involved in Ziv's 1959 science fiction series for CBS, *Men into Space*. The show starred William Lundigan as Colonel Edward McCauley, an astronaut involved in the U.S. space program during its beginnings. Episodes involved the first orbiting of the moon, first landing and exploration of the moon, building a space station, and other way-out exploits.

Ziv assigned producer Lewis J. Rachmil to develop the series. As he explained, "We're doing everything to make *Space* honest and accurate. ...Our scripts are approved in Washington D.C. Even the space suits Bill and the other actors wear were made by the New England firm which has the government contract to manufacture space suits for the Air Force."[18]

In 1959, Frederick Ziv sold 80 percent of his production company for $14 million to a group of Wall Street investors. The following year, United Artists purchased Ziv for $20 million including the 20 percent share held by Ziv and the president of the firm, John L. Sinn. At the time, Ziv felt that the TV networks were taking control of the medium, leaving little room for independent producers such as himself. Ziv became a professor in the Division of Broadcasting at the University of Cincinnati, College Conservatory of Music. He died at age 96 in 2001.

CHAPTER 9

Edward Lewis

A Pioneer of Back-Door Pilots

At age 15, Edward Lewis attended Bucknell University in Pennsylvania and began writing songs and dramatic material. During the Second World War, he became a captain in the Special Services corps, which brought him to Hollywood to seek talent for tours of Midwestern military hospitals. After the war, Lewis settled in Hollywood and became a screenwriter and producer of movies including *The Lovable Cheat* and *The Admiral Was a Lady*.

In 1950, Lewis and Marion Parsonnet formed Palisades Productions. Parsonnet had been a program director in radio and then a screenwriter and subsequently became an advertising consultant for Pepsi-Cola. Palisades Productions' first project was a 15-minute interview show starring Faye Emerson.

The company then attempted *A Hollywood Affair,* a detective series with Lee J. Cobb and Adele Jergens. It concerned a disbarred lawyer who becomes a private investigator. The original stories, adapted by Rip Van Ronkel, were written by attorney Louis Blatz. While this pilot didn't sell, a new one, made with Melvyn Douglas in the lead, became the 1952 series *Hollywood Off-Beat,* also known as *Steve Randall,* which was produced by Parsonnet.

Lewis and Parsonnet soon split with each forming their own production company. In 1951, Parsonnet started Parsonnet Studios, which later became Parsonnet & Wheeler.

In that same year, Edward Lewis Productions made *Washington Lady* starring Ann Harding and John Litel. Harding played *"the"* Washington D.C. hostess in this projected series. As Harding noted to columnist Erskine Johnson, "I guess I'm supposed to be Evelyn Walsh MacLean."[1] Mrs. MacLean was an heiress and socialite and the last private owner of the Hope Diamond. The storyline of the pilot centered on a crusading Congressman who finds that much of running the country is done away from the capital with lovely ladies who take great interest in politics.

Schlitz Playhouse of Stars

In 1951, Lewis planned to produce a 52-week series of filmed dramas hosted by movie star Joan Bennett, to be called *Joan Bennett Presents*. Bennett dropped out of the project after her husband Walter Wanger shot and wounded her agent Jennings Lang, because Wanger believed the two were having an affair. Charged with assault with a deadly weapon, Wanger served some months in prison.

Irene Dunne took over as hostess for the dramas incorporated into *Schlitz Playhouse of Stars*. Lewis hired Luther Davis to pen Dunne's introductions and epilogues for the episodes as well as write several of the episodes themselves.

As described below, virtually all of the Lewis-produced episodes were actually back-door pilots for possible series. Some were pilots for new anthologies, while others were for planned "continuing character" shows with supporting actors, character actors and some leading actors, mainly from B movies, wanting to become TV stars. Lewis was among the first producers to use an anthology series as a showcase for potential series. Following is a description of the Lewis-produced pilots for *Playhouse of Stars*.

1. "A Quarter for Your Troubles," May 30, 1952

Lewis attempted a series about a skip tracer with movie supporting actor Richard Haydn as the main character, Wilbur Peddie. Peddie worked in a department store's credit unit tracking down delinquent account holders. He becomes a murder suspect when a customer who was delinquent on his account, is killed. Wilbur tracks down the real killer.

Oliver Crawford scripted this episode. Previously, he had done scripts for *The Stu Erwin Show, Boston Blackie* and *Terry and the Pirates*.

There were a couple of attempts to revive this projected series. One in 1952 had Edward Everett Horton as Wilbur Peddie in a planned series of 13 episodes. The second, in 1954, was to feature Thelma Ritter as the skip tracer. Presumably, in the latter case, the character's first name would be changed to reflect a female skip tracer.

2. "Souvenir from Singapore," June 6, 1952

This episode of *Playhouse of Stars*, the pilot for the syndicated series *The Affairs of China Smith*, featured Dan Duryea as Irishman

William Smith, accused of treason in his home country and now living in Singapore. Smith had experience in the ways of the Orient and provided his services to the highest bidder. Following is a description of China Smith:

> He was lanky and sardonic and wore a white fedora and matching suit. China Smith liked to smoke cigarettes and drink hard liquor. When he hunched his shoulders and smirked with glee, it was usually to deliver a sardonic conclusion to an ironic turn of events for his chief adversary. It was all done in the lyrical tones of an Irish brogue. China Smith was lazy but enterprising, shifty yet truthful, and braved any odds if it meant pleasing a beautiful woman with dubious intentions or dealing with ancient mysteries that challenged him to come and fight it out in the jungle.[2]

Robert Dennis, who created Hal Roach Jr.'s *Passport to Danger*, wrote the pilot.

3. "Dress in the Window," June 12, 1952

Teresa Wright starred in a series pilot to be titled *By-Line*, about newspaper reporter Terry Hagen. She is instructed by her editor Steve (John Ridgely) to dig up information about the 17-year-old girl in an apartment with her boyfriend, wanted fugitive Frankie Farrell (Brett King), as police surround the building. Terry interviews police and other people about the fugitive and his girlfriend. The girlfriend's mother says her daughter's name is Mary Connor (Delores Mann). The mother gives Terry a letter she has written to her daughter, and the police allow Terry to deliver it to Mary. Terry attempts to convince Farrell to let Mary go. Mary tells the reporter that she had wanted to purchase a new blue dress in order to marry Frank before the police located him, hence the name of the pilot episode, "Dress in the Window." Terry and the girl leave as the police shoot and kill Frank.

Commenting on the making of the pilot, columnist Walter Ames wrote that the confusion and helter-skelter of backstage television began to unnerve the actress when an old prop man told her, "Don't worry about a thing. Nothing will be all right."[3] Wright controlled her nerves and gave what she considered to be a top performance. The pilot was based on a story by columnist Adela Rogers St. Johns.

4. "Say Hello to Pamela," June 20, 1952

This *Playhouse of Stars* installment was a pilot for an anthology titled *My Most Frightening Moment*. The theme of the anthology was to present both comic and dramatic scary moments in a person's life. Based on stories from *Coronet* magazine, the pilot featured Barbara Britton and Leif Erickson in a tale about a traveling salesman stopping to say hello to an acquaintance's girlfriend.

5. "The Von Linden File," June 27, 1952

During a lull in her movie career, Joan Leslie starred in this episode, a pilot for a series to be called *The Girl from Maiden Lane*. She and Steve Brodie played insurance investigators assigned to learn if a diamond brooch has been lost or stolen. Leslie goes undercover to date a ladies' man who reported the missing brooch. One of his former girlfriends reveals that the jewelry was actually given to another of the man's female friends.

This was the second pilot for the planned series. An earlier pilot aired live on July 27, 1951, on *Hollywood Theatre Time*. Sheila Ryan starred as an insurance investigator tracking down stolen jewels. She was employed by a company headed by Tom Neal. Aben Kandel wrote both the *Theatre Time* and *Schlitz Playhouse* episodes.

6. "The House of Death," July 4, 1952

This installment, a pilot for a planned anthology to be called *Purple Playhouse*, featured Boris Karloff as kindly Charles Brandon, whose niece (Toni Gerry) arrives from England for a stay and begins receiving death threats. Vincent McConnor, who authored scripts for *Lights Out*, wrote the pilot.

7. "A Southern Lady," July 11, 1952

Starring Jane Wyatt as Mattie Smith and written by Luther Davis, this installment concerned the Wyatt character's life disrupted by a visit from her nephew, looking for money. The episode was apparently a pilot for what could have been an anthology titled *Alarms in the Night*.

8. "Early Space Conquerors," July 18, 1952

Bobby Driscoll starred as a teen who, with his young friends, constructs a rocket to travel into space. Driscoll's "Captain Sherman" supervises the building of the rocket. The Driscoll character along with his youthful scientist associates feel sure that the rocket will bring them glory in the world of nuclear physics. But "Flight Experiment No. 1" is not successful over New York's Prospect Park. Luther Davis scripted this episode.

9. "A Man's World," July 25, 1952

This *Playhouse of Stars* installment featured Pat O'Brien as a widower taking care of four sons. O'Brien described the proposed series as a "male *I Remember Mama*. ...I've got plenty of material of my own for a series like this because I've got four kids of my own—two boys and two girls—and almost any evening that the whole family is home would make another chapter for the TV show."[4]

The title of the series was to be the same as the episode title. In the pilot,

Dad Matson deals with his son Buddy, apparently not the handsomest of his sons, overcoming his shyness to ask a girl out on a first date.

In the same year, Lewis also attempted to produce *Your Neighborhood*, a series of human interest stories based on the short stories of William Cox as a possible vehicle for O'Brien. No series emerged from the proposal.

10. "Crossroads," August 1, 1952

This episode featured Sir Cedric Hardwicke as a cynic whose attempt to be on both sides in the French Revolution leads him into a trap. This installment of *Schlitz Playhouse* was a pilot for an anthology to be called *Crossroads* dealing with the crucial points in a person's life where a decision must be made. Adrian Gendot, who had written for the radio series *Crime Correspondent*, scripted the pilot.

11. "So Help Me," August 8, 1952

Jean Wallace played a nightclub star who meets and marries a millionaire and then informs him that she married him for his money. The episode grew out of a story by Nelson Algren, a writer noted for his novel *The Man with the Golden Arm*.

12. "Double Exposure," August 15, 1952

John Beal appeared as Mel Creighton, an attorney who deals with problems that cannot be solved by the police or others. Valerie Jeans (Amanda Blake), the wife of a university professor, suspects that her husband Clifford (John Brown) wants to kill her. Clifford comes to Creighton with the notion that Valerie wants to murder *him*. A Ben Hecht story served as the basis for this installment.

13. "The Trubbles," August 22, 1952

This episode is also known as "Mr. and Mrs. Trouble." Real-life husband and wife Willard Parker and Virginia Field played a couple who do detective work and find themselves in the middle of a heist. Parker was the lead in several Columbia B pictures during the 1940s.

During the same year that *The Trubbles* failed to become a series, Parker and Field were slated to star in the NBC comedy *Boss Lady*, but they were replaced by Lynn Bari and Glenn Langan when a shampoo sponsor of the series found that Field had earned $5000 for endorsing a rival shampoo.

14. "Port of Call," August 29, 1952

This installment starred Victor McLaglen as a character who runs a hotel in Boca del Rio. In the episode, he does a favor for the Duchess (Gertrude Michael) in exchange for a stolen camera. A *Saturday Evening Post* story by Bud Hutton served as the basis for the episode.

15. "Homecoming," September 5, 1952

An insufferable egotist, Sam Sargent (Leif Erickson) lives on the glory of his long-ago college days as a football player. He returns to his campus for the annual homecoming celebration and tries to prove he is still a big shot. He cannot face growing older until he meets a woman who refuses to age. Richard De Roy, who scripted the episode, later wrote episodes of *Surfside 6* and *77 Sunset Strip*.

16. "The Marriage of Lit-Lit," September 12, 1952, "The Trail," September 26, 1952, and "The House of Pride," November 14, 1952

Edward Lewis produced these three episodes in Mexico in conjunction with Mutual Television Productions for the proposed anthology series *Jack London Theatre*. The three installments aired on *Schlitz Playhouse of Stars*.

a. "The Marriage of Lit-Lit" starred Don DeFore as John Fallon, the manager of a general store, Frank Silvera as Snettishane, and Rita Moreno as Lit-Lit. Snettishane is looking to marry off his young Native American daughter Lit-Lit. Fallon, a widower with two children, wants her to be his wife. Snettishane agrees to the marriage provided he receives a large dowry in store goods. After the marriage, Snettishane instructs his daughter to leave her husband after ten days so the father can receive more goods in exchange for returning her. Lit-Lit doesn't obey her father's instructions. Snettishane makes the sounds of a raven at night, beckoning his daughter. Fallon grows suspicious and fires buckshot at the old man. He then invites Snettishane to come to his home once a week to dine and take back gifts.

b. "The Trial" featured Lon Chaney Jr. Not much about the storyline is known except that it involved a gold miner's greed and the murder of his partners.

c. "House of Pride" starred Robert Hutton as the iron-handed ruler of a Hawaiian estate who has just married Coleen Gray. He orders a man and his ailing mother off the estate because they know too much about his family's past. However, the family doctor discloses that Hutton is really an orphan and has no lineal rights to the estate. Hutton walks down to the lagoon and commits suicide by plunging into the water.

17. "I Want to Be a Star," September 19, 1952

After his movie career fizzled, James Dunn became a character actor on television. In this episode, he played a father who complains about his daughter's movie magazines and desire to be a star until he

is discovered by a talent agent. The husband-and-wife team of Dale
Eunson and Katherine Albert scripted the episode. If the pilot had been
turned into a series, Dunn would have continued to portray a character
beset by the problems of raising a teenage daughter.

18. "Come What May," October 3, 1952

This *Schlitz Playhouse* installment starred Wallace Ford as the
smartest man in a small town. He becomes involved with a housing project and learns that a gun is a poor problem-solver. Robert
Riley Crutcher, who wrote the radio comedy *Fabulous Dr. Tweedy*,
authored this back-door pilot. Ford had been a lead actor in films
in the 1930s and '40s but transitioned to character actor roles in the
1950s.

19. "Trouble on Pier 12," October 10, 1952

This pilot for an anthology to be called *Ring* was titled "Ship from
Macabao" before it was called "Trouble on Pier 12."

The suspense drama related the story of a ship's captain (Akim
Tamiroff) who hires a private detective (John Howard) to provide
him with an alibi for a murder he committed. After the police have
been convinced that the murder was in self-defense, the private eye
becomes suspicious. The sea captain decides to kill him along with his
own girlfriend (Elena Verdugo). The private detective's wife (Rochelle
Hudson) prevents the two from being murdered by the captain.

Lewis produced this pilot in association with Primrose Productions.
As columnist Louella Parsons put it in her February 24, 1951, column,
"Money is where you find it, I always say. John Ireland and his attorney,
Albert Pearlson, found it with Joyce Primrose Lane, local society
woman. She's angel-ing Primrose Productions, Inc., John's independent
company." In addition to Ireland, his attorney and Lane, also on the
board of the company were Richard Morley and cinematographer
Kemp Niver.

Ring was the firm's first TV project. Lou Stoumen was signed to
write the scripts for a series of 13 episodes with several to star actor
John Ireland. Stoumen and Val Lindberg co-wrote the pilot.

20. "This Plane for Hire," October 17, 1952

Another pilot for a possible series. Dean Reisner scripted this
episode, which starred Lloyd Bridges as the boss of a wildcat airline
who becomes embroiled in trouble with the Mexican underworld.
Before "The Plane for Hire," Bridges had supporting roles in major
films and leading parts in B movies. Reisner is probably best known for
writing the screenplays for Clint Eastwood movies, including *Coogan's
Bluff* and *Dirty Harry*.

21. "Drawing Room A," October 24, 1952

While on a train, psychiatrist William Bishop treats a beautiful woman suffering from amnesia. This episode's writer Sam Locke, then just starting his TV career, went on to script *McHale's Navy* and *The Brady Bunch*. Bishop had starred in several B Western films.

22. "Enchanted Evening," October 31, 1952

Lewis and actor Eddie Albert made a family comedy pilot, *The Cherry's,* starring Albert and his wife Margo. Filmed in October 1951, "Enchanted Evening" featured the entire Albert family with Eddie as Dick Cherry, a former GI, Margo as his wife, and their children all living in a modest home. Al Laszlo and Laszlo Gorog wrote the script with Albert who, after leading roles in features, became a character actor and host on TV. Albert financed the pilot using his own money.

An enchanted evening is supposed to be spent by Mr. and Mrs. Cherry entertaining a major client of Dick's boss. The evening takes on nightmare qualities when the Cherrys' kids lose the tickets to the Broadway show *South Pacific.*

23. "Tango," November 7, 1952

Cesar Romero and Ann Savage played dancers who become involved in a mystery. The ex-king and queen of the tango are on the skids both in their act as well as in their personal relationship because of Romero's jealousy. While dancing in a broken-down Panama club, they have the chance to return to the big time, but the old difficulties plague them.

24. "The Pussyfootin' Rocks," November 21, 1952

This *Playhouse of Stars* episode was written by Luther Davis. The pilot, originally titled *Calamity Jane,* was changed to "The Pussyfootin' Rocks" when it aired as an episode of the *Schlitz* anthology.

In this attempt to introduce a series based on the Western sharpshooter, Blondell appears as Calamity Jane along with Buddy Ebsen. (Tom Ewell originally was announced for the part but Ebsen took over for him.) It was directed by Robert Aldrich and shot in Mexico City.

The storyline had Blondell meeting smuggler Ebsen, who is transporting aliens into the U.S. He explains to Jane that the rocks she sees moving are really immigrants covered with canvas. A gang of masked robbers captures Blondell, Ebsen and the immigrants. Blondell manages to escape as the U.S. Border Patrol comes to the rescue.

As she aged, Blondell had played mainly character and supporting roles in the movies. Kathleen Freeman appeared as the robbers, the Ripplehissian brothers, and also as their mother.

After the Lewis-produced episodes of *Playhouse of Stars*, Meridian Pictures made subsequent installments with, as *Variety* reported, an accent on story instead of stars.[5] Irene Dunne no longer introduced each episode. That task was left to the actor appearing on each episode.

China Smith and Brass McGannon

As noted above, the only pilot made by Lewis for *Schlitz Playhouse of Stars* to become a series was *The Adventures of China Smith.*

A noirish hero, China Smith was well-suited to be the self-styled private eye in a B television series. He became involved in murder, robbery, smuggling and missing persons cases.

First-run episodes of the series, which took place in Singapore, lasted for one season. Douglass Dumbrille as Inspector Hobson and Myrna Dell as Madame Shira were regulars on the show. Smith handled cases such as "The Kaprielian Caper," written by series creator Robert C. Dennis. Smith is asked by a Mr. Roshid to locate Max Kaprielian. After visiting Inspector Hobson and Madame Shira, Smith learns that Kaprielian had a multi-faceted personality. Marchella St. John informs Smith that the mystery man died in prison five years ago. Mr. Roshid wants to know every detail of Kapreilian's life. A man writing a book about Kaprielian tells Smith that Max escaped from prison but later died in a mental institution. When Smith revisits Marchella, she reveals that Max led an expedition to Tibet. She gives Smith a paper Kaprielian gave her along with a photo. From the photo, Smith deduces that Roshid is really Kaprielian. After suffering a mental breakdown and having amnesia, Max wanted to find out about his life in order to recover a fortune in jewels that he once hid. Smith advises the man to forget about the jewels. In the end, Kaprielian is murdered by someone looking for the fortune.

In 1954, National Telefilm Associates (NTA) resurrected the series as *The New Adventures of China Smith* and aired a season of first-run episodes. Instead of being set only in Singapore, Smith's cases took him to other cities in the Orient. In "The Yellow Jade Lion," Smith is in Hong Kong where he is hired by banker Mr. Savoy to find out who is stealing gold shipments intended for the bank. The Yellow Jade Lion, a pirate, is receiving advance notice of when the shipments are being made. Smith finds that someone at the bank is leaking information through encoded messages on watercolor paintings displayed in a store window. The store is owned by the father of Mei Lin, Mr. Savoy's secretary. Mei Lin says that her father's life had been threatened, which is why she divulged the information. Smith finds that Mei Lin is the real Yellow Jade Lion and has her reveal the location of the stolen gold.

Working with Ralph Branton Productions in 1951, Lewis attempted a series about an advance man for a traveling circus: *Brass McGannon—Advance Man* starring Preston Foster in the lead role and featuring Clancy Cooper. John and Gwen Bagni, radio writers, scripted the pilot.

McGannon scheduled locations around the country for a traveling circus to perform. In the pilot, "The Bogus Green," McGannon is accused of circulating counterfeit money in a town named Cedarville. Professing innocence, he is permitted to return to the circus to find out who really is passing the bogus money. On a train back to the circus, he encounters Tina (Martha Vickers), a former performer in the show, returning to visit her dad Alonzo (Don Beddoe), an alcoholic. Circus manager Sam Hackett (Clancy Cooper) suspects Nick Helmereck (Bill Boyett), who helps raise the circus tent. Helmereck divulges that he is actually an undercover Treasury agent working on the case. He ends up with a knife in his back. Alonzo is found drunk with a stash of the bogus bills and reveals that his daughter Tina married a counterfeiter who is now in prison, and that she is the one passing the funny money in cahoots with the circus worker who killed Helmereck. Tina pulls a gun on Brass, who slugs her.

Despite this pilot's storyline of murder and counterfeiting, at least the hero was someone other than a detective or cowboy.

Tales of the Vikings

Edward Lewis later worked with Kirk Douglas' production company, Bryna Productions: In his role as vice-president, he helped produce such classic films as *Spartacus*, *Seven Days in May* and *Grand Prix*. He also executive-produced the period adventure series *Tales of the Vikings* (originally called *King of the Vikings*), an outgrowth of *The Vikings* that took advantage of the movie's costumes, model ships and villages.

Syndicated during the 1959–60 season, the show starred Jerome Courtland as Viking captain Leif Ericson, Buddy Baer as Haldar and Walter Barnes as Finn. The three sailed to various European countries for their adventures which involved hunting for treasure, exploring new territories, fighting evildoers and rescuing innocent victims. In "The Merchants of Venice," Leif, Finn and Haldar come upon an abandoned ship and its load of pepper. A young woman on the ship says that her father, the captain, was killed by mutineers who then ran off to Venice. To help the woman, the Vikings sell the pepper at a good price to a merchant who turns out to have been behind the mutiny. The mutineers return to the ship and take the woman and the Vikings hostage. The three Vikings challenge the mutineers to a swordfight, and the Vikings come out victorious.

Science Fiction and Western Series Attempts

While a Bryna executive, Lewis became involved in executive-producing some pilots for the company. One planned series in 1958, *Ray Bradbury's Report from Space*, a science fiction entry, was based on the work of the author. Two of his books, *The Illustrated Man* and *The Martian Chronicles*, served as the basis for the planned series.

The pilot script, "And the Moon Be Still as Bright," focused on residents of a neighborhood inhabited by astronauts. One resident was Janice Smith, the first woman to go to Mars, marry and have a baby there. Captain Jonathan Wilder, his wife and son also live there. Stories were to deal with the space adventurers in the neighborhood, the first rocket trials, and the problems leading up to the flights to Mars. According to the script, Mars is apparently similar to Earth but with thinner oxygen.

Producer Edward Lewis (center) working with Kirk Douglas (right) and an unidentified actress. Lewis went from producing backdoor pilots on *Schlitz Playhouse* to making TV series based on Kirk Douglas movies.

Wilder flies to Mars with Spender, an archeologist, Biggs, Hathaway, Gibbs and Cherokee. On Mars, the men find that the planet's original inhabitants were wiped out by chicken pox brought by the first Earthlings to visit the planet, much like the European settlers in America brought disease to Native Americans. Spender goes off on his own. A week passes and the other crew eventually find him reading a book left on Mars by its original inhabitants and claims he has deciphered the Martian language. When Biggs strikes the book from Spender's hands, Spender shoots and kills him. Thinking that the crew will destroy Mars, Spender threatens to kill the rest of the crew.

The crew goes after Spender. Upon locating him, Wilder seeks a truce. After delving deeper into Martian literature, Spender has become a more peaceful individual. He wants the rest of the crew to learn what he has discovered about non-violence. Wilder says that Spender is being unrealistic. As Wilder leaves, Spender begins firing at the other men. Spender is killed by Wilder. Speaking softly, Wilder says he hopes he can build Mars the way Spender wanted him to: the best of the past and the best of the new.

Lewis was also involved with another proposed series while at Bryna. Based on the Kirk Douglas film *The Indian Fighter*, a treatment and script were developed for a TV Western with the same title, set in 1869 Indian territory and featuring 22-year-old Jimmy Hawk, whose parents had been murdered by the Apaches, and his sidekick Zeb Underwood, who would also narrate each episode. The Hawk character was apparently never cast, but Zeb Underwood would have been portrayed by Arthur Hunnicutt. Hawk, an employee of Colonel H.B. Wyncoop, commissioner of Indian Affairs, worked out of Fort Kearny, Nebraska.

Stories would deal both with the mistreatment of Native Americans by white people as well as settlers moving West. Hawk's favorite weapon was the tomahawk. In a pilot script written by Christopher Knopf, four young Sioux braves raid a farmstead, killing the owner. Hawk is ordered to bring them to justice. He and Zeb travel to the Sioux encampment where they find that the perpetrator is the chief's son. The chief challenges Jimmy to a fight over a knife in the ground. If the chief wins, his son will not return with Jimmy. If Jimmy wins, the chief will permit his son to leave. Naturally, Jimmy wins the contest and takes the son back for trial.

One of the last projects Lewis produced was the 1983 TV miniseries *The Thorn Birds.* He passed away at age 99 on July 27, 2019.

Chapter 10

Albert Gannaway

Early Country and Western TV Producer

Born on April 3, 1920, in Charlottesville, Virginia, Albert Gannaway grew up in Arkansas and attended the University of Arkansas. During World War II, while serving in the Army, he was captured by the Germans but subsequently escaped. He became head of the "Soldier Show Company" which entertained the troops. Returning to civilian life, he ventured into radio, syndicating *Captain Starr of Space* and *Mike Molloy*, among other programs.

Initial Ventures into Television

Gannaway sought to produce a number of TV series of various genres during the 1950s. One of his first endeavors was *The Music World*. His Telco Productions in collaboration with Normandy Productions planned a series of 13 episodes of interviews with singers whose records were played with the performers commenting on their works.

In 1951, he formed a company with Henry Morgenthau to make *Al Gannaway's Half-Pint Party*, televised late afternoons on ABC in New York. The kids' program involved young children of about seven participating in a variety of games. As *Billboard* wrote, "Host Gannaway, a personable young man with collar-ad good looks, took the small fry over a variety of game hurdles, including a seesaw session and a pin-the-mustache-on-Gannaway contest."[1]

Later in 1951, Gannaway re-joined the Army and produced a series called *The Big Picture* depicting the activities of the U.S. military. When he was again out of uniform, he sought to resurrect *Half-Pint Party* on CBS Saturday afternoons in 1952. Later that same year, the producer moved to California and attempted to launch the children's series *It's a*

Albert Gannaway (center) with children in an episode of *Half-Pint Party*. On the series, Gannaway asked children about their favorite clothes, songs, etc.

Small World, produced by Filmcraft Productions. Gannaway joined that firm as director of programming.

Mike Molloy

In 1953, Gannaway formed Mike Molloy Productions with Film-craft production manager Glenn Miller, actor Steve Brodie, MGM scenarist Fred Eggers, cinematographer Virgil Miller and Tom Hubbard, one-time director of productions for Liberty Network. The new company wanted to produce a detective drama titled *Mike Molloy* starring Brodie, with Ken Christy as Lieutenant Berg and George Berkeley as "The Professor."

Malloy is a cop turned private eye who left the force over bureaucratic red tape. In the pilot, he is on the trail of the killer of a friend of his—a cop who was working on a narcotics case. As he interviews informants including "The 'Professor,'" a jazz pianist, and Sheila (Patricia Joiner), an undercover cop, he is being tracked by his friend's killer,

Orville (Phillip Monsour). Orville has been hired by mob boss Raddock (Burt Topper). Raddock's henchmen kidnap Malloy. Raddock wants Molloy to work for him, but the private eye declines. Orville tries to kill Molloy, but the private investigator gets the upper hand as the police close in.

The unsold pilot's theme song was "Sweet Molly Malone," whistled by Molloy during the show.

Early Country and Western Variety Shows

After *Mike Molloy* failed to become a series, Gannaway worked with Flamingo Films of New York to bring the iconic Country and Western radio music series *Grand Ole Opry* to TV in 1954 through syndication. Gannaway made 96 half-hours of that series. Performances by rising stars Faron Young, Carl Smith and Marty Robbins on the series led Gannaway to feature them in subsequent TV and movie projects.

Gannaway continued in the country music vein. In 1956, he syndicated *The Country Show* featuring *Grand Ole Opry* stars Young, Smith, Robbins and Webb Pierce. Twenty-six episodes of the 30-minute series were filmed in color featuring songs and some comedy routines. Gannaway also attempted to launch Smith and Young each in their own self-titled half-hour variety show.

In the late 1950s, Gannaway planned to make *The Judy Canova Caravan* with the comedienne, known for her singing, yodeling, guitar-playing and persona as a likable country bumpkin. Canova was set to play a traveling carnival entertainer in a 30-minute musical series produced by Caravan, Inc., a company formed by Gannaway and Canova.

In the pilot directed by Charles Lamont, the carnival caravan arrives in another small town. A young Mexican boy has stowed away in the caravan and causes problems when he won't leave. When this music project was not picked up as a series, Gannaway and Canova sought to make a movie starring the comedienne in Cuba. But then along came the Cuban revolution, and the movie was never made.

Western and Adventure Projects

In 1955, the producer launched yet another production company, Gannaway-Ver Halen Inc. with Charles Ver Halen to make two TV pilots, *Young Sheriff* and *Tramp Steamer.*

Gannaway sought to make male Country and Western singers

Richard Arlen and Faron Young (right) in *Hidden Guns*. Young's biggest country hits were "Hello Walls" and "It's Four in the Morning."

into TV Western heroes. Gannaway–Ver Halen signed Faron Young to appear in several proposed projects, one of which was a TV series about a peace officer who takes over law and order duties from his father.

Young was one of the stars of a Gannaway–Ver Halen B Western movie, *Hidden Guns*, which seems like a "pre-pilot" for the planned radio and TV series featuring the singer. Young plays himself as Deputy Faron Young whose father, Ward (Richard Arlen), is the sheriff of Youngstown, somewhere in the West.

The town is under the thumb of the hotel-saloon owner, Stragg (Bruce Bennett), who runs crooked card games and intimidates or shoots anyone who questions his power. Stragg has the town council change its charter to have the sheriff's position appointed rather than elected. Before the charter becomes effective, Ward Young vows to bring Stragg to justice. Stragg hires gunman Snipe Harding (John Carradine) to take care of the situation. The elder Young seeks a witness who saw Stragg shoot an unarmed man to testify. Snipe has the witness killed. He then conspires with Stragg on a plan to kill the sheriff. Ward is an expert gunman. Knowing that he would lose a fair gun duel with the sheriff, Stragg has Snipe hide in his office with a rifle to shoot the sheriff when Stragg fires at him in a duel. The plan works. The sheriff is not killed, but his gun-drawing hand is severely injured, meaning that he can no longer participate in a gunfight. When Faron discovers the rifle slug taken from his father, he suspects a sniper was involved in the shooting. Stragg and Snipe plan to use the same tactic with Faron, but when Stragg shoots at the deputy, he moves to the side, avoiding the sniper shot. Both Stragg and Snipe are killed, and presumably Young becomes the new sheriff, taking over his father's job.

The other planned pilot, *Tramp Steamer*, to be made by Gannaway and Ver Halen, apparently never materialized despite reports that Ray Milland was considering it as a starring vehicle. The proposed series would have focused on a tramp steamer captain carrying cargo to various ports of call.

Gannaway followed up *Hidden Guns* with another film that served as a pilot for a proposed TV series, *Daniel Boone—Trail Blazer* with Bruce Bennett as Daniel Boone.

The precursor to the planned TV series was a movie, with many songs, made in 1955. In it, Boone establishes the Kentucky fort and trading post known as Boonesboro. On his way to meet his father, Daniel's son James is killed by renegade Shawnees headed by Simon Girty (Kem Dibbs). Girty, allied with the British, is giving the Indians guns in return for scalps. The same renegades abduct a group of settlers traveling to Boonesboro. Daniel and his men free the settlers. In the process, Daniel becomes separated from his men as the renegades come after him. He goes to the Shawnee village whose chief, Blackfish (Lon Chaney Jr.), is Boone's blood brother. Before Blackfish will discuss peace with Daniel, he challenges him to run a gauntlet of Indian braves with tomahawks. Boone survives the gauntlet. When one of Blackfish's sons is killed by the renegades, the chief thinks the settlers murdered him. Boone saves the chief's other son and takes him to Boonesboro to recover from injuries. When Blackfish's tribe attacks the fort, Boone and the settlers beat back the initial onslaught. After the chief's other son dies, Boone asks the chief to pretend that his son is still alive and talking to his father so that Girty reveals himself as the leader of the group that murdered Blackfish's sons. When Girty shows himself, he is killed by the chief.

Gannaway tried again to launch Country-Western stars in their own series. This time the producer came up with a vehicle called *Western Musketeers* based on *The Three Musketeers*. The three stars would be Marty Robbins, Carl Smith and Webb Pierce.

As he did with *Hidden Guns* and *Daniel Boone—Trail Blazer*, Gannaway made a movie, *Buffalo Gun*, to introduce audiences to Robbins, Smith and Pierce as actors. Produced in 1957 but not released until 1961, the film, set in 1875, had Pierce playing a federal agent with Smith and Robbins as his deputies.

Pierce, Smith and Robbins are working undercover as cattle drivers to find a stolen cache of buffalo guns. They are driving cattle to an Apache reservation to feed the Native Americans since the buffalo gun has decimated the buffalo herds. While on the cattle drive, the three are attacked by rustlers. Smith finds that one of the rustlers left behind a buffalo gun, meaning that, if they find the culprits, they will also find the men who stole the buffalo guns. Pierce, Smith and Robbins discover that the local Apache Indian agent, Sam Roeca (Wayne Morris), is behind the theft of the guns as well as the cattle rustling. Roeca hopes to sell the guns to the Indians. The three "Western Musketeers" round up Roeca and his gang and locate the stolen guns.

The movie, produced and directed by Gannaway, had all the elements of a B Western: romance, fistfights, gunplay, square dancing, cattle stampedes, and a comical sheriff who looked like Gabby Hayes. Songs were performed by Pierce, Smith and Robbins, while Elvis Presley's back-up singers, the Jordanaires, sang the theme song as the three stars rode off into the sunset.

Anthology Attempts

Gannaway sought to produce two anthologies in 1956. *Medal of Honor* would dramatize the lives of the recipients of the medal. *Battle of the Century* would use Army film in depicting great American battles. Neither project resulted in a series.

Other Series Attempts

The producer partnered with Magazine Management to syndicate a series based on its *Jungle Girl* comic books, to be shot in Acapulco, Mexico. The series would focus on the Brazilian Indian Protection Service.

After purchasing Charles Ver Halen's interest in the production company which then became Gannaway Productions, Gannaway planned another series in the late '50s, *Calamity Jane,* which would present stories about the fictional adventures of the Western heroine. This project was seen as the successor to the Gene Autry–produced *Annie Oakley* Western (see Chapter 13) which performed very well in reruns. Apparently, other producers were also trying to launch a series based on Calamity Jane including Warner Brothers and Doris Day's Arwin Productions. None of these attempts resulted in such a series.

Gannaway joined forces with comic Pinky Lee to organize Pinky Lee Inc. to film 39 half hours of the planned series *The Perils of Pinky*. In this combination adventure-comedy series (with the emphasis more on the latter), Lee was to play a messenger who got in and out of trouble.

In 1962, in association with Colorvision Corporation, Gannaway sought to produce a jungle adventure series called *Aba of the Jungle*, later titled *Tongoloa*. CBS Films planned to syndicate 39 color half-hours of the show starring a young actor named John Carroll in the lead role of a juvenile living on a South Seas island; he got there when a plane carrying him and his parents crashed and his parents died. Other actors in the project included Wayde Preston and Jil Jarmyn. The pilot for the never-realized series was filmed around Acapulco, Mexico.

One of Gannaway's final TV projects was creating a pilot for a proposed adventure series starring Gerald Mohr. In *Holiday for Hire*, Mohr planned to star as a globetrotting travel agency manager. The 1964 pilot "Rendezvous in Acapulco" was filmed at the Hilton Hotel retreat in the Mexican city. If the pilot had become a series, subsequent episodes were to be made at Hilton Hotels all over the world. The pilot storyline had Mohr searching for the runaway daughter of a millionaire.

Gannaway spent his later years producing and directing B movies such as *Man or Gun* (1958) and *Plunderers of Painted Flats* (1959). He died in 2008 at age 88.

Chapter 11

Leon Fromkess

The Master of the Adventure Genre

After graduating from Columbia University in 1926, Leon Fromkess worked on Wall Street for an international banking outfit. This led him to Columbia Pictures, where he handled the refinancing of the studio's debt. Later, he served as treasurer and coordinator of distribution and production for Monogram, which he was instrumental in founding. In 1939, he organized Producers Releasing Corp. and, as its president, he made over 200 films. A few years later, in 1945, Fromkess joined Samuel Goldwyn as vice-president of production, making movies like *The Best Years of Our Lives*, *The Bishop's Wife* and *My Foolish Heart*.

The Adventures of Kit Carson

In 1950, Fromkess ventured into television in charge of MCA's TV subsidiary, Revue Productions. He worked on Revue's anthology *Stars Over Hollywood*, and, like several early TV producers, he launched a Western, *The Adventures of Kit Carson* starring Bill Williams in the title role with Don Diamond as his Mexican sidekick El Toro. "Kit" (short for Christopher) was always on the side of justice, thwarting bad guys.

Eric Taylor scripted several *Kit Carson* episodes in 1951 and 1952. In the 1920s and '30s, Taylor wrote stories for pulp magazines such as *Black Mask*, *Clues* and *Dime Detective*. He later became a screenwriter for Republic and Columbia, writing for mystery series (including the *Crime Doctor* and *The Whistler*). Furthermore, he worked for Universal on *Son of Dracula* and *The Ghost of Frankenstein*. Besides authoring scripts for *Kit Carson*, Taylor scripted episodes for TV's *The Roy Rogers Show* and *Ramar of the Jungle*.

"Enemies of the West" was one of Taylor's earliest *Kit Carson* scripts. Carson and El Toro are escorting a lawyer, Mr. Spence, to deliver the pardon of Daly, who is about to be hanged for killing a judge. Evidently, Daly's wife provided information to California's governor that cleared her husband of the crime. Some bad guys want to prevent the arrival of the pardon. Spence pledges to find the judge's real murderer. Kit and El Toro are taken hostage by men working for the real killer. The two escape their captors, save Spence from death at the hands of the judge's killer, who is turned over to the authorities.

In addition to scripting several *Kit Carsons*, Taylor developed some treatments for the series that appear to have never been filmed, perhaps because of the writer's early death in 1952 at the age of 55. One treatment, "California Vendetta," dealt with Don Anselmo Mendoza, a land owner who has been put on trial for murdering a cattle rustler. The rustler's brother testified that the land owner killed his brother, who was trying to collect a gambling debt from Anselmo. Carson pledges to find Anselmo's son, who is away, to have his testimony exculpate his father. Kit and El Toro discover that another land owner, Hernandez, is holding Anselmo's son hostage. Hernandez is behind Anselmo's troubles. He wants Anselmo's son to marry his daughter to gain possession of Anselmo's land. Carson and El Toro rescue the son. The false testimony against Anselmo is exposed, and Anselmo is freed.

The other treatment Taylor wrote for the series, "In Old Mariposa," concerned a California land owner, Mr. Bolton, and his daughter Margarita. Kit and El Toro find Bolton's stagecoach driver dead and tell Bolton. At Bolton's ranch, Bill Edmunds says that Bolton has sold him the property and left the area. Carson feels that Bolton may be prisoner in his own house. He sneaks into the dwelling and discovers Bolton gagged and tied in a chair. Bolton knows that Edmunds and his thugs have kidnapped his daughter. He doesn't want to be freed, thinking that Margarita will be killed. He explains that he will be released when he signs a bill of sale for the ranch. Edmunds comes into the room and, in a fight with Kit, is knocked unconscious. When he comes to, he reveals where Margarita is being held. Edmunds' two thugs return to the ranch. Kit flees with the two men in pursuit. El Toro sees what is happening and rides out after them. Kit and El Toro apprehend the men and then go to an inn where Margarita is behind held. Based on evidence provided by Carson, Bolton and Margarita, Edmunds and his bunch are brought to justice.

In making the series, Fromkess employed technical experts to check details on recreating exactly the frontier flavor of the 1840s and 1850s when Carson fought bandits and hostile Indians. The producer hoped to make the series an educational tool for parents and teachers, saying, "If we can teach the kids a bit of history without their realizing it, I think it's worthwhile."[1]

While the settings in the Southwest and the accoutrements used on the series may have been accurate for the time period, the stories were not based on the actual exploits of Christopher Horton Carson who, among other endeavors, was a guide for John C. Fremont in his explorations of California and Oregon, an Indian agent, and a Civil War Army officer. However, that is not unusual for B television series whose titular heroes were named after real-life Western legends but whose stories were fiction. *The Adventures of Kit Carson* was syndicated for five seasons, from 1951 to 1955.

Arrow Productions Adventure Series

After leaving Revue, Fromkess formed his own TV production company, Arrow Productions, which launched the syndicated series *Ramar of the Jungle* starring Jon Hall.

As *Billboard* pointed out in its review of the pilot, "Traditionally, jungle pictures have been top box-office draws. As a matter of fact, it's generally agreed that there hasn't been a jungle picture made that lost money."[2]

Hall played Dr. Tom Reynolds, a physician who travels to Africa to study the methods of tribal witch doctors. Ray Montgomery appeared as his assistant Howard Ogden, a chemist. "Ramar" is an African title referring to a white medicine man. The concept for the syndicated series was created by Hall in consultation with executive producer Rudolph Flothow. Fifty-two episodes were made and syndicated from 1952 to 1954.

The pilot, "Evil Trek," introduced the Dr. Reynolds character. Reynolds and Ogden want to meet the "white goddess" who may have the secret to eternal youth. They venture into the jungle to locate her, but their native guides desert them when they come to "taboo land." The duo is captured by native warriors and taken to the village of the "white goddess." She speaks English, having learned the language from a missionary's book. The woman ingests a special plant that apparently keeps her young. Reynolds and Ogden are able to free themselves from captivity, go to the witch doctor's hut and take samples of the special plant. Dr. Reynolds pledges to examine the specimens he took to see if indeed they have youth-maintaining properties.

Footage shot in Africa was combined with film shot outside Los Angeles at an estate that had foliage similar to the African jungles to give the series an authentic flavor. African-American college football players appeared as African tribesmen and film of animals fighting one

A scene from *Ramar of the Jungle* with (left to right) Ray Montgomery, unidentified actor and Jon Hall.

another was shot in Mexico. The series was rerun multiple times by the stations that purchased it. Its staying power was due to the fact that it gained a new viewing audience every year because as it lost kids growing up, it gained an entirely new audience of children who liked the show.

Fromkess cobbled together episodes of *Ramar* into feature-length films to be shown in movie theaters. As the producer indicated in a *Billboard* article, "The scripts were so prepared that serialization and feature film re-editing would be possible and still retain a storyline continuity. We were also careful to keep the production values of the series as high as possible so that the product itself could be marketable for theatrical use abroad."[3]

After *Ramar of the Jungle* ended, Jon Hall sought another starring vehicle in a tale of adventure titled *Knight of the South Seas*. He played Captain Jim Knight in this seafaring series attempt. Charles Mauu played Tula, a shipmate; Stanley Adams was the first mate, Roxy; and Salty the Chimp played himself. With money he made from *Ramar*, Hall formed Lovina Productions with George Bilson to film the series. "Lovina" was Hall's mother's name.

When the three episodes that were made failed to result in a series, they were released together in 1957 as the film *Hell Ship Mutiny*. John Carradine, Mike Mazurki and Peter Lorre co-starred. It concerned a gang of thieves headed by Malone (Carradine) who are forcing the natives of a tropical island to dive into deep waters for pearls. Many of the natives die in the attempt. Trying to unite an island chief with his daughter, Captain Knight arrives on the island and encounters Malone and his two henchmen. They force him to dive for pearls, but he frees himself from their clutches and subdues Malone and his men.

In the second part of the film, Malone and his gang free themselves from their shackles and take over Knight's boat. They force Knight's crew to abandon ship and order Knight to take them to New Zealand. Knight sails in circles and takes them back to the island where they were stealing the pearls. A French commissioner (Peter Lorre) arrives on the island to conduct a trial for Malone and his men. However, the commissioner is conspiring with Malone to obtain the pearls from Knight as well as retrieve a recently discovered treasure from a sunken ship. Knight foils their plans.

Jon Hall's father Felix Locher, then 75, played the island chief in the first episode of the planned series.

Fromkess' Arrow Productions sought to launch other series but these attempts did not prove successful. In late 1952, the production company announced that it intended to film 26 episodes in color of *King Arthur and the Knights of the Round Table* in England. The cost of each episode was estimated at $25,000, high at the time because of the costs of period costumes and sets. Errol Flynn was at one time rumored to have been in contention for the lead role. The series, set to begin production in early 1952, never came to fruition.

Ringside, the pilot for a potential series about the world of boxing, was initially to be produced in June 1953 with Mike Mazurki playing a fighter. Pat O'Brien was considered for the lead on the show as a fight manager. When this casting didn't work out, executive producer Fromkess attempted to sign Barbara Stanwyck as the fight manager. She rejected the role even with a deal to share in the profits. Fromkess abandoned the project without making a pilot.

A third project envisaged by Arrow was to be called *Arabian Knights* which was to begin production in September 1953. However, in July 1953, Fromkess ran into financial complications when beginning production on another 13 episodes of *Ramar of the Jungle*. His chief financial backer stepped out. Edward Small and Milton Gordon stepped in to fill the void.

Television Programs of America (TPA)
Mystery and Crime Series

Gordon and Small, president and vice-president of Television Programs of America, bought Arrow Productions with Fromkess becoming executive producer for the TV series the company developed. Fromkess also served as vice-president and executive producer of Norvin Productions (Norman and Irving Pincus), created in 1953, to produce *Mystery Is My Business* (aka *Adventures of Ellery Queen*) as well as serving in the same capacities for Hall Productions which made a CBS comedy series, *Halls of Ivy,* starring movie actor Ronald Colman and his wife Benita Hume.

The fictional detective Ellery Queen had been created in 1928 by Frederic Dannay and Manfrid B. Lee and was the central character in several mystery novels, movies and a radio series. In 1950, the DuMont Television Network brought Ellery to the small screen in a live series which lasted until 1952. When Norvin and TPA decided to resurrect the series for TV, actor John Ireland was their initial choice for the lead role, but Hugh Marlowe ended up playing the detective on the series. In March 1954, Ireland sued TPA for breach of contract, stating that he had been discharged without cause or excuse. According to his complaint, TPA slandered him as "politically unacceptable" to advertising agencies and prospective sponsors.

In a statement for Norvin Productions, Fromkess declared that negotiations for the actor to star on the series had never been concluded and that no derogatory remarks about Ireland were made to or about him. "We had ascertained that Ireland, contrary to his representations to us, recently entered into an agreement with a nationally known tobacco company, endorsing its product, thereby making it impossible to sell any TV program on which he might appear to competitive tobacco concerns."[4]

In May 1954, Ireland received a cash settlement and a statement clearing him of any suspicion of disloyalty for which he agreed to withdraw his $1.7 million+ breach of contract and slander suit against TPA, Norvin and Fromkess, among others.

Adventures of Ellery Queen was a standard mystery series usually involving a murder with the culprit eventually identified as the least likely person the viewer would have thought. Florenz Ames co-starred on the syndicated series as Ellery's father, Police Inspector Richard Queen.

In a typical episode, "Once a Killer," Ellery is on vacation with his father in Acapulco where they encounter a newlywed couple, the Harveys. Richard thinks he has seen Mr. Harvey before but can't remember where. After a redhead is murdered, Richard recalls that when he was in New England, he read about a case involving the attempted murder of a wealthy woman by her intended, who pleaded insanity and was institutionalized. He believes Mr. Harvey is the man from that case. The Queens question Harvey about his past with his wife overhearing. Mrs. Harvey then informs the Queens that she thinks her husband is on the verge of a breakdown. Mr. Harvey spoke to the redhead right before she was killed and thinks he dropped his cigarette lighter at the spot. Ellery goes looking for the lighter but can't locate it. Later, Mrs. Harvey plants her husband's lighter at the murder scene to incriminate him. Ellery finds Mr. Harvey looking for his lighter and instructs him to discuss the situation with his wife. Harvey accuses his spouse of murdering the redhead and trying to frame him. She confesses that she did kill the woman, who was attempting to blackmail her because Mrs. Harvey was already married to another man. The Queens overhear Mrs. Harvey's confession.

Created by writer Earl Derr Biggers in the mid–1920s, Oriental detective Charlie Chan had been featured in several motion pictures of the 1930s and 1940s. TPA's take on this character, *The New Adventures of Charlie Chan,* was syndicated beginning in 1957. As with most actors who played Chan in the movies, a Caucasian actor, J. Carrol Naish portrayed the knowledgeable detective in the TV show. James Hong appeared as Barry Chan, Charlie's Number One son, who was always arriving at the wrong conclusion concerning the guilty party. The first five episodes were filmed in the United States; the balance were made in England. The standard plot had Chan becoming involved in a criminal investigation with a number of suspects and then, near the end, gathering the suspects and identifying the culprit, with the guilty party always being the least likely suspect.

In an episode, "The Great Salvos," set in Washington, D.C., files for a secret jet engine are stolen from Charlie's friend Douglas Fenton. While Charlie is having dinner at a nightclub with the Fentons and Dr. Kruger, a brother-and-sister mind-reading act, the Great Salvos, perform. They take Charlie's pocket watch to use in the act and surreptitiously slip microfilm of the plans into his watch, thinking the detective is flying to Madrid later that evening. But Charlie is asked to delay the trip to determine who stole the files. Chan learns that the Great Salvos are being forced by a foreign spy organization to do its bidding. Charlie invites Dr. Kruger and the Fentons to again dine with him and his son the next night. Barry displays his father's watch, which is stolen when the lights go out. Chan's watch was taken by Mrs. Fenton, who is revealed as the head of the spy organization.

Another project to be executive-produced by Fromkess was *Mr. Digby* with William Demarest as a sardonic and dour newspaper photographer who likes to solve crimes. The never-realized series was to be based on the *Saturday Evening Post* stories of Douglass Welch. Robert "Happy" Digby worked for the *Central City Daily Informer*. In one Welch story, "Time and a Half for a Hero," Digby inadvertently takes a photo of an auto accident with three men exiting from the vehicle and running away. Digby learns that the three men in the photo included the head of an organized crime gang, one of his henchmen, and the mayor's nephew, who were all fleeing from the site of the bombing of a laundry building that the gang was trying to take over. The photo is published on the front page of Digby's newspaper along with a lengthy article about the gang.

For the planned television series, Digby got a young assistant named Jimmy Brown and two daughters, 18-year-old Janet and 14-year-old Midge. Scripts were written for at least three episodes, but apparently none were filmed. In the first script, "Mr. Digby and the Fare Hike," Digby and Jimmy uncover corruption in the city bus company and correct the situation. Also, Jimmy and Janet Digby become friendly with each other.

One of the last TPA series executive-produced by Fromkess was 1958's *New York Confidential*, another syndicated program. This one, based on a book of the same title by journalists Jack Lait and Lee Mortimer, supposedly described the real New York City. The book also served as the basis for a 1955 film produced by Edward Small, co-owner of TPA, about a New York crime boss and his family.

On the TV series, Lee Tracy starred as investigative reporter Lee Cochran. The first story concerned the plight of an orphaned immigrant who loses his sponsor and faces deportation. The show, filmed in New York, presented not only human interest stories but also standard crime dramas like "Crime Cradle," in which a detective searches for the leader of a crime school for children. This episode served as a pilot for a crime drama chronicling the career of real-life New York City detective John H.F. Cordes. Cordes was the only policeman to twice win the NYPD's highest award, the Medal of Honor. Gary Merrill would have portrayed the detective in a series to be called *Johnny Cordes*.

Halls of Ivy

Halls of Ivy, the TV adaptation of a gentle radio comedy of the same name, concerned the life of a college president, Dr. William Todhunter

Hall (Ronald Colman), and his spouse Victoria (Benita Hume). In the opener, Hall awaits the verdict of the school's Board of Governors to extend his term as president for five years while he reminisces about his previous tenure at the college. The comedy was a departure for Fromkess in that it was not an adventure show nor could it be considered B television. The series was expensive for TV at the time, costing $50,000 per episode. The comedy did not deal with slapstick or misunderstandings as its basis for laughs. Instead, it was a warm comedy dealing with interpersonal relationships. For instance, in one episode without a laugh track, a former English professor--advanced in years and without much money—returns to campus to see it one last time before he dies. Hall has the Board of Governors approve a project for the retired professor to begin writing a history of Ivy College.

Commenting on the dialogue used in the series, Colman remarked, "Sometimes we use more than three syllables. The public is ready for adult, quality entertainment on TV."[5] Up against the Milton Berle, Martha Raye and Bob Hope variety series on NBC, the CBS show was canceled after one season.

Lassie, Fury and Other TPA Adventure Series

In the fall of 1954, Fromkess supervised the production of *Lassie*, a TV series about a female collie and her owners, filmed by Robert Maxwell and Associates. The CBS program starred Tommy Rettig as Jeff Miller, Jan Clayton as his widowed mother Ellen and George Cleveland as his grandfather.

In the opener, "Inheritance," Jeff and his mother attend a reading of a will for a deceased neighbor, farmer Homer Carey, who bequeathed his dog Lassie to Jeff. Depressed over his master's death, the dog is unresponsive to Jeff. When Jeff takes her home, the dog returns to the Carey farm. Gramps and Jeff go to bring her back, but that night, she leaves again. The second time, the dog encounters Carey's crooked farmhand, who is trying to find $2000 that his boss had saved. When Jeff goes to retrieve Lassie again, he discovers the hidden money. Jeff is interrupted by the farmhand. Lassie attacks the man and pursues him as the local postman arrives and subdues the hired hand. Lassie then begins her new life with the Millers.

In many episodes of *Lassie*, the canine helped rescue Jeff or others from dangerous situations. In "The Feud," Gramps and neighbor Matt Brockway argue over their weekly checker game, and then both men forbid Jeff and his friend Sylvester "Porky" Brockway from visiting each other's farms. Jeff and Porky come up with a plan to have Gramps and Mr. Brockway reconcile, but it backfires. Jeff and Porky then run away into the woods where Porky falls into quicksand. Lassie is sent for help. Working together, Matt and Gramps rescue Porky and the two men settle their differences. Sheldon Leonard directed this episode.

Robert Maxwell and Associates originally wanted to produce *Lassie* in color. Fromkess was opposed to color filming because of its expense. He also felt that when color film was viewed on a black-and-white TV set, the black-and-white quality was inferior.

Jack Wrather bought the rights to *Lassie* from TPA and Robert Maxwell in September 1956. However, TPA had syndication rights to its original episodes, which they sold to local stations under the title *Jeff's Collie*.

With the success of *Lassie*, TPA launched another adventure series about a boy and his pet, aimed at juvenile viewers. It starred Peter Graves as Jim Newton, whose wife and son had been killed by a drunk driver; Bobby Diamond as Joey, a young orphan whom Jim befriends, and William Fawcett as Pete, Jim's right-hand man. Also featured was a black stallion called Fury, the name of the series. Loosely based on *The Adventures of Black Beauty*, *Fury* debuted in October 1955 on NBC's Saturday morning lineup.

In "Joey Finds a Friend," Jim and Pete, after trying for several years, entice a wild black stallion to the Broken Wheel Ranch, when they capture the herd of wild horses that the stallion led. Pete comments that the stallion is full of "fire and fury." Hence the name of the horse.

In town one day, Jim befriends a young orphan who is about to be sent to juvenile hall and takes him to the ranch. Joey attempts to stop a ranch hand from whipping Fury; the boy is knocked unconscious and Fury escapes. Jim enlists the help of teacher Helen Watkins (Ann Robinson) to care for Joey while he recovers. When Jim doesn't believe Joey's story of the incident with the ranch hand, Joey runs away. Jim goes looking for him. Joey finds Fury, who has a cut on one leg. With Jim's help, the horse is nursed back to health.

Fromkess signed a new two-year contract with Television Programs of America in early 1956 to continue as vice-president and executive producer of all its shows. The deal put an end to rumors that Fromkess would join Screen Gems to produce specials for CBS.

In 1956, TPA premiered the adventure series *The Count of Monte Cristo*, based on the Alexandre Dumas novel and set in 1834 France. It was initially developed by Fromkess' Arrow Productions in 1953; originally the program was to star Anthony Dexter. When the series premiered, the lead character Edmund Dantes was portrayed by George Dolenz, the father of future *Monkees* star Micky Dolenz.

The initial 12 episodes were filmed at Hal Roach Studios with the succeeding 27 installments made in Britain with the assistance of producer Harry Alan Towers. The switch in production location served to reduce costs since British labor worked at wage rates lower than American labor. The 39 episodes were sold to local stations across the country.

In the opener, "Affair of the Three Napoleons," Dantes is asked by Albert Morrell's daughter to investigate his murder. Three Napoleon gold coins were found in her father's possession in a small snuff box. Dantes' sidekicks are Macho (Fortunio Bonanova) and Jacopo (Nick Cravat). All wear masks during their adventures to correct injustice. The count asks an informer to explain the significance of the three gold coins. They turn out to be a password identifying a group seeking to overthrow the king. Dantes uses the coins to meet the conspirators and learn their names. He finds that Morrell's murderer is the fiancé of Morrell's daughter. Dantes engages in a swordfight with the killer. Naturally, he is triumphant, and the murderer is arrested by the king's soldiers.

TPA and the Canadian Broadcasting Company executed a deal in 1956 to create a joint venture, Normandie Productions, to make TV series in Canada to broadcast on both the CBC and on stations in the United States. One of the first series to result from this venture was *The Adventures of Tugboat Annie* featuring the characters of Annie Brennan (Minerva Urecal), the captain of the *Narciscus*, based in the Pacific Northwest, and rival skipper Horatio Bullwinkle (Walter Sande) of the *Salamander.*

TPA spent 13 months trying to find the right actress for the role of Annie. According to columnist Vernon Scott, "An actress testing for the role had to be in good physical condition for climbing tugboat ladders. She had to know how to handle her dukes for fight scenes with Annie's traditional adversary Horatio Bullwinkle. And she needed to be enough of a sailor not to get seasick. Finally, all aspirants had to have a voice like a fog caller and a figure built along the lines of a scow."[6]

Tugboat Annie was a character-driven comedy-adventure with the plot of several episodes similar to that of a regular adventure series. On one installment, assassins target the queen of a small European country when she visits America. Annie is hired as the queen's double because of her resemblance to the monarch. On another episode, Annie's tugboat is hired to bury a corpse at sea. However, the coffin really contains an infamous bank robber hoping to escape to Canada. On another episode, Bullwinkle is romanced by beautiful young Lydia—but Lydia and her real boyfriend are trying to transport illegal cargo on the *Salamander.*

Suspicious of Lydia's motives, Annie follows Bullwinkle's ship, climbs aboard and finds Bullwinkle being held at gunpoint. Aware of Lydia's extreme allergies, Annie has brought some ragweed and wrestles the gun away from Lydia when the latter has a sneezing attack.

The Adventures of Tugboat Annie lasted for one season in first-run syndication.

Hawkeye and the Last of the Mohicans, based on the James Fenimore Cooper stories, was an adventure show produced by Fromkess in 1957. Set in 1757 when England still ruled the American colonies, the premiere had Hawkeye, aka Nat Cutler, and his Indian companion Chingachgook (the last of the Mohicans) returning to upstate New York to visit Hawkeye's mother. Near the mother's cabin, an Indian guide, Ugaro (Michael Ansara), shoots a Redcoat messenger. The messenger turns out to be Hawkeye's younger brother Tommy. While his mother takes care of Tommy, the English want to arrest him for supposedly warning the Huron tribe about the dispatch he was carrying. Tommy subsequently dies of his wounds. Ugaro, a Huron spy masquerading as a Mohawk, wants to lead the Hurons against the British. Hawkeye tells the English captain about Ugaro, but the captain is also a traitor. Hawkeye shoots the captain and is arrested. The Hurons attack the English fort. Hawkeye escapes to help fight the Indians and kills Ugaro.

The syndicated series was shot in Canada through Normandie Productions. John Hart, who had played the Lone Ranger for one season in 1953, appeared as Hawkeye, while Lon Chaney Jr. played Chingachgook.

TPA attempted an adventure series, *The Mysterious Island*, based on the Jules Verne trilogy about five prisoners of the Civil War who escape in a balloon and land on an uncharted island. Pirates arrives, and the five men are saved from death at their hands by a waterspout that drowns the buccaneers. A volcano then erupts, submerging the island. The men escape again only to encounter the submarine *Nautilus* and Captain Nemo.

Fromkess indicated that the story would be divided into 39 episodes with the series to be made in color—a departure from the producer's previous reluctance to use color. While the cast, which was never announced, and the crew would be from America, filming was to take place in Australia and New Zealand.

TPA also planned other series for the 1957–58 television series that never took flight. One project, *Dude Ranch*, would have focused on life at a contemporary dude ranch in the southwest, featuring the owner of the ranch and his teenage daughter, with guest stars playing visitors to the dude ranch each week.

A second planned series, *The Enchanted Forest* (aka *Thunder Ridge*) was to be made by *Lassie* producer Robert Maxwell, about an orphaned youngster living on his uncle's farm, interacting with both farm animals and wildlife. The pilot eventually aired on *Best of the Post* under the title "Thompsons of Thunder Ridge" with Charlotte Greenwood as Aunt Martha, Jay C. Flippen as Uncle Hank and Charles Herbert as Tommy. In the story, Tommy is saved by a raven, a deer, a skunk, a raccoon and a squirrel.

Although *The Enchanted Forest* never became a series, producer Robert Maxwell created an adventure series called *Cannonball* about two truckers. It premiered in the fall of 1958 and ran for one season. Produced through Normandie Productions, the show starred Paul Birch as "Cannonball" Mike Malone and William Campbell as his partner Jerry Austin. Both worked for C&A Transport out of Toronto and encountered various adventures on Canadian and Northeast United States highways. In one episode, Mike and Jerry are hauling a load of explosives when one of their tires blows; in others, they help stop a runaway gasoline truck, transport valuable but dangerous radioactive material, and find a stowaway who pulls a knife on them.

TPA's Anthology and Melodrama Series Attempts

One False Step was to have been an anthology produced by John Guedel, who had made such series as *You Bet Your Life* and *People Are Funny*. The series would feature a different cast each week in stories about people who make a mistake and break the law. Guedel initially attempted to launch this series in 1952 with the airing of a pilot on ABC's *Personal Appearance Theatre*. The anthology would have featured stories of first-time offenders and people who got in trouble by accident. The pilot starred Hugh Beaumont, Steve Dunne and Veda Ann Borg in a story about counterfeiting.

In "The Captain Kenesaw Story," a *New York Confidential* installment executive-produced by Fromkess, an elderly man strikes it rich on a quiz show. With his winnings, he buys the home for the aged where he lives. His daughter-in-law then attempts to have the man declared incompetent. This episode was for an unsold anthology series called *Turning Point*, about the effect that winning big on a quiz show has on people's lives.

Another back-door pilot shown on *New York Confidential* was "Airline Hostess," the debut for a potential series of the same title. Marcia Henderson starred as a senior flight attendant dealing with the problems of other hostesses as well as with airline passengers. In the unsold pilot, Henderson contends with a younger hostess, disillusioned in love, who goes home and risks losing her job since she is on immediate call. Outdoor scenes were filmed at Los Angeles International Airport. If the concept had become a series, additional location filming would take place in England and the Far East.

One of the last pilots contemplated by Fromkess while at TPA was a supernatural anthology series, *The Witch's Tale*, which had aired on radio for several years. Alonzo Deen Cole, who created *The Witch's Tale*, was to serve as consultant and story supervisor of the planned series.

The radio version of the series presented stories of suspense and horror such as "The Mannequin," about the lifelike female mannequin an artist purchases for a model. The figure seems to understand what the artist says. The artist's wife thinks she hears the mannequin sigh and tells her husband that she will leave him if he doesn't discard it. The artist later learns that he resembles a sculptor from several years ago and that the mannequin looks like the sculptor's wife. When she died, the sculptor encased her body inside the mannequin. The figure is opened up, revealing a skeleton inside.

An actress portraying a witch introduced each radio episode. On the proposed TV version, Jeanette Nolan would have played the witch.

Milton Gordon purchased the interest held by Edward Small in TPA in 1957. At the time, Gordon also announced a new plan where both stars and producers had the opportunity to share not only the profits of their series but also in TPA's overall profits. Fromkess continued as the company's vice-president in charge of production. Later in that year, he was among three TPA vice presidents named to the company's board of directors.

In September 1958, the Jack Wrather organization and Associated Television Ltd., a British program contractor, formed ITC, which purchased Television Programs of America. Three months later, Fromkess left the company. In the early 1960s, he formed a partnership with Sam Firks to make features, including *Shock Corridor* and *The Naked Kiss*.

Fromkess died of a heart attack on March 11, 1977, in North Hollywood, California, at age 75.

CHAPTER 12

Walter Wanger

From Films to TV and Back to Films

Unlike the producers profiled in the preceding chapters, film producer Walter Wanger was unable to launch a successful TV series despite numerous attempts.

Wanger was born on July 11, 1894, as Walter Feuchtwanger in San Francisco. His mother shortened the family name to Wanger in 1908. Attending Dartmouth College, he developed an interest in amateur theater. During World War I while serving in the Army, he began producing propaganda films directed at the Italian public.

After the war, Wanger obtained jobs at Paramount and then Columbia. He married actress Joan Bennett in 1940. As noted in Chapter 9, he gained infamy in December 1951 when he shot and wounded his wife's supposed paramour, agent Jennings Lang.

Aladdin's Lamp and Other Adventure Series Attempts

Wanger entered the field of television in 1950, proposing an Oriental fantasy-adventure series to ABC titled *Aladdin's Lamp*. The pilot starred Johnny Sands as Aladdin, Patricia Medina as Princess Jasmine and Richard Erdman as Mirza. ABC provided $10,000 of the financing for this project, and Wanger put up $22,000. The pilot was filmed in color at Hal Roach Studios in the fall of 1950. The network attempted to find a sponsor for the potential adventure series but could not.

When the pilot didn't sell, Wanger started discussions with Steve Broidy, head of Monogram, to expand the television pilot into a feature film. The movie, with a screenplay written by Howard Dimsdale and Millard Kaufman, was released in 1952 as *Aladdin and His Lamp*.

The motion picture, a little over one hour in length, focused on

Producer Walter Wanger with his wife Joan Bennett. Despite the Jennings Lang incident, Wanger and Bennett remained married for many years.

the love affair of Princess Jasmine and Aladdin, a talented pickpocket. Aladdin breaks into the princess' chambers and kisses her. Later, he is instructed by Mohmud, a magician, to retrieve a magic lamp. When Aladdin rubs the lamp, a genie (Charles Horvath) appears. The genie will grant Aladdin's wishes but vows to try to kill him (or anyone who possesses the lamp) in order to permanently free himself. Aladdin's wish for power and wealth is granted so that he can impress Princess Jasmine. Initially the princess is not persuaded to marry Aladdin but then changes her mind even though the genie takes away Aladdin's wealth and power.

Prince Bokra (John Dehner), who wants to take over as caliph of Bagdad from Jasmine's father, asks Jasmine to marry him, but she refuses. Aladdin saves the princess from Bokra's men. The two escape only to be captured by a slave trader who is unaware that Jasmine is a

Johnny Sands and Patricia Medina in a scene from the movie version of the *Aladdin's Lamp* **pilot. Sands gave up acting in 1953, moved to Hawaii and became a realtor.**

princess. After more adventures, Bokra takes possession of the lamp, but the genie kills him and frees himself. The genie tells Aladdin that another genie will take his place.

In 1950, Wanger, Rudolph Abel and Howard Dimsdale formed Craftsman Productions to make an adventure series called *Captain Scarlett* featuring a hero fighting injustice. It was filmed in Mexico with Richard Greene as Capt. Carlos Scarlett, Nedrick Young as Pierre DuCloux, Leonora Amar as Princess Maria and Mondo Fabregas as the Duke de Corlaine.

After the fall of Napoleon, Capt. Scarlett, dressed in a red cape with a red feather in his hat, returns to France and learns that his estate has been confiscated and that injustice rules the land. His first act of valor is to rescue Princess Maria from highwaymen. Subsequently, he finds that she doesn't want to marry her intended. Before he can help her, he is taken prisoner. In prison, he meets Pierre, whose lands have also been appropriated. He and Pierre escape and free the princess. The princess joins Scarlett and Pierre as they fight for justice.

When the series didn't sell, the first episode was paired with two others and released as a motion picture. The second part of the film had

A scene from the *Captain Scarlett* pilot with Richard Greene as the title character and Leonora Amar as Princess Maria. Greene later played Robin Hood in TV's *The Adventures of Robin Hood*.

Scarlett taking up the cause of peasants who are unable to pay their taxes. Capt. Scarlett and his two compatriots fight the Duke de Corlaine, who is levying the taxes and living in Scarlett's estate. The duke sends an undercover operative to set a trap for the captain. Scarlett recognizes the trap and escapes.

In the final part of the movie, the princess is captured when trying to evade the duke's soldiers. The duke will execute her if Capt. Scarlett doesn't surrender to him. Disguised as old peasant women, Scarlett and Pierre enter the town where Maria is being held and free her with help from the villagers, all dressed in red capes to lure away the soldiers.

Wanger also worked on a project for ABC to star Dorothy Lamour. Presumably, the planned series would have starred Lamour in a role similar to one she originally played in *The Jungle Princess* in 1936 and subsequently satirized in several *Road* movies with Bing Crosby and Bob Hope as the beautiful "Sarong Queen." The Wanger project, titled *The Jungle Princess* or *Queen of the Jungle*, doesn't appear to have gotten off the ground. It would have been produced by Television Enterprises with common stock divided among Walter Wanger (50 percent), Lamour (40 percent) and Wynn Rosemore (ten percent).

Dynamite, a contemporary adventure series proposed by Wanger, was set in different locales around the world but, unlike other shows set abroad, it did not deal with foreign intrigue but rather with a family-owned construction company that undertook large projects in exotic locales. Jeff Bentley owned the company with his son Judd working for him on various engineering and construction projects. In the proposed pilot, "The Testing of Judd," the firm builds a road through mountains to a mine in a South American country at the behest of the country's leader. Put in charge, Judd faces problems like interference from the government's opposition. Other storylines envisioned for the planned series were constructing a pipeline in the desert, building a dam in Pakistan, a bridge in Mexico, and an airbase and military installation in the South African jungle.

In 1957, Wanger sought to produce a series called *Stagecoach,* set before the Civil War and before the completion of the railroad, about two brothers who run the McGovern stage line between Missouri and California. Fred McGovern and his brother John managed stagecoaches carrying mail, passengers and freight. Fred was the administrator of the business, John the hands-on operator. Other characters slated to appear in the series included Jesse Tate, a stagecoach driver, Elmo Hatfield, a circuit judge, Mary Jane Reilly, manager of a traveling stock company of female entertainers, and Ramon Valles, an outlaw.

In the 1957 treatment for the proposed series, John McGovern travels incognito on a stage driven by Ted Robinson to evaluate how well the stage line is working. McGovern fires Robinson when he discovers that the driver is lining his pocket by transporting contraband whiskey. McGovern drives the stage to Indian Springs where he encounters Jesse Tate, whom he instructs to take the coach on to its destination. In Indian Springs, McGovern sees that Matt Farkos, a stage line supervisors, lives in an expensive, newly built house. McGovern asks him bluntly how much graft has he taken to build such a residence. Knowing that he won't have his job for long, Farkos tries to bribe McGovern with favors from his mistress. When John rejects the offer, Farkos has his two gunmen hijack the stage Tate is driving, beat up Tate, and try to burn down the way stations. McGovern goes after the gunmen, killing one and wounding the other. When Farkos learns what happened, he tries to flee as his mistress runs to McGovern to tell him about Farkos. Farkos shoots her, and McGovern kills him.

Like Wanger's other television projects, *Stagecoach* never became a series.

The Quest—An Anthology Attempt

In 1956, Wanger attempted to sell to Irving Briskin Productions *The Quest,* a TV series concept created by writer Daniel Mainwaring. The idea presumably was for an anthology with religious overtones. The Mainwaring treatment focused on John Evans, an ex-convict who accompanies Pete Howe, a friend of the prison chaplain, on an expedition to Algiers to search for ancient documents about the Moors preserving learning during the Dark Ages. In Algiers, the two become involved in the war for independence between France and Algerian nationalists. John finds strength in his religious faith when he is able to prevent a specific conflict between the French and Algerians.

A Different Kind of TV Series

In the late 1950s, Wanger sought to launch a series other than a B level adventure. His concept involved rewarding scholarships to students for college. Wanger's initial idea was titled *Planet Earth,* a public affairs program dealing with subjects like democracy, education and large corporations. As part of the show, four-year $10,000 scholarships would be awarded to students. This idea evolved to a slightly different idea called *Radar 1956* which would be an electronic review of what is occurring all over the universe. *Radar 1956* would be an entertaining international news magazine with sketches and music with well-known stars discussing world problems and solutions. When this idea didn't sell, Wanger proposed a quiz show called *The Biggest Job in the World.* Top personalities would give their ideas on how to run the United States. The incentive for people like Eleanor Roosevelt, Edward R. Murrow and Harry Truman to appear would be the awarding of four scholarships each week to boys and girls from the different sections of America. Scholarships worth $25,000 each would be given to take each individual through four years of college. The master of ceremonies would be the "Secretary to the President" of the week with experts being cabinet members arguing different points proposed by the president. At the end of a season, viewers would be able to send in ballots with the president receiving the most letters being awarded the grand prize of $500,000 for 20 extra scholarships. As with the other concepts, no network wanted to turn the idea into a series.

After his experience in television, Wanger returned to producing movies, including the original *Invasion of the Body Snatchers* (1956), *I Want to Live!* (1958) and *Cleopatra* (1963). He passed away at age 74 on November 18, 1968.

CHAPTER 13

Movie Star Production Companies of B TV

Some More Successful Than Others

Bing Crosby Enterprises

Founded in 1946 by singer-actor Bing Crosby, this company produced Crosby's radio show and then entered the field of television in the early '50s. It was headed by Everett Crosby (Bing's brother) and vice-presidents Basil Grillo and Charles Brown. Everett was reportedly instrumental in getting the company into TV production by risking $2 million on the initial endeavor.

In 1950, BCE signed a contract with Proctor and Gamble to produce episodes of NBC's anthology *Fireside Theatre,* one of TV's first filmed series. After episodes aired on *Fireside Theatre,* they were rerun as episodes of the syndicated *Royal Playhouse* as well as airing on the DuMont network.

Episodes produced by BCE were melodramas and light comedies. For example, "Hope Chest" concerned a beautiful young girl with an overly possessive mother who wants her daughter to marry for money. The daughter does eventually find her "knight in shining armor." "Leather Heart" told the story of a confirmed bachelor who had fun reorganizing a boot-making business when he joined forces with a competent and attractive bookkeeper. Most *Fireside Theatre* episodes were directed by Frank Wisbar.

Everett Crosby explained how he ensured that episodes of this anthology were produced at low cost. "A TV film can be made for $15,000 up, depending on the nature of the drama. We rent space from a Hollywood movie studio and, with the use of their mechanical facilities, complete shooting a picture in two and a half days. Casting is a big factor in determining a show's budget. The players we hire have had only bit part experience. We couldn't afford to pay top stars."[1]

BCE produced several other early TV series and unsold pilots. *The Chimps*, actually produced by Courneya Productions under contract with BCE, was made at Thousand Oaks Jungle Compound and featured two chimpanzees in a comedy-mystery series satirizing Sherlock Holmes and Dr. Watson.

In 1951, *Kandid Kids* was BCE's effort to develop a show for children with a panel of youngsters discussing toys and other new inventions. Hy Averback served as the moderator. Hal Goodman and Ruth Stevens developed the concept.

Rebound (1952–53), a melodramatic anthology, first appeared on ABC and then on the DuMont network. Stories were mostly in the mystery-suspense genre with ironic endings. The series was advertised as "Gripping Shows of Plain People." "Thrilling! Intense! Surprise! Impact!" In one installment, a man kills his wife and attempts to pin the crime on the wife's lover. But the lover was a fiction that the wife made up, to get her husband jealous. On another episode, three bank robbers are holed up in a mountain cabin surrounded by police. The robbers discover a vein of gold that would make them all wealthy just before the police wipe them out. Columnist John Crosby (no relation to Bing Crosby) pointed out, "All these dramas are characterized by Hollywood know-how.... All the know-how, in fact, of 1000 B pictures, the corner cutting, the false economy, the clichés of acting and writing, the absence of imagination, show only too well how pictures lost so much of their audience to TV...."[2]

Gloria Swanson began hosting her own melodramatic anthology series in 1952, the syndicated *Crown Theatre*. Swanson acted in four of the 26 episodes, several of which were filmed in Mexico. In "My Last Duchess," she appeared as Eleanor Hallam. The show reminded some of Swanson's *Sunset Blvd.*: She starred as a once-famous actress who is now giving acting lessons to make the money she needs to pay her nephew's college tuition. Her agent indicates that the long-running Broadway play in which she appeared, *My Last Duchess*, has been purchased by Frank Lord, a director and former actor. When Lord played opposite Eleanor in the show, she had him fired because of his poor acting. Eleanor visits Lord to plead for a part in the film. If she admits that she kicked him out of the play on a whim, he will give her the role. She refuses to admit that but, because of her honesty, she receives the role anyway. In her second *Crown Theatre* episode, "If Speech Be Silvern," a salesman no longer wants to live when an accident causes him to lose his voice. His wife (Swanson) attempts to restore his faith in himself.

In a "Choice of Weapons," the actress appeared as an adventuress who falls in love with a stranger. The last episode in which Swanson acted, "Short Story," dealt with a famous female novelist searching for a short story idea to complete a collection. She comes up with the tale of her falling in love with an aging busboy. Like Edward Lewis' *Schlitz Playhouse of Stars*, *Crown Theatre* featured several episodes that served as pilots for possible series.

A handsome young Frenchman sits at a Parisian sidewalk café and relates his adventures to viewers on the planned 30-minute series *A Chair on the Boulevard*, written and directed by Walter Doniger and based on the works of writer Leonard Merrick, known as the British O. Henry.

In the pilot, *La Voix Parisienne*, a Paris newspaper trying to increase its circulation, offers a reward to whomever identifies one of their employees wandering around the city waiting for someone to recognize her. The editor selects a smudgy photo of a young female reporter to be printed in his paper with a prize of one million francs as the prize for the first stranger who says to her, "Pardon, are you Mademoiselle Girard?" After two weeks, the reward is raised to two million francs. Writer Georges (Claude Dauphin), who has been following the story, becomes acquainted with Jeanine, a young woman dining at the same restaurant as he is. After some subtle hints from the woman, he identifies her as Mademoiselle Girard. She confesses that, to be honest, she had wished that they had met three weeks hence because by then, the reward would increase to four million francs. The man agrees not to divulge to the paper the fact that he found the mademoiselle for another few weeks so he can win the larger prize. In the meantime, he agrees to support her and allows her to stay in his boarding house while he lodges elsewhere. Georges promises her that every day of the next three weeks will seem like Christmas to her. He brings her food and gifts. Right before the end of the three weeks, Jeanine disappears. He thinks the concierge identified her and collected the prize money. Georges goes to the newspaper and speaks with the editor, who informs him that Mademoiselle Girard had really been identified yesterday evening by the wife of a piano tuner who discovered her working in a store's corset department.

A Chair on the Boulevard, if it had been turned into an anthology, would have debuted in fall 1952.

Corney Johnson starred Richard Rober as a Damon Runyon–type character working out of a shoeshine stand as an office. Co-starring in the pilot were Barbara Billingsley, Henry Slate and Robert Osterloh. In the *Crown Theatre* episode that aired June 9, 1953, "Half the Action," Corney transacts a deal wherein he receives half-interest in a magician as collateral for his loan to a friend. Rober died in an automobile accident shortly after the pilot was made.

BCE advertised the planned *Corney Johnson* series as the story of a beloved town character who, while never quite doing anything in particular, always does something singular and is therefore the topic of local talk through the years. *Variety*'s reviewer wrote, "The late Richard Rober did as well as he could with an impossible part, and the same goes for Barbara Billingsley, Henry Slate, Robert Osterloh and others in the lineup."[3] This unsold pilot was made by Lancer Productions, a BCE subsidiary formed by Basil Grillo, Bernard Girard and Richard Dorso.

Louis Bromfield, a writer now perhaps better known for his conservation efforts than for his novels, provided the stories and narrated *Louis Bromfield Presents,* an anthology effort. The pilot, "Up Ferguson Way," eventually aired on *Crown Theatre.* Told in flashback style, it starred Frances Rafferty as a gentle young woman who "wouldn't hurt a fly." She is tormented by bandits but insists there will be no violence around her farm. She lives alone waiting the return of her boyfriend who has gone west seeking his fortune. One night she hears a noise at the door and, without waiting for identification, she aims her trusty .44 and kills her returning, long-lost boyfriend.

The projected anthology would have premiered in the fall of 1952. Bromfield planned to introduce each installment from Malabar, his ranch home.

BCE also attempted to launch a series starring child actor Bobby Driscoll via a pilot titled "The Best Years," written by D.D. Beauchamp and co-starring John Litel and Barbara Woodell. It's a story told in flashbacks about a boy, his father and his aunt living on a farm. The boy, Ben Risteen (Driscoll), loves his horse whom he thinks of racing in the county fair. His father Adam (Litel), who is having financial problems with the farm, is thinking of selling the horse to the cavalry to raise some money. Very reluctantly, Ben allows his horse to be sold but, seeing how unhappy his son is, the father wants to give the money to his son. Ben refuses to take it. A few days later, Adam presents his son with a new horse and a colt. At first, Ben says that he wants his original horse returned but then starts bonding with the new animals.

Another planned anthology from Bing Crosby's production firm, *Rose Colored Glasses* (originally titled *Dreams of Glory*), concerned various individuals' dreams of a different life. The pilot "Hemingway" dealt with a sporting goods store clerk, Wendell Taylor (Robert Nichols), who yearns for bigger things in life. When he helps wealthy Louise Osborn (Mary Shipp) start her foreign car, she is impressed with him and thinks he is a man of position. Wendell allows her to continue to believe this. When Louise invites him to her family's hunting lodge for a weekend, he begins to realize that his dream is over. Nevertheless, he still thinks that in the future he will be presented with a similar situation and will rise to the occasion.

A proposed dramedy about small town American life, the pilot for *Those Were the Days*, titled "The Crystal Set," aired on *Crown Theatre* on February 10, 1952. The episode, made by Lancer Productions, starred Charles Winninger as Will; Arthur Q. Bryan as Fred; Ted Thorpe as Herb; Doris Singleton as Will's daughter Peggy; Howard Erskine as Peggy's boyfriend Stanley, and Harris Brown as Ben.

The anticipated series was described as keeping viewers of all generations "chuckling from start to end."[4] Furthermore, BCE indicated that the stories would weave the nostalgia of bygone years into episodes filled with warmth and charm.

The show took place in December 1922 in Canfield, population 7000, established in 1835. Will Stevens, now retired but formerly the owner of the local hardware store, insists that, with a good antenna, he can be the first man in town with a working radio—and he does succeed in picking up a radio station from Springfield. To the chagrin of Ben, editor of the local newspaper, many of the town's citizens begin asking Will for the latest weather report from the radio instead of reading it in the paper. Will's battle with the editor continues over items like the latest sports scores and breaking news.

One story the townsfolk are following concerns a young boy named Bobby Downey, suffering from leukemia; everyone hopes he will live to open his gifts on Christmas Day. Ben is concerned that the radio will put his paper out of business since it has up-to-the-minute news. Will tries to ensure him that it will not. On Christmas Day, Will learns that Bobby passed away the day before but refuses to tell anyone so as not to spoil their holiday. Walking down the street, Will notes the headline on the local newspaper, "Bobby Downey Lives for Christmas." Ben walks out of his newspaper office and sees Will. They exchange greetings for the day but say nothing more.

CBS Television Film Sales attempted to find a buyer for the proposed series with no luck.

Bing Crosby Enterprises also made other unsold pilots not aired on its anthologies. Based on short stories by William Cox and featuring sports personalities who would act as narrators, the anthology *The Show of Champions* would feature tales of sport accomplishments. Heavyweight boxing champion Jack Dempsey appeared in the pilot as both narrator and as an actor playing himself. Figures under consideration for future episodes had the series sold were baseball's Joe DiMaggio, tennis player Jack Kramer, wrestler Gorgeous George and golfer Ben Hogan. The pilot was screened in March 1951 in New York City for the National Brewers Association in hopes that they might sponsor the series, but to no avail.[5]

In spring 1952, BCE filmed a pilot featuring novelist Erle Stanley Gardner's iconic lawyer Perry Mason. The planned series was to be syndicated to local TV stations. Actor George Macready was under consideration to portray Perry Mason, as was John Larkin, who voiced the character on the radio. The characters of Della Street and Police Lt. Tragg were also in the pilot.

Based on Gardner's *The Case of the Crimson Kiss* as adapted by Walter Doniger for television, the pilot begins with a man named Carver Clement being found poisoned in his apartment, a lipstick mark on his forehead. Perry Mason becomes involved when an aunt of Fay Allison's finds Fay and her roommate, Anita Bonsal, both unconscious from too many sleeping pills. Perry and Della go to the roommates' apartment, located below the Clement apartment, where a doctor says both will recover. Fay will soon marry Dane Grover, who previously had dated Anita. In Fay's purse, Della finds a key to the Clement apartment. Lt. Tragg discovers items such as a toothbrush and glasses with Fay's fingerprints in the deceased's apartment. Fay is arrested for the murder.

During the trial, Perry proves that the lipstick mark on Clement's forehead was not made by Fay's lips. He also shows that Anita, who had given her roommate sleeping pills, planted evidence in Clement's place while Fay was asleep and put Clement's key in Fay's purse in order to make it look as if Fay was having an affair with the deceased. Bonsal hoped that Grover, her former boyfriend, would decide against marrying Fay. However, the real murderer is Clement's neighbor Shirley Tanner, who was in love with him. Tanner saw Anita enter the Clement apartment to plant evidence and concluded that he was having an affair with her and, out of jealousy, poisoned him.

Gail Patrick, who later became the executive producer of the *Perry Mason* series with Raymond Burr, was an associate producer on this effort in conjunction with her husband Cornwell Jackson, a literary agent for *Perry Mason* creator Gardner.

Another unrealized series from BCE, *Trauma*, planned to present psychological suspense dramas. Scheduled to be shot in spring 1952, the pilot, titled "The Chase," was written by Bernard Girard and Richard Dorso. James Agee, who helped write the screenplay for the movie *The African Queen*, was to adapt the story for the potential TV series.

Bing Crosby Enterprises evidently also produced a reboot of an early live NBC comedy, *The Hank McCune Show*, in 1952. *The Citizen-News* of Hollywood, California, reported on May 13, 1952, that *Hank McCune* began shooting on May 12 for BCE. In June 1952, BCE advertised the show as "[a]n entirely new situation comedy series featuring HANK (Ears) MCCUNE whose remarkable rating on NBC-TV a couple of seasons ago proved viewer desire for more Hankomania!"[6] CBS-TV film sales represented BCE in the sale of this series for syndication.

The Hank McCune Show was really more a comedy sketch series than a situation comedy. One of the filmed shows included sketches about soap operas and moviemaking with lanky, jug-eared McCune introducing each segment in character as a TV host. The soap opera spoof, called *Everything Is Peachy*, starred Larry Keating dealing with the trials and tribulations of being the head of a family whose daughters have run off with various delivery men. His young son, played by McCune, comes home with his report card saying he got an "A" in spelling. Looking at the card, Keating responds that his son failed spelling, to which the son says, "That's because I put an 'A' in the word, 'spelling.'"

In 1956, Bing Crosby decided to close down his company, saying that production costs were too high and that there was no point in trying to compete with all the old movies being released to television. Later in the 1950s, Bing Crosby Productions succeeded Bing Crosby Enterprises and, in the early 1960s, made such series as *Ben Casey* and *Hogan's Heroes*.

Bracken Productions

Actor Eddie Bracken, best known for his comedy films from the 1940s including *Hail the Conquering Hero* and *The Miracle of Morgan's Creek*, formed a production company in 1947 to make films starring himself. In 1950, he attempted to produce TV series. In one of his first projects, *This Is Our Home*, also known as *Family Album*, he starred along with Jane Darwell, Sonny Tufts and Jimmy Conlin.

Bracken sought to produce 78 *This Is Our Home* episodes, chronicling the history of an American family over a period of three years. Bracken's own children were drafted for the initial episodes. The series was to be filmed in color. Only a pilot appears to have been made.

Another project Bracken undertook in the early 1950s was called *Picture Platters*. His company made about 32 such mini-films, somewhat similar to music videos. Each installment was a filmed story fitting the lyrics of a song. For example, for the Bing Crosby song "Among My Souvenirs," Bracken featured a girl on a park bench opening her handbag and taking out a photo showing her and her boyfriend kissing. She then examines souvenirs like a wedding ring, a draft notice and a "We regret" letter from the military.

Bracken Productions also made a syndicated children's show called *Willie Wonderful* with hand puppets, set at a carnival. In the pilot, Willie, a young blond boy voiced by Bracken, helps his foster father save the circus from foreclosure. Willie talks with the animals in the carnival and has a fairy godfather who takes after W.C. Fields. Sixty-five 15-minute episodes were made. Willie Wonderful Productions, formed by Robert C. De Vinny, purchased the *Willie Wonderful* series from Bracken in 1957. After this transaction, the Bracken production company appears to have ceased operation.

Bracken's TV efforts were not related solely to his own production company. He also starred in a pilot for NBC: *Mr. Breger.* Along with Everett Crosby, Dave Breger originally proposed a radio series to NBC based on his *Private Breger* comic strip. The radio show would have dealt with Breger, who had previously served in the Army, being drafted again and, thinking that he knows everything about soldiering, blundering through basic training.

The network decided, instead of a *Private Breger* radio series, that perhaps a *Mr. Breger* TV situation comedy might be more appealing. The pilot concerned Breger, now a civilian, meeting a young girl named Michelle, an orphan whom he had met during World War II in France when she was eight years old. When she arrives in America as his ward, he is surprised that she is now an attractive young lady. Mrs. Breger is jealous of the new arrival. Michelle becomes involved in a TV quiz show and wins the grand prize.

The pilot aired on December 26, 1952, as an episode of *Gulf Playhouse.*

Joseph Cotten's Production Companies

In 1948, Joseph Cotten, known for movies such as *Portrait of Jennie* and *The Magnificent Ambersons,* joined with Daniel T. O'Shea of Vanguard Films and radio scripter-producer Stuart Ludlum to form 29:30 Incorporated, to produce radio and television shows. The company began business making radio dramas and syndicating them. "29:30" is the time allotted to a half-hour radio show.

The company's first television effort was *Peter Hunter, Private Eye.* The proposed syndicated 15-minute series featured Frank Albertson as tough detective Peter Hunter (also sometimes referred to in *Variety* as "Keith Hunter"). Cotten directed the pilot with Stuart Ludlum writing the script. The pilot, mostly filmed outdoors near Pacific Palisades, was shot over four days for $2000, which was about $5000 under the then-current average cost for such a project. It was marketed to TV stations for $7500. The pilot was initially scheduled to be filmed in three days, but another day was added when the script was found to be too short.

The test show, titled "The Fingerprint That Wasn't There," consisted of voiceover narration provided by Albertson over scenes from his investigation, filmed without dialogue—an inexpensive way to make a TV pilot.

The show opens with Albertson remarking, "Sometimes a whisper speaks louder than a shout. The same goes for evidence. As in the case of the fingerprint that wasn't there. It was murder in the modern way."

Bachelor Mike Towers is found murdered with only a slug from a .45 and a little black book as evidence. Hunter identifies several suspects: a jealous woman, Betsy Bardow (Wendy Waldron), who didn't like it that Towers was seeing other women; Hank Sargent (Richard Crawford), Towers' underpaid handyman, and Johnny Todd (James Baker), a man who likes his .45. Hunter finds that Sargent committed the murder. Sargent took Todd's .45 and substituted the barrel from the gun he used to kill Towers in an attempt to frame Todd for the killing. Sargent was very careful to leave no prints on the gun barrel.

The company subsequently attempted to sell a second TV series, *George Fisher in Hollywood*, an interview-type program featuring CBS announcer Fisher talking with celebrities

Joseph Cotten later narrated and occasionally starred in *On Trial*, a 1955 series based on famous historical court cases. It was produced by Fordyce Enterprises Productions, a firm owned by the actor, producer Collier Young and writer Larry Marcus. In the series debut, Cotten starred as Edward Pritchard, a Scottish physician accused of poisoning his wife and mother-in-law. Did the doctor really commit the murders or was the murderer the couple's maid, taking seriously a remark the doctor had made to her about marrying the maid if he were free? Poison, found in the bodies of the victims when they were exhumed, led the jury to convict Pritchard, who was subsequently hanged.

As with several crime series described in this work, the episodes *On Trial* were based on authentic court room transcripts. To ensure the series' authenticity, a member of the New York State Bar served as a technical adviser.

Fordyce Enterprises also made several pilots that never resulted in series:

1. *The House of Seven Garbos* concerned seven aspiring actresses living in a boarding house. The proposed series would chronicle their private lives as well as their careers. Other unsuccessful attempts to turn the concept into a series were made in 1956 and again in 1959.

2. *The Nowhere Boys*, a comedy–Western starring David Wayne.

3. *Rescue*, focused on real stories of amazing rescues.

4. *Wish You Were Here* followed an American adventurer in his travels around the world.

Evidently *On Trial* was the only successful series produced by Fordyce Enterprises.

Gene Autry's Flying A Pictures

Western movie star Gene Autry, "America's Favorite Cowboy," established Flying A Pictures in 1950 to produce his self-titled cowboy series.

Flying A made several Western series mainly aimed at young TV viewers. The first, *The Gene Autry Show*, premiered on CBS on July 23, 1950, and ran until 1956. The singing cowboy starred astride his horse Champion. CBS owned a 50 percent share of the series.

Pat Buttram portrayed the typical TV Western sidekick, lending comic relief to the series. As Autry wrote in his autobiography, Buttram and Andy Devine from *The Adventures of Wild Bill Hickok* organized "The Exalted Order of Sidekicks." They printed membership cards and established a set of rules:

1. When a Sidekick is thrown in a water trough, the water must be heated.

2. Ice thrown in the face of a Sidekick must come from the bar of the Brown Derby.

3. The Sidekick gets the girl in every tenth picture.

4. The Sidekick must be reimbursed for money he has loaned the star.

5. The Sidekick must be reimbursed for coffee he has purchased to sober up members of the cast, including himself.[7]

The Gene Autry Show was the consummate B TV Western with a lot of action (gunfights and fisticuffs), comedy by Buttram, and songs by Autry. On the series, Autry also introduced stars who would appear on his other shows as well as having one of the first TV spin-offs. Gail Davis, who would play Annie Oakley in a Flying A series, appeared

Cowboy actor Gene Autry was also a very successful businessman. He invested wisely in hotels, TV stations, radio stations and real estate and owned the California Angels, a major league baseball team.

several times in guest roles on the *Autry* Western. In "Blackwater Valley Feud," she played Lila Carson, daughter of the owner of the T-C Ranch. The latter wants to sell the property to farmers, much to the consternation of Autry's boss Mr. Meachem, who doesn't want the adjoining property divided into farm plots. To get back at Carson, Meachem instructs Autry to no longer give the Carsons the right of way to a road that runs across the Meachem ranch. When Carson is shot and killed, suspicion falls on Meachem. Gene finds that one of Carson's men actually killed his boss to force Lila to sell the ranch to him. During the episode, Gene sings "That's My Home."

The unique aspect of the Autry series was that each episode was like a mini-movie with Gene's character having a different occupation in each installment. In some, he played a rancher or a ranch boss, in others a sheriff or border agent. Also, his relationship with sidekick Pat Buttram could be different in various episodes. For instance, in "The Black Rider," Autry's character is described as a "former Texas Ranger turned rancher." He comes to a Western town to help a sheriff capture a murderer known

as the Black Rider. The Black Rider has been killing men who were part
of a posse as well as part of the jury who convicted Rocky Dexter, who
was subsequently hung. Dressed all in black and riding a white horse, the
Black Rider leaves a gold peso as his calling card. Unusual for Western
series at the time, the Black Rider turns out to be Shelia Dexter (Sheila
Ryan), a female who is avenging her brother's hanging.

Different about this episode is that Autry meets a bearded Pat Buttram who is playing a gold prospector studying to be a detective. When
they first meet on the installment, Pat calls Gene "Gene Artery."

Next, Autry's production company introduced *The Range Rider*
starring Jock Mahoney in the title role. This syndicated series was one
of the first, if not the first, TV Western series created specifically for
the new medium and had all the elements of a B Western. The Mahoney
character, like other Western heroes in early TV series, fought injustice
wherever he encountered it. He had no name other than the Range Rider
and had a horse named Rawhide. Young Dick West played by Dick Jones
was the Rider's trusty sidekick. Jones later starred as Buffalo Bill Jr. in
another Autry production. However, unlike other sidekicks in many B
TV Westerns, Dick West was not primarily for comic relief but, given
his age, was meant to attract juvenile viewers who could vicariously
identify with his adventures. West rode a horse named Lucky.

Despite the fact that this series was syndicated, CBS also owned a
50 percent share of it. The series lasted for 78 episodes.

"Home on the Range" was *The Range Rider*'s theme song. The
hero starred in adventures the announcer said were like those of Davy
Crockett and Daniel Boone. Sidekick Dick West was described as an
"all–American boy." Above all else, episodes emphasized action. For
example, in "The Buckskin," the Range Rider engages in a swordfight
with one of the badmen while both are on horseback.

The Dick West character first meets the Range Rider in an episode
written by Lawrence Hazard and titled "The Range Rider." The Rider
brings a gambler who attempted to steal Rawhide into the town of
Whetstone to turn him over to the sheriff. West learns that the gambler,
John Rivers, is his father. The sheriff kicks Rivers out of town and then
asks the Rider to deliver money to a neighboring town. West decides to
catch up with his father to get to know him. They meet at the same place
that the Rider stops after capturing two men, sent by the express agent
Hannigan, who attempted to steal the money from him. West and his
dad decide to take the money from the Rider. West has second thoughts,
and the Rider talks him out of it. The Range Rider unmasks Hannigan as
the man behind the money shipment robberies. West decides to become
the Rider's partner, and they ride off together.

Flying A next produced the first two seasons of the iconic Western anthology series *Death Valley Days* that began running in syndicated in 1952. The series ran until 1970 with different production companies making episodes after the 1953–54 TV season.

Death Valley Days had a lengthy run on radio that ended in 1944. The TV version initially used the same writer. Based on library research, Ruth Woodman wrote her first script for the radio series before ever traveling to the California desert region. She recalled how she came up with ideas for the series when visiting Death Valley: "Mr. Cahill, my guide, would stop at the most prosperous-looking bar in town and announce to the bartender that the author of *Death Valley Days* was there. The bartender would poke his head out of the door and holler up and down the street. Pretty soon people would start to drift in and tell us wonderful stories of the past."[8]

Woodman began writing the radio series while working at an advertising agency as a copywriter. Her employer asked her to create a trial script for the Pacific Borax Company, sponsor of the series on both radio and TV.

Ruth Woodman wrote the initial episode of the television version of this Western anthology, "How Death Valley Got Its Name." During the California Gold Rush of 1849, some families decide to take a short-cut to the gold fields through the valley. While many are forced to turn back, a few wagons proceed through the desert, lightening each wagon's load as they go. Eventually they come to an insurmountable mountain range. After their horses run off, two men from the group go on foot to find help. They come upon a ranch near an oasis. Loading up on supplies, the duo returns to the families they left behind and lead the group out of what they call "Death Valley."

A character known as "The Old Ranger," played by actor Stanley Andrews introduced and narrated each episode. In later seasons, the host was Ronald Reagan, and after that, Robert Taylor.

One of a very few TV Westerns with a female lead, the syndicated *Annie Oakley* made its bow in January 1954. Gail Davis appeared in the main role with Billy Gray and then Jimmy Hawkins playing her younger brother Tagg and Brad Johnson, who had appeared in the *Death Valley Days* pilot, portraying Deputy Sheriff Lofty Craig. Canada Dry sponsored the show. While Annie Oakley was a real figure in the West, the series was pure fiction.

Phoebe Ann Mosey was the real Annie Oakley, adopting her stage name when she became a sharpshooter in Buffalo Bill's Wild West Show. Among other media, the Annie Oakley character appeared in a 1951-53 comic strip. In 1952, Autry's production company acquired the

TV and radio rights to the Annie Oakley character and created a TV series with its heroine similar to the one portrayed in the comic strip.

Before *Annie Oakley* premiered, Autry remarked,

> Little boys have always had their idols—Tom Mix, William S. Hart, Buck Jones, me, and, pardon the expression, Roy Rogers. The little sisters in recent years have had to tag along with their brothers in this respect. ...When I was a kid, the girls had heroines in Pearl White, Ruth Roland and all the other serial queens. And they were big box office, too. I think we've got something in Gail [Davis].[9]

The series was initially titled *Annie Oakley and Tagg*, which was the title of the comic strip that predated the TV series.

Davis had roles on several of Autry's movies as well as on *The Gene Autry Show*. On her series, Annie was described as a hard-ridin', straight-shootin' gal, but she left the fisticuffs to her sidekick Lofty Craig. She used her shooting skills to subdue the bad men.

In "Annie and the Six of Spades," the heroine is concerned that a young man, Bucky Donovan (Gary Gray), has fallen in with a bad influence, Mace Carver (Jimmy Murphy), who considers himself a fast gun. Bucky's brother Steve (Dick Jones) takes Bucky's gun away from him. Mace gives Bucky another gun and they hold up a stagecoach. Annie witnesses the robbery. Mace and Bucky hide in a cabin. When Mace attempts to flee, Annie, using her sharpshooting talents, fires at him and he surrenders.

Besides co-starring on *The Range Rider*, Dick Jones guested on other *Annie Oakley* episodes before starring as Buffalo Bill Jr.

In 1954, Flying A began making episodes of DuPont's *Cavalcade of America*. One of the initial episodes produced by the company, "Plume of Honor," concerned the Marquis de Lafayette, hero of the American Revolution who had been imprisoned in Austria. An adventurous young American and a young German physician attempt to free him from a dungeon of the Castle Olmutz. They communicate with Lafayette through the use of lemon juice as invisible ink in books sent to him as reading material. Another installment, "The Absent Host," depicted the night of June 3, 1781, when Jack Jouett rode from his father's tavern in Cuckoo, Virginia, to warn Thomas Jefferson and the Virginia Assembly of approaching British soldiers attempting to seize Jefferson and Assembly members.

Dick Jones starred as Buffalo Bill Jr. in the Western of the same name syndicated by Flying A in 1955. Nancy Gilbert appeared as his sister Calamity and Harry Cheshire as their guardian, Judge Ben Wiley, the founder of Wileyville. Judge Wiley found Bill and his sister after Indians had attacked a wagon train and killed their parents; Bill was holding his sister wrapped in a buffalo robe which gave rise to his name "Buffalo Bill, Jr."

Autry decided to star Jones in his own series based on his popularity from *The Range Rider* and guest appearances on *Annie Oakley*. According to the series introduction, Buffalo Bill Jr., a trick horse rider, was the "greatest fighter of them all." Jones reminisced about the creation of the series:

> Gene would get together people for brainstorming sessions and I imagine that they came up with the name, came up with the judge, came up with the little girl to attract the feminine side of the audience. Then they wanted somebody handy so they wouldn't have to stop the camera to get a double to make it look like he knew how to ride. Since they wanted somebody handy and I was still under contract, they said that's what Dick can do.[10]

The series had a trial run on Tucson, Arizona, television in 1954 to test public reaction before debuting nationwide in syndication in 1955.

On the premiere, "Fight for Geronimo," Bill overhears a plot to free the Apache chief from a train on his way to a Florida prison. The plotters want to free the chief so that he can be captured again and they would receive the reward. With the help of an Indian friend, Bill foils the plot.

Geronimo was not the only Western legend on whom *Buffalo Bill Jr.* episodes were based. During the series run, Bill, the judge and Calamity Jane also encountered Billy the Kid, Johnny Ringo, Wyatt Earp and Jesse James.

Ordinarily, TV series spin-offs involved taking a supporting character and creating a new show around him or her. Autry attempted this by spinning off his horse Champion from his series into a Western called *The Adventures of Champion* with a theme song performed by Frankie Laine titled "Champion, the Wonder Horse." *The Adventures of Champion* actually began on radio in 1949, featuring Ricky West and his Uncle Smoky. The TV adaptation lasted from September 1955 to early February 1956. On the series, the horse was owned by 12-year-old Ricky North (Barry Curtis), the only person the horse allows to ride him. Ricky also had a German shepherd named Rebel whose real name was Blaze. The boy lived on his Uncle Sandy's (Jim Bannon) ranch. Champion was now a wild stallion leading a herd of horses. Ricky rode him bareback.

Most episodes depicted Ricky becoming involved in some dangerous situation with Champion and/or Rebel rescuing him. On an early episode, "Saddle Tramp," Ricky befriends a geezer named Will Calhoun while Uncle Sandy is off trying to track down rustlers. Based on the tall tales Calhoun tells Ricky, the boy goes after the rustlers by himself.

Ricky almost falls off a cliff, hanging by dear life to some rocks. Calhoun finds him, ties a rope around his waist and has Champion pull the boy up. Later, Rebel mauls the rustlers so they can be arrested. CBS replaced *The Adventures of Champion* with another horse drama, *My Friend Flicka.*

Flying A also made several pilots that never went to series. Some of the pilots departed from the Western genre.

George Raft agreed to do an adventure series for CBS based on a radio program called *Rocky Jordan.* Jordan, a café owner, would become involved in stories of crime, mystery and beautiful women. However, in a dispute with Flying A Productions, plans for the series were abandoned when Raft demanded story and director approval. The production company felt that Raft's demands would lead to budget problems.

Calling All Cars (aka *Squad Car*) featured Lamont Johnson and Jack Moyles. The unsold pilot, based on a radio series from the late 1930s, chronicled the cases of two police detectives. In the pilot, written by Jackson Gillis, Sergeant Drexel and his partner Murray are called to a hotel where a man is threatening to jump from a ledge. Andy Kroll is distraught because a girl he likes has abandoned him. A fireman using a rope tries to climb down from the hotel's roof to attempt to grab Andy. Drexel falls off the ledge but is saved by the rope that was holding him. In the process, the detective tears off Kroll's coat. In a pocket he finds a photo of a waitress and goes to the diner where she works. The waitress, Cora, has apparently left town with another man. Drexel learns that Jerry, the diner owner, was jealous of her flirtation with Andy.

Drexel subsequently finds that Cora has been murdered. The police locate Jerry, who says that the man she planned to leave town with killed her. Drexel returns to the hotel where Andy is still contemplating jumping and informs him that Cora is dead and that he needs Andy's help in identifying the murderer. Drexel then points the finger at Kroll as the real killer. Kroll jumps, but his life is saved by the net firemen had set up on the ground.

Fred Harman, who drew the *Red Ryder* newspaper comic strip, arranged a deal with Autry's company and CBS to make a pilot based on the Red Ryder character. Stephen Slesinger, in 1951, made the first attempt at turning the *Red Ryder* comic strip into a TV series. The pilot starred Jim Bannon as Red Ryder; Don Kay Reynolds as Little Beaver, Red's Navajo Indian companion; Olive Carey as the Duchess; Jean Dean as Lindy, a girl who is infatuated with Red; and Patty Ann Garrity as Pigtales, the daughter of the local newspaper editor. Red Ryder, a cattle rancher, lived in the Colorado Rockies with his ranching partner, the Duchess. They resided near a town called Devil's Hole. Red named his horse Thunder and throughout the pilot, one hears the catchphrase "Roll, Thunder" as Red gallops away.

In the 1951 pilot, the local Cattlemen's Association want to insure that they receive the money for the sale of their animals given the number of recent robberies. They ask Red Ryder, so-named because of his red hair, to take charge of the cattle shipment. After the cattle are delivered to Clay City, Red gives the money to his friend Pat Collins, who will take it back on the train and stagecoach. When Red arrives in Devil's Hole, Collins has disappeared with the money. Red learns that Collins has been shot and the cattle payment stolen. Martin (Lyle Talbot), the head of the Cattlemen's Association, is behind the theft and the death of Collins. Red recovers the money and the cattlemen each receive their share.

Starring in the 1955 pilot ("Gun Trouble Valley") were Rocky Lane as the lead character, Louis Lettieri as Little Beaver, and Lizz Slifer as the Duchess. Lane had starred as Red Ryder in several Republic movies about the Western hero. The storyline gave the Duchess a new neighbor: Mr. Killgore (Bill Henry), whose men are stealing her hay and taking down fences. Killgore picks a fight with Perry Cochran (James Best), who doesn't fight back. Because of this, his fiancée Kathy (Sally Fraser) calls off the wedding. Red hires Perry to look out for Killgore and his men trespassing on the Duchess' ranch. In the inevitable showdown, Red and Perry successfully fight the gang with Perry being wounded in the shoulder. Perry explains that years ago, he shot a man in self-defense and subsequently decided to never again participate in a gun battle. After Kathy reconciles with Perry, they are married.

This *Red Ryder* pilot also failed to become a series. Rocky Lane later voiced the horse Mister Ed on the TV series of the same name.

In 1955, Flying A sought to make a pilot based on the newspaper comic strip *King of the Royal Mounted*. The comic strip, which debuted in 1935, was another project by Stephen Slesinger. Zane Grey created the character of Dave King, a Canadian Mountie. Grey's son Romer and Slesinger collaborated on many of the stories for the strip. A movie featuring the Dave King character was produced in 1936, and two movie serials made in the early '40s. However, evidently, the planned pilot for the series never got off the ground.

A year later, Flying A attempted to launch a Western anthology series about the early pioneers. Titled *Winning of the West*, after a 1953 Autry film, the program would have been similar in content to *Death Valley Days*. A pilot was scheduled to be filmed in November 1956 but apparently it never was.

In 1957, the production company sought to introduce another

anthology, *Ticket of Fate*, about what happens to individuals who possess a pawn ticket. This project never resulted in a series. Also in 1957, Autry attempted to launch a TV version of his long-running radio show *Melody Ranch*. The intended series would have been a 15-minute variety show featuring Gail Davis and including Country and Western songs.

Gene Autry passed away in 1998 at the age of 91.

Mickey Rooney Enterprises

Mickey Rooney, best known for his MGM films as a child actor, entered television in 1954 with his own NBC situation comedy, *Hey Mulligan* aka *The Mickey Rooney Show*, which lasted one season (September 4, 1954–June 7, 1955). Rooney appeared as Mickey Mulligan, a page at the network IBC (International Broadcasting Company), who wants to become an actor. Also on the series were Claire Carleton as his mother, a former burlesque dancer; Regis Toomey as his father, a cop who wanted his son to become a police officer; and John Hubbard as the boss, Mr. Brown. The comedy, up against CBS's *The Jackie Gleason Show*, got clobbered in the ratings.

The pilot, written by Blake Edwards and Richard Quine, aired August 24, 1954, a week before the series' formal debut. Mickey is part of a theater group, the Jonathan Swift Academy of Drama and Theater Arts, but has never appeared on stage. He understudies the other actors and spends most of his time painting sets and sweeping up. When the lead actor in an original play shows up at dress rehearsal with laryngitis, the director reluctantly has Mickey fill in. On opening night with his parents, his girlfriend Pat (Pat Walker) and Mr. Brown in the audience, Mickey is ready to go on but the lead actor recovers. Mickey's dad, disappointed that his son will not be appearing, substitutes liquid adhesive in the star's throat spray, making the actor incapable of doing the play. Mickey appears but encounters numerous problems. Upon entering, his cloak becomes stuck in the door, the doorknob comes off in his hand, a painting falls off the wall, Mickey slips on the floor, and he messes up his lines. However, the next day, back at work, Mr. Brown compliments him on giving a nice comedy performance.

Despite its low ratings, Pillsbury, one of *Hey, Mulligan*'s sponsors, wanted to renew the show for another season if NBC found a better time slot for it. However, at an anniversary celebration for the Pillsbury company, Mickey insulted the president of the corporation and the Pillsbury family itself, and the series ended after its first season.[11]

Rooney attempted to produce a second comedy series, *Male Sec-*

retary, starring Keefe Brasselle as the title character, reporting to a female boss played by Janis Paige. No pilot appears to have been made of this 1954 reversal of sex roles in the business world.

Rooney sought to produce series other than comedies through his production company. One such attempt, *Dateline Tokyo*, featured Dane Clark as Ken Wayne and Philip Ahn as Yoshio Yamada. This NBC pilot, based on Japanese police files, was dubbed "Dragnet in Tokyo" because the script was written by Kitty Buhler, who authored many *Dragnet* scripts. The series was to follow the work of an Army Criminal Investigation Department agent (Clark). Peter Lorre was originally sought for the series lead.

The crime drama opens with Ken Wayne flying to Tokyo with the airplane's pilot and co-pilot describing the city as loaded with intrigue, dames, booze, chaos and crime. Wayne is going to Tokyo to replace a murdered Army Criminal Investigation agent. He breaks up a black-market gang responsible for the agent's murder. After Wayne solves his first case, the ending of the pilot is like the conclusion of a *Dragnet* episode with an announcer stating that the suspects were brought to trial before the American Provost Court in Tokyo. After a commercial break, the results of that trial were revealed.

Commenting on the project, Rooney remarked, "I plowed another $30,000 into a pilot called *Dateline Tokyo*.... The pilot starred Dane Clark. It said goodbye during the introduction."[12]

Daniel Boone was another unsuccessful endeavor by Mickey Rooney Enterprises. The pilot starred Mike "Touch" Connors as Daniel Boone. Connors later played Joe Mannix in the Desilu-produced detective series. This first attempt at turning the exploits of legendary frontiersman Daniel Boone into a television series was scheduled to be filmed in November 1954.

Actor Don Barry was under consideration for the series but the producers found him "unacceptable." In response, Barry said, "If I'd put up $12,500, I'd have been 'acceptable.' They wanted me to finance half the pilot."[13]

Authored by Jack Laird and Kitty Buhler, the pilot script "Westward Ho" begins in 1774 Richmond, Virginia, where Daniel takes on the task of making peace with the Cherokee Indians, laying the foundation for a road through the wilderness into the Kentucky territory. Another script appears to have been done in October 1954 titled "The Gun Runners"; it featured Daniel Boone along with a character named Michael Stoner, played by Ed Hinton. That script dealt with a merchant, Jonathan Hanley, wanting Boone to lead him to Cherokee chief Oconostata, in order to trade guns for the Cherokees' furs. Daniel rejects the job offer and subsequently meets with the governor about the situation. The governor instructs Daniel and Michael to travel to Kentucky to stop Hanley from providing guns to the Native Americans. When the two arrive at Oconostata's encampment, they find that a man representing Hanley has already been there encouraging the tribe to go to war with the Shawnee. Daniel meets with the chief and his war council and pledges to travel to the Shawnee to determine if they intend to go to war. But before he can begin his trip, Daniel and Michael come upon Hanley's cache of weapons and substitute sand for gunpowder. When the Cherokee see that the guns do not fire, the tribe refuses to trade their furs.

Reminiscing about the pilot, Rooney wrote, "I came up with an idea for a series on the life of Daniel Boone. I put $30,000 into a pilot film. Then I found out that no one knew who Daniel Boone was. They all thought he was Davy Crockett."[14]

In 1956, Rooney sought to produce a TV series in conjunction with Screen Gems, this one based on the adventures of Calamity Jane. Filming of the first of 39 episodes was set to begin around July 1, 1956, but evidently never took place. One actress who wanted to play the part was Rose Marie, who later co-starred as Sally on *The Dick Van Dyke Show*.

Mickey also attempted a series starring Sabu, based on stories from the Arabian Nights. In the pilot, Sabu, a stable boy taking care of an elephant, finds a ring on the ground. He rubs it and a genie named Ubal (William Marshall) appears. Mazufar (Peter Mamakos), the Caliph's prime minister, plots to steal the ring with the help of a magician. To get the ring, the magician tells Mazufar to kidnap Sabu's female friend Zumila (Daria Massey) so that Sabu will conjure up Ubal to find her. Ubal forces the magician to break the spell on Zumila and sends the magician to the South Pole.

In a second episode produced for the planned series, Mazufar continues to pursue Sabu for the magic ring. Sabu overhears that Mazufar is poisoning the Caliph. Sabu finds that a goose has swallowed the magic ring which Zumila finds in a goose egg. Zumila then becomes Ubal's mistress and has him make Sabu a prince so he can enter the palace in disguise where he warns the Caliph of the plot to kill him. Sabu saves the caliph from death.

When this comedy-adventure series did not sell, the two episodes were spliced together s a feature film under the title *Sabu and the Magic Ring* and released in 1957 by Allied Artists. This was the final production made by Mickey Rooney Enterprises.

CHAPTER 14

Early Female TV Producers Who Sought to Make B TV Shows

Commodore Productions

Originally established in 1942 to produce radio shows, Commodore Productions, owned by Walter White Jr. and his wife Shirley Thomas, ventured into TV in the early 1950s. Thomas, who divorced White in 1952, had married him three times in three years. The couple had eloped in May 1947 and then for personal reasons married again in January 1948. Thomas had always wanted a church wedding and so a third marriage ceremony was held in February 1949.

Shirley Thomas, an early pioneer in television, related to a journalist, "I was busy with television back in 1937 to 1940 on the experimental Don Lee station in Los Angeles (which later became KNXT). I did everything from acting to sweeping out the studio. We did full-length Shakespearean productions and we even did original plays for TV."[1]

After Thomas married White and formed Commodore Productions, they produced such popular radio series as *Hopalong Cassidy*, *Clyde Beatty* and *Tarzan*. In the mid–40s, Commodore was offered a show that had been rejected by several radio producers. Thomas thought it had promise, and so Hopalong Cassidy, portrayed by William Boyd, was given a chance for a comeback. When transferred to TV through Boyd's movies, it became a hit on TV as well.

In summer 1951, Commodore Productions was to begin filming 13 half-hour episodes of *The Andy Clyde Show*, a family comedy starring Andy Clyde and Renie Riano as his wife. Clyde is best known for his comedy shorts produced by Columbia, for his portrayal of Hopalong Cassidy's sidekick in movie Westerns, and for playing assorted "old codger" roles on TV including Walter Brennan's friend George MacMichael on *The Real McCoys*. Renie Riano appeared in many films, most notably portraying Maggie in the late 1940s *Jiggs and Maggie* films based on the comic strip *Bringing Up Father*.

Nothing is known about the plot of the proposed television series, but it very well could have been similar to *Bringing Up Father* with Clyde playing a character who always wants to go to the local tavern and drink with his friends, while the Riano character seeks to be a model of decorum and wants her husband to act accordingly.

Circus owner and wild animal trainer Clyde Beatty starred in a planned series focusing on his adventures in Africa, adapted from Beatty's radio series produced by Commodore. Stanley Farrar co-starred as Grant Cunningham. At least two pilots were made since it appears that when the series didn't sell, the producers edited the pilots into a one-hour feature titled *Perils of the Jungle*.

The character of Grant Cunningham, who accompanied Beatty on his safaris, narrated the picture. The first part chronicled Beatty's safari in the Belgian Congo where he and Cunningham come upon an estate owned by Josephine Carter (Phyllis Coates) that includes a zoo. Jo, who inherited the estate from her father, deals in wild animals. Her father's former partner, Gorman (John Doucette), is her major competitor. When the zoo is destroyed by fire, she has no insurance to rebuild. Gorman makes an offer for the property which she refuses. With Beatty's help, she decides to capture a wild gorilla to put her back in business (gorillas go for big bucks on the wild animal market). Jo, Clyde and Cunningham search for a gorilla and are followed by Gorman and his men. Beatty is able to capture a gorilla. When Gorman, who also wants such an animal, is attacked by one, Beatty has to shoot the gorilla to save Gorman's life.

The second part of the film had Beatty and Cunningham in southern Rhodesia on the hunt for black-maned lions. Clyde comes upon a pride of lions and ends up killing one that attacks him. Cunningham falls ill from the bite of a tsetse fly. Beatty takes him to a hospital through territory controlled by dangerous natives. Clyde comes upon an Australian named Grubbs (Leonard Mudie) who has lived with the native tribe ever since he saved the king's son from a crocodile attack. Beatty and Cunningham are captured by the tribe where they witness a trial of native girls accused of stealing gold (actually stolen by Grubbs). Clyde is able to capture the king and Grubbs and flee. He frees the king to go back to his tribe as he and the others find a boat to escape down the river.

After divorcing her husband, Shirley Thomas had her own radio show called *The Hollywood Story* through the Columbia Pacific Radio

Network. Her career then took a radical turn. She turned her attention to space flight, writing several books on aerospace, including an eight-volume series on astronauts titled *Men of Space*. In 1967, she earned her doctorate in Communications from the University of Sussex and became a professor at USC in the Master of Professional Writing Program.

Virginia Kellogg and Mary Ross

Retired Los Angeles policewoman Mary Ross and screenwriter Virginia Kellogg collaborated on a TV pilot called *Policewoman, U.S.A.* with Jeanne Cagney in the title role. Ross used her knowledge of past investigations in which she had been involved as a basis for the potential series. Both Ross and Kellogg produced the show. Kellogg is best known for scripting the films *White Heat* and *Caged*.

Presented in documentary style, the pilot, which aired January 17, 1951, on *Hollywood Theatre Time*, related the story of the investigation of the Red Rose murder case with filmed scenes of the actual crime site inserted in the live presentation. The Red Rose murder evidently involved the stabbing of a young woman in December 1939; her nude body was found in a vacant lot in Los Angeles with a crushed rose under her head. Los Angeles Police Chief William H. Parker introduced the TV presentation.

Cagney reprised the role of Mary Ross on another installment of *Hollywood Theatre Time* airing May 16, 1951. This one, titled *Mary Ross, Private Investigator*, focused on Ross' post–police force career as a private eye.

Ross and Kellogg originally proposed a radio series called *Policewoman USA* to CBS in 1950. After an audition tape was made, the network did not turn it into a series. Later that same year, consideration was given to making a motion picture called *Badge 23* with Eleanor Parker in the lead role about the exploits of Ross, but this venture did not materialize.

Ross and Kellogg were also involved in other projects but not for television. Unrealized projects included *Her Name Was Grace*, written by Kellogg and based on information provided by Ross, to be produced as a feature film by Abner Greshler, and *Towne Street*, a play to star Patricia Neal. Ross provided the story for *Towne Street*, which concerned a Los Angeles schoolteacher who visits jails with welfare work in mind. When she contracts polio, her fight against the disease becomes the central theme of the story.

Grace Gibson Productions

One of the few female producers in the 1950s, Grace Gibson, an American living in Australia, made several hours of radio programs for that country. They were syndicated to other English-speaking lands like New Zealand, South Africa and Canada.

Born in El Paso, Texas, Gibson started her career in the United States working for the Radio Transcription Company of America, as a distributor of radio shows. While visiting the U.S., Alfred Bennett, general manager of an Australian radio station, recruited Gibson to help him establish American Radio Transcription Agencies to sell American radio programs throughout Australia.

In 1952, Gibson came up with the idea of doing a TV pilot, *Adventures of Al Munch* starring Charles Tingwell, filmed in Australia in two days but intended for American television since, in the early 1950s, Australia had yet to implement the new medium. Her creation concerned an American G.I. who had been stationed in Australia, and, after World War II, decided to remain and become a private investigator. Filmed in Sydney, the pilot, "I Found Joe Barton," dealt with Munch being hired by a Hollywood film producer named Krenkov to locate Joe Barton, an American mobster living in Australia. Krenkov had made a movie about Barton after being told by police that the mobster had died. Subsequently, he received a letter from Barton demanding $50,000 in return for signing a release for the movie.

Munch contacts a lawyer named O'Leary to try to find Barton. After the lawyer is murdered, Barton's estranged wife Florea tells Munch that she overheard his phone conversation with O'Leary and that she wants to locate Barton as well. She makes arrangements with a ship's captain (who says he knows where Barton is hiding) to take her and Munch to the mobster. After the captain brings the two near where Barton lives, Munch goes alone to see the man. The mobster signs the release and Munch gives him the money. Nevertheless, Barton won't allow the private detective to leave alive. They fight, and Florea shows up holding a pistol. She shoots and kills Barton. Munch figures out that the murdered man is not the real Joe Barton, but someone Barton hired to pose as him and to kill O'Leary. Shots ring out with Munch and Florea taking cover. The shots are being fired by the ship's captain, who turns out to be the real Joe Barton apparently in an elaborate disguise so as to hide his identity from his wife. Munch is able to wrest the gun from Barton and knock him unconscious. The police then take over.

While the pilot never sold, it eventually was syndicated to TV stations as a stand-alone episode under the title "I Found Joe Barton."

Grace Gibson continued to make radio dramas until 1971. Her later radio projects were for South Africa, the last English-speaking country to adopt television. She passed away in 1989.

Joan Harrison and Ella Raines

Joan Harrison worked with legendary director Alfred Hitchcock on his films *The Lady Vanishes* (1938), *Rebecca* (1940) and *Suspicion* (1941) and also produced her own movies, including *Phantom Lady* (1944), *The Strange Affair of Uncle Harry* (1945) and *Nocturne* (1946). She then entered the world of television production.

In association with Hal Roach Jr., Harrison produced a female-centric melodrama called *The Female of the Species*. This proposed anthology in 1952 had Harrison as its host. Harrison and Roach contemplated making 13 episodes.

The concept of the melodrama involved a character named Margo (Amanda Blake) relating a story to viewers about women she has known. The episode would relate the story in flashbacks. The pilot, "Sunday Night," starred William Ching as Avery Morgan and Geraldine Brooks as Laurie Hillman in a tale of a suicidal model whose relationships always fall apart and the man whom she desperately loves. At the start of the show, Blake appears and introduces Joan Harrison, who tells viewers that the story takes place on a Sunday night. Laurie takes an overdose of sleeping pills. With Avery and Margo discussing his relationship with Laurie over drinks, flashbacks reveal the reason for Laurie's suicide attempt. After Avery meets Laurie at a dinner party, she falls in love with him. Laurie soon wants to marry Avery but he doesn't think he is ready for marriage and so ends the relationship. After discussing the affair with Margo, Avery decides to phone Laurie but doesn't get an answer. When he tries again, the line is now busy. He goes to Laurie's apartment and finds medics taking an unconscious Laurie to the hospital. An errand boy had become concerned about Laurie when he attempted to deliver a dress but got no response and so called the police.

The stars of each episode would appear with Harrison at the conclusion of the installment to talk about possible endings for the story. In the pilot, Ching, Blake and Harrison discuss what the future will hold for Avery and Laurie.

When the pilot didn't sell, Harrison joined actress Ella Raines, star of *Phantom Lady*, to produce Raines' syndicated series *Janet Dean, Registered Nurse*. Formed in 1953, Cornwall Productions was a joint project of Raines and William Dozier, then a CBS executive producer in charge of dramatic programs. Raines was president of the company, Dozier vice-president. The name "Cornwall" came from the house Raines and her family occupied at Cornwall-on-the Hudson. The series was filmed in New York.

On *Janet Dean, Registered Nurse*, Raines appeared as a private duty nurse assigned to various cases in the New York area. Dean became a nurse after her fiancé was shot down during World War II and passed away. She was also a member of the U.S. Air Force Nurse Corps reserve. As with many drama series covered in this book, the episodes were based on actual stories.

In the 1950s, actresses mostly appeared as the main character on comedy series; rarely were they a lead continuing character on a contemporary dramatic series. *Janet Dean, Registered Nurse* was an exception to the rule. The series' melodramatic stories dealt with Dean's interaction with her patients and their families. In one episode, she is assigned the case of a Korean War veteran suffering post-traumatic stress syndrome.

The man's mother interferes with his recovery by isolating him from the outside world, in particular from his fiancée. Dean takes it upon herself to visit the fiancée and arrange a luncheon with her and her patient while his mother is out of the house. There is a reconciliation, and the mother is told to be less possessive. In another case, Dean takes care of a blind woman whose daughter-in-law, a woman with extravagant tastes, is attempting to kill her to inherit her estate. Dean foils his plans by switching poisoned coffee cups.

Gore Vidal wrote an episode under the pseudonym Cameron Kay. In "The Jinx Nurse Case,"

Actress Ella Raines, producer and star of *Janet Dean, Registered Nurse,* **continued acting off and on until 1984. Her final appearance on television was on an episode of the detective series** *Matt Houston.*

Dean remembers her days as an Air Force nurse in England during World War II and a young nurse who dated several pilots who were later killed in action. The series lasted for 39 episodes during the 1954–55 television season.

Cornwall Productions attempted to follow-up *Janet Dean* with a combination melodrama–crime story series starring Darren McGavin: *Jeff Kincaid, Probation Officer* would have featured stories about a probation officer and the cases he handled. McGavin had appeared in two *Janet Dean* episodes, "The Gomez Case" and "The Van Horn Case."

Kincaid's wife had been killed in a traffic accident, leaving him to care for his young daughter. He worked for the New York County General Services Court. In the pilot script, written by Stanley Niss, Kincaid is assigned the case of wealthy 22-year-old playgirl Judith Mason Lowell, who has pleaded guilty to second degree manslaughter after a hit-and-run accident which killed an old man. Kincaid has to investigate Judy's background and make a sentencing recommendation to the judge. He interviews Judy, her divorced parents (who basically abandoned Judy when she was 13), her maid and her ex-boyfriend. Although Judy's mother thinks that her daughter is looking forward to prison, Judy tells Kincaid that she really doesn't want to be incarcerated. Kincaid meets with the judge, who is reluctant to accept his recommendation of probation given the press publicity the case has generated. At the sentencing, the judge gives Judy two and a half years in prison but suspends the sentence and puts her on probation providing that she agrees to not drink or drive for the period of the sentence and agrees to remain in the court's jurisdiction.

At the end of the pilot, Darren McGavin talks to viewers about the planned series emphasizing that it will reveal the full scope of a probation officer's responsibilities.

Joan Harrison went on to produce several suspense anthologies such as *Alfred Hitchcock Presents* and *Journey into the Unknown*.

M&H Productions

Marion Davies partnered with Russell Hayden in M&H Productions in 1954. Davies was a former actress and mistress of William Randolph Hearst. Evidently she invested some of the wealth she inherited from the Hearst estate along with her own money, earned while a film actress, in M&H Productions. Davies' husband Horace Brown, whom she married after Hearst's death, also had a position in the company.

The company attempted to launch a comedy called *Meet the*

Family featuring Arthur Lake, his wife Patricia and their children Arthur Jr. and Marian. Walter Catlett played Grandpa and Harley Stafford appeared as Arthur Lake's boss. Patricia Lake was Davies' niece or, according to some accounts, her illegitimate daughter with Hearst.

Arthur Lake indicated that the idea for the comedy came about because he thought that too many TV shows for children were frightening and designed for nightmares instead of relaxation. This 1954 sitcom attempt written by Lake and Davies was directed by Russell Hayden. Lake played a bumbling character very similar to the character of Dagwood Bumstead that he had portrayed in the movies. He worked for an irascible boss, Mr. Hotchkiss. His wife's father, who liked to dabble with his own inventions, lived with the family.

The storyline had Lake intending to order 143 surf balls (beach balls) for his company but ending up with that number of surfboards. His boss demands that Lake dispose of the surfboards or else he will charge him $50 for each. Hotchkiss lines up a potential buyer for the items: hotel owner Carlos Martinez (Hans Conried), who may want the surfboards for his guests. The entire Lake family goes to the beach with Martinez to demonstrate how the boards work. All of his family members master surfing except for Arthur. Martinez refuses to purchase the lot, thinking the boards would be dangerous for his guests. Later, Hotchkiss wants Arthur to attend a charity raffle on his behalf. When Lake breaks the glass coffee table his boss has donated to the affair, he makes a replacement table using a surfboard. Martinez is impressed with the creation and wants to purchase the surfboard tables for his hotels.

Lake had ideas for additional episodes of *Meet the Family*, saying:

> Maybe we can tie in something about travel, or some of the places in the country that youngsters ought to know about. There really must be something we could do with a Williamsburg (Virginia) background. Maybe bowling on the Palace Green—or that maze in the Palace Green. That's a natural location for comedy—you know, me getting lost in the maze while the wife and kids go on a tour of the buildings, and every time I think I'm out of the thing, I make a wrong turn and get mixed up again.[2]

Meet the Family was initially pitched to the networks as a series. When no network picked it up, the potential series was to be syndicated via Screencraft in the East and Jack Russell Associates in the Midwest and West, but that never happened.

Meet the Family was Davies' only foray into TV production. Her partner Russell Hayden produced other TV series, including *Judge Roy Bean* and *26 Men*.

Notes

Introduction

1. Tim Brooks and Earle Marsh, *The Complete Directory to Prime Time Network and Cable TV Shows: 1946–Present*, Ninth Edition, New York: Ballantine, 2007, 169.

2. Allen Glover, *TV Noir: Dark Drama on the Small Screen*, New York: Abrams, 2019, 62.

3. Christopher Anderson, *Hollywood TV: The Studio System in the Fifties*, Austin: University of Texas Press, 1994, 56.

4. "On Gold Mine Made in State," *Arizona Republic*, June 17, 1948.

5. "Tele Film Parade Passable but Bit Too Grisly," *Variety*, May 10, 1948.

Chapter 1

1. "Roach Calls Off 6 MGM Pix," *Variety*, December 22, 1948.

2. Louella Parsons, "Famous Directors to Travel from Italy with Contract for Ingrid Bergman," *The San Francisco Examiner*, December 2, 1948.

3. Thomas M. Pryor, "Movies for Video Produced Quickly," *The New York Times*, August 21, 1951.

4. David C. Tucker, *Gale Storm: A Biography and Career Record*, Jefferson, North Carolina: McFarland, 2018, 115.

5. Walter Ames, "Joe E. Brown Signed for Hal Roach TV Series; NBC Gets Go-Ahead on New Studio Plans," *The Los Angeles Times*, March 18, 1952.

6. "Blondie Soon to Appear on Television," *The San Francisco Examiner*, May 13, 1951.

7. Erskine Johnson, "Hollywood," *The Manhattan Mercury*, May 19, 1955.

8. Richard Lewis Ward, *A History of the Hal Roach Studios*, Carbondale: Southern Illinois University Press, 2005, 146.

9. Larry Wolters, "TV Deals for Laurel and Hardy," *Chicago Tribune*, August 10, 1955.

10. "Newest TV Star Is Sonja Henie," *The Evening Sun*, March 2, 1955.

11. Erskine Johnson, "Hollywood Today," *The Pomona Progress Bulletin*, April 7, 1955.

12. Evelyn Rudie, private communication with author, May 6, 2021.

13. Steven H. Scheuer, "Love That Jill Debuts This Week," *The Birmingham News*, January 18, 1958.

14. Erskine Johnson, "'Ghosts' of 'Topper' Back on TV with 'Love That Jill' Show," *Muskogee Times-Democrat*, January 22, 1958.

15. John Crosby, "Hal Roach Jr. Likes Money; Critics Dislike 'Oh, Susanna,'" *The Times Tribune*, October 12, 1956.

16. Charles Mercer, "Behind the TV Camera," *The Evening Times*, July 11, 1956.

17. John Crosby, "May Be Charlie's Whole Show Is a Mistake," *Detroit Free Press*, July 9, 1956.

18. "ABC Television Network ad," *Variety*, March 10, 1954.

19. "ABC ad," *Variety*, March 10, 1954.

Chapter 2

1. Jack Gould, "Billy Rose Gives First Show on TV," *The New York Times*, October 4, 1950.

2. Gene Fowler, *The Great Mouthpiece: A Life Story of William J. Fallon*, New York: Grosset & Dunlap, 1931, 148.

3. *Ibid.*, 163.

4. *Ibid.*, 165.

5. Guy V. Thayer, Jr., "The Case for Hollywood," *Broadcasting*, January 11, 1954.

Chapter 3

1. Walter Ames, "Jack Chertok Grinds Out TV Films with a Production Line," *The Los Angeles Times*, July 19, 1953.

2. Leon Morse, "Sky King," *Billboard*, May 10, 1952.

3. "Stafford's Telepic Pilot Reel in NY for Agency Eyeing," *Variety*, October 25, 1950.

4. Francis M. Nevins, *Paul Landres: A Director's Stories*, Lanham, Maryland: Scarecrow, 2000, 22.

5. *Ibid.*

6. Joe Hyams, "'The Lawless Years' May be a Winner," *Tampa Bay Times*, April 16, 1959.

7. Jack Chertok, "Secrets of Success Is Like an Open Book," *Billboard*, February 13, 1954.

8. "Susie McNamara Celebrates Fourth Birthday as 'Private Secretary,'" *The Crowley Post-Signal*, February 17, 1956.

9. Marie Torre, "Radio and Television," *The Marion Star*, March 7, 1957.

10. Erskine Johnson, "Coulee Region Visited by Martian, Ch 8 Feature Finds Ready Welcome," *The La Crosse Tribune*, October 5, 1963.

11. Julie Newmar, conversation with author, June 9, 2021.

12. Harry Harris, "Many Series Lose 'Regulars,'" *The Philadelphia Inquirer*, January 12, 1965.

Chapter 4

1. *Daily News* (Los Angeles, CA), July 14, 1947.

2. "Anybody Wanna Buy TV Pix?" *Variety*, September 1, 1948.

3. Ed Sullivan, "Little Old New York," *Daily News*, May 25, 1951.

4. Walter Ames, "Whodunit Tonight on KTTV; TV Gets Singer Film Test," *The Los Angeles Times*, March 2, 1951.

5. Marie Torre, "Radio & Television," *The Marion Star*, July 3, 1958.

6. "States of the Union," shooting script, Jerry Fairbanks Productions, Inc., Collection, Charles E. Young Research Library, UCLA, February 1948.

7. John J. Simmons, "Sports Fictional Theatre" script, Jerry Fairbanks Productions, Inc., Collection, Charles E. Young Research Library, UCLA, undated.

Chapter 5

1. John Crosby, "Big Story Praised as Best TV Program," *Oakland Tribune*, December 22, 1950.

2. Dwight Newton, "Day and Night with Radio and Television," *The San Francisco Examiner*, October 26, 1953.

3. "NBC Trade News," September 23, 1952.

4. "Soap Opera Bubbles Up in TV," *Variety*, February 1, 1954.

5. John Dunning, *On the Air: The Encyclopedia of Old-Time Radio*, New York: Oxford University Press, 1998, 685.

6. "Conne-Stephens Future in Doubt," *Variety*, October 24, 1956.

Chapter 6

1. Jerome Coopersmith, private communication with author, March 24, 2021.

2. *Ibid.*

3. Buffalo Bob Smith and Donna McCrohan, *Howdy and Me: Buffalo Bob's Own Story*, New York: Penguin, 1990, 29–30.

4. *Ibid.*, 42.

5. *Ibid.*, 24.

6. *Ibid.*, 39.

7. Coopersmith, private communication with author.

8. Donald Kirkley, "Look and Listen," *The Baltimore Sun*, October 1, 1956.

Chapter 7

1. Tom E. Dawson, "TV and Radio Notes," *San Pedro News-Pilot*, May 31, 1951.

2. Lou Larkein, "Inside Radio & TV," *The Mirror*, June 2, 1950.

Chapter 8

1. Isobel Silden, "Gene Barry Derby-Hatted Dude in TV Role as Bat Master-

son," *St. Louis Post-Dispatch*, October 5, 1958.

2. Bill Ladd, "The 32-Hour Raid that Became a 39-Week Series...," *The Courier-Journal*, September 21, 1958.

3. "Dick Powell, Ziv in Talks," *Billboard*, April 4, 1953.

4. Larry Wolters, "TV Star's 'Easy Day': 4:15 A.M. Until 8 O'clock," *Chicago Tribune*, November 6, 1955.

5. Leo Mishkin, "Screening TV," *The Philadelphia Inquirer*, April 3, 1953.

6. Steven H. Scheuer, "Television Program News," *The Capital Times*, August 15, 1956.

7. Charles Mercer, "Radio-TV," *The Ithaca Journal*, May 31, 1958.

8. Hal Erikson, *Syndicated Television: The First Forty Years, 1947–1987*, Jefferson, North Carolina: McFarland, 1989, 72.

9. Cy Wagner, "Vic and Sade," Radio and Television Program Reviews, *Billboard*, July 30, 1949.

10. Quoted in David Weinstein, *The Eddie Cantor Story: A Jewish Life in Performance and Politics*, Waltham, Massachusetts: Brandies University Press, 2018, 220.

11. Dave Kaufman, "Syndication Bigger 'Than the Both of Us,' Carlson Avers," *Variety*, December 21, 1955.

12. Irv Broughton, *Producers on Producing: The Making of Film and Television*, Jefferson, North Carolina: McFarland, 1986, 17–18.

13. *Ibid.*, 21.

14. Steven H. Scheuer, "TV Keynotes," *The Troy Record*, August 26, 1959.

15. Pete Rahn, "Dane Clark on a 'Bold Venture,'" *St. Louis Globe-Democrat*, January 29, 1959.

16. TV Key, "TV KEY Notes," *The Times*, April 27, 1955.

17. Hal Humphrey, "Viewing TV," *The Tampa Times*, August 18, 1958.

18. Rita Ashe, "Have Long Johns—Will Space Travel," *The Orlando Sentinel*, September 27, 1959.

Chapter 9

1. Erskine Johnson, "Menjou Loses His Moustache; Ann Harding Keeps Her Long Hair," *The La Crosse Tribune* (La Crosse, Wisconsin), November 3, 1951.

2. Joseph Fusco, *Dan Duryea: A Career Appreciation*, Albany, Georgia: Bear Manor Media, 2017, 166.

3. Walter Ames, "Actress Tells of Wisecrack Saving Scene; Films of USC, UCLA Games Set for KTTV," *The Los Angeles Times*, September 22, 1951.

4. Hal Humphrey, "Pat O'Brien Refuses Crime Show Offers," *The Pittsburgh Press*, June 22, 1952.

5. "To Emphasize Story on New Schlitz Series," *Variety*, October 25, 1952.

Chapter 10

1. June Bundy, "Al Gannaway's Half-Pint Party, Television-Radio Reviews," *Billboard*, March 10, 1951.

Chapter 11

1. "Kit Carson Series Employs Outdoor Sets for Realism," *Hartford Courant*, December 2, 1951.

2. "Ramar of the Jungle," TV-Film Reviews, *Billboard*, September 27, 1952.

3. Leon Fromkess, "A Financing Slant: Developing Foreign Income from TV Series," *Billboard*, January 17, 1953.

4. "TPA, Others Sued by Actor Ireland," *Broadcasting*, March 8, 1954.

5. "Halls of Ivy Will Return, But on TV," *The Sacramento Bee*, May 1, 1954.

6. Vernon Scott, "Bellowing 'Tugboat Annie' Set for New TV Series," *The Indianapolis Star*, April 8, 1956.

Chapter 13

1. Kay Gardella, "Televiewing & Listening In," *New York Daily News*, January 15, 1952.

2. John Crosby, "Writer Says TV Better Stop Copying Hollywood—Or Else," *The Sacramento Bee*, March 10, 1952.

3. "Half the Action," Telepix Reviews, *Variety*, June 11, 1953.

4. "Four Top Drawing Cards!" *Variety*, October 23, 1952.

5. Walter Ames, "Jack Dempsey in Pilot Film for Sporting Series; Travel Bug Bites Orchestra Leader," *The Los Angeles Times*, March 27, 1951.

6. "Bing Crosby Enterprises, Inc.," *Broadcasting*, June 14, 1952.

7. Gene Autry with Mickey Herskowitz, *Back in the Saddle Again*, Garden City, New York: Doubleday, 1978, 111.

8. Ray Kovitz, "Author Wrote Death Valley Script before Seeing Region; Now She's Leading Authority," *The Los Angeles Times*, August 18, 1952.

9. James Bacon, "Gene Autry to Air TV Series for Little Girls," *Asheville Citizen-Times*, November 8, 1953.

10. Quoted in Ann Snuggs, *Dick Jones: Where the Action Was*, Albany, Georgia: Bear Manor Media, 2015, 138.

11. Richard A. Lertzman and William J. Birnes, *The Life and Times of Mickey Rooney*, New York: Gallery, 2015, 320–322.

12. Mickey Rooney, "Of $100,000 Earnings He Gets $8700!" *The Mickey Rooney Story* excerpt, *Philadelphia Daily News*, May 21, 1966.

13. Dave Kaufman, "On All Channels," *Variety*, September 14, 1954.

14. Mickey Rooney, "Of $100,000 Earnings He Gets $8700!" *The Mickey Rooney Story* excerpt, *Philadelphia Daily News*, May 21, 1966.

Chapter 14

1. Jack Gaver, "Up and Down Broadway," *The Daily News-Journal*, June 14, 1951.

2. Edith Lindeman, "Films' 'Dagwood' Eyes TV Series with Family," *Richmond Times-Dispatch*, June 27, 1953.

Bibliography

Books

Anderson, Christopher, *Hollywood TV: The Studio System in the Fifties*, Austin: University of Texas Press, 1994.

Autry, Gene, with Mickey Herskowitz, *Back in the Saddle Again*, Garden City: Doubleday, 1978.

Brooks, Tim, and Earle Marsh, *The Complete Directory to Prime Time Network and Cable TV Shows: 1946–Present*, Ninth Edition, New York: Ballantine, 2007.

Broughton, Irv, *Producers on Producing: The Making of Film and Television*, Jefferson, North Carolina: McFarland, 1986.

Dunning, John, *On the Air: The Encyclopedia of Old-Time Radio*, New York: Oxford University Press, 1998.

Erikson, Hal, *Syndicated Television: The First Forty Years, 1947–1987*, Jefferson, North Carolina: McFarland, 1989.

Fowler, Gene, *The Great Mouthpiece: A Life Story of William J. Fallon*, New York: Grosset & Dunlap, 1931.

Fusco, Joseph, *Dan Duryea: A Career Appreciation*, Albany, GA: Bear Manor Media, 2017.

Glover, Allen, *TV Noir: Dark Drama on The Small Screen*, New York: Abrams, 2019.

Lertzman, Richard A., and William J. Birnes, *The Life and Times of Mickey Rooney*, New York: Gallery, 2015.

Nevins, Francis M. *Paul Landres: A Director's Stories*, Lanham, MD: Scarecrow, 2000.

Smith, Buffalo Bob, and Donna McCrohan, *Howdy and Me: Buffalo Bob's Own Story*, New York: Penguin, 1990.

Snuggs, Ann, *Dick Jones: Where the Action Was*, Albany, GA: Bear Manor Media, 2015.

Tucker, David C., *Gale Storm: A Biography and Career Record*, Jefferson, North Carolina: McFarland, 2018.

Ward, Richard Lewis, *A History of the Hal Roach Studios*, Carbondale: Southern Illinois University Press, 2005.

Weinstein, David, *The Eddie Cantor Story: A Jewish Life in Performance and Politics*, Waltham, MA: Brandies University Press, 2018.

Periodicals

Billboard
Broadcasting
Variety

Archival Collections

David Victor Collection, Wisconsin Center for Film and Theater Research, Wisconsin Historical Society.

Jerry Fairbanks Productions, Inc., Records, UCLA Library Special Collections, Charles E. Young Research Library, University of California, Los Angeles.

Kirk Douglas Collection, Wisconsin Center for Film and Theater Research, Wisconsin Historical Society.

Mrs. Omar N. Bradley (Kitty Buhler) Scripts, University of Texas at El Paso Library.

Steven H. Scheuer Collection of Television Scripts, Yale Collection of American Literature, Beinecke Rare Book and Manuscript Library, Yale University.

United Artists Collection, Wisconsin Center for Film and Theater Research, Wisconsin Historical Society.

Vincent J. Donehue Papers, New York Public Library for the Performing Arts.

Walter Brennan Papers, Dickinson Research Center, National Cowboy and Western Heritage Museum, Oklahoma City, Oklahoma.

Walter Wanger Collection, Wisconsin Center for Film and Theater Research, Wisconsin Historical Society.

William Dozier Papers, 1941–1977, American Heritage Center, University of Wyoming.

Index